From Innocence to
IMPUDENCE

Library and Archives Canada Cataloguing in Publication

Jaggernath, Awadh, 1942-, author
        From innocence to impudence / Awadh Jaggernath.

Issued in print and electronic formats.
ISBN 978-1-77161-198-5 (paperback).--ISBN 978-1-77161-199-2 (html).--ISBN 978-1-77161-200-5 (pdf)

1. Jaggernath, Awadh, 1942- --Childhood and youth. 2. Jaggernath, Awadh, 1942- --Family. 3. Trinidad and Tobago--Biography. 4. Trinidadian Canadians--Biography.

     I. Title.
F2121.J332016   972.983'03092   C2016-901103-8
                                                C2016-901104-6

No part of this book may be reproduced or transmitted in any form, by any means, electronic or mechanical, including photocopying and recording, information storage and retrieval systems, without permission in writing from the publisher, except by a reviewer who may quote brief passage in a review.

Published by Mosaic Press, Oakville, Ontario, Canada, 2016.

MOSAIC PRESS, Publishers

Copyright © 2016 Awadh Jaggernath

Printed and Bound in Canada

Designed by Courtney Blok

ONTARIO ARTS COUNCIL
CONSEIL DES ARTS DE L'ONTARIO
an Ontario government agency
un organisme du gouvernement de l'Ontario

We acknowledge the Ontario Arts Council
for their support of our publishing program

We acknowledge the Ontario Media Development Corporation
for their support of our publishing program

Funded by the Government of Canada / Financé par le gouvernement du Canada

MOSAIC PRESS
1252 Speers Road, Units 1 & 2
Oakville, Ontario L6L 5N9
phone: (905) 825-2130
info@mosaic-press.com

www.mosaic-press.ca

From Innocence to
IMPUDENCE

To: Jamuna — a blessed soul.

Have dreams that are greater than memories.

Awadh N. Jaggernath
AWADH JAGGERNATH
July 11/2016

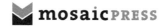

To
My Grandparents
And
Parents

Life is short, live it
Love is rare, grab it
Anger is bad, dump it
Fear is awful, face it
Memories are sweet, cherish it

- Unknown

What lies behind you and what lies in front of you, pales in comparison to what lies inside you.

- Ralph Waldo Emerson

ANCESTRY

It was neither the best of times nor the worst of times. It was a time either to follow the pathways of promising opportunities for a better life, or miss them altogether. If followed, it could mean the end to the bane of unemployment, the scourge of financial hardships, the injustice of privileged education, and the daunting curse of social degradation.

Towards the very end of the 19th century in the sub-continent of India, my ancestors stood at such crossroads looking at these pathways. It was also a time for the intrepid, the courageous, the resolute and the astute risk-takers to make new beginnings.

This memoir relates their true life stories as narrated to me by my two grandfathers and my father. It also included my personal life experiences while living, growing up and maturing with them during my childhood and adolescence.

After successfully completing my studies at the Elementary School in the rural Village of Chauhan, in Trinidad, I furthered my education at Excelsior College. This was a private college for boys operated by the Catholic parish priest in Benevolence Village. There our teachers came from Ireland, Scotland, England and the nearby villages. Our courses of study were prescribed by Cambridge University in England under the supervision of the British Ministry of Education and the Ministry of Education in Trinidad and Tobago. The final examinations were set by the University of Cambridge and were graded there. During British colonial rule that was the education model for the students in Trinidad and Tobago. Those students who successfully passed the British designed examinations could apply for admission to any university in the British Isles. Excelsior College admitted any boy who wrote and successfully passed the College's entrance examination. The boys had to be older than eleven years but less than thirteen. Most interestingly, the College accepted boys from any religious denomination, any colour, any class, and any socio-economic background. As soon as we entered the College's compound, however, we were obliged to obey Catholic teachings, and respect the School's code of behaviour and conduct. Regardless of our religious beliefs at home, whether Hinduism, Islam, Sikhism, Buddhism or any other Christian denomination, we were required to memorize the prayers, sing the selected hymns, study the Gospels, the Life and Teachings of Christ, and attend mass once a week. We observed all Catholic religious celebrations during school time.

The college had a very strict dress code. Each one of us felt privileged to honour and respect that code. The boys in the junior forms wore uniforms, short khaki pants, blue short sleeved shirt, crested gold and blue tie, and black leather shoes with knee high Oxford blue socks. The senior boys wore long khaki pants, white shirts, crested gold and blue tie, Oxford blue knee high socks and black leather shoes. On formal occasions we wore an Oxford blue felt cap bearing the Excelsior crest and an Oxford blue tweed blazer with the Excelsior monogram on the upper left blazer pocket. Our school motto was *Palma non sine pulvere*, which meant "No reward without effort."

We all looked very erudite and distinguished when we milled around in the school yard. We were also very proud to wear our school uniform in the village. Our teachers were always immaculately dressed. They all wore the school tie with their Oxford blue tweed jacket.

*****

When I was in Form Three, I had already befriended many of the boys, not only from my class, but also from other classes. They came from various parts of this British ruled island, situated in the Caribbean.

One rainy day, as we were sitting in our classroom having lunch, one of the boys, Krishna Maharaj, from Preysal Village questioned me. He asked, "Mitra! What is your caste?"

"What do you mean, Krishna?" I responded.

He continued his inquisition, "Are you a high class East Indian or a low class East Indian?"

"I do not understand your question. Can you please explain what you are talking about? In our home, no one speaks about caste or anything like high class East Indian or low class East Indian," I calmly replied.

Krishna continued the discussion by taking out a blank page from one of his notebook and slowly sketched a diagram of a pyramid. His drawing showed Brahmins at the top of the pyramid with Sudras at the base. Immediately below the Brahmins were the Kshatriyas and above the Sudras were the Vaishas. Krishna started to explain the annotations that he made on the diagram.

"You see, the Brahmins are the elite of the East Indians from India. They are pundits, scholars, professors and teachers. The warriors and soldiers are Kshatriyas. They are second class East Indians. The Vaishas are the shop-keepers, merchants, and the professionals like lawyers, doctors and nurses. The real low class Indians are the Sudras. These are the coolies. They work as labourers and servants."

"Krishna, why are you asking these questions? Why are you telling me all these things? What has all this talk to do with me? Are you claiming to be a high class Indian from a Brahmin family because your name is Maharaj?"

"Yes, I am a Brahmin, a first class East Indian. I want to be your friend, I like you Mitra."

"Krishna, why do you want to be my friend? You don't even know anything about me."

"Mitra, you have to be high class. I have watched how you conduct yourself in all the classes. The teachers are very interested to hear what you have to say. You are always answering the questions that nobody else in the class can answer. Sometimes our mathematics and geography teachers would send for you to answer questions in the higher forms. How come you are so neat, clean, punctual, always prepared for all subjects and forever smiling? Even Mr. Franklin is calling you 'Smiley' instead of Mitra Roshan. You have to be a high class East Indian."

"Krishna, I will try to discuss this question with my family on the weekend when everyone is at the lunch table," I said politely.

The bell rang, signaling the end of lunch time and the beginning of the geography class. We always had to remain standing until our teacher for the next class arrived. When the teacher came into the classroom, a prayer was recited by the prefect, after which the lesson commenced.

*****

On Sunday during lunch, I told Papa (my father) and Ajah (my paternal grandfather) about the conversation I had with Krishna. They looked at each other, smiled and started to laugh.

I asked, "What is so funny that you are laughing? This is a very important question and I need to respond to Krishna when I return to school on Monday. He wants to be my friend. He is one of the smartest boys in my class. He wants to know to which class I belong, whether I am a high class East Indian or a low class East Indian."

"Tell Mitra who we are," my stepmother, Tanty Seloni interjected.

Papa said, "Mitra, my son, this boy has been influenced by his family's caste prejudice. We are 'Aahir Gwalvanse' from Uttar Pradesh. We do not believe in any caste system. Your grandparents left India to escape that discriminating and unjust system. They deliberately indentured themselves for five years, so that they could work their way to freedom.

You would have to talk to your surviving grandfathers, your Nana (maternal grandfather) and your Ajah, to learn more details about their experiences in India, as adolescents and young adults, under the caste system."

Papa said that he had tried on several occasions to inquire about his parents living conditions during their early childhoods, their adolescent lives, and their early adulthood. He also said that my biological mother had made the same requests. Neither he nor she received any meaningful answers from anyone of their parents. Maybe their parents were too embarrassed to disclose their trials and tribulations. Papa added that, since I was their first grandson, they should be most willing to reveal their life stories to me, and I might be very surprised, if and when I learned about their secret lives.

"Tell Krishna that we do not believe in any caste system. If he thinks that you are a high class East Indian, then you are. Tell him that you are from the highest of the high classes. You are as good as any one of them and better than most of them in many ways. Let him find out who we are." Papa then hugged and squeezed me.

Papa continued: "We are a friendly, honest, forgiving, compassionate, hardworking and magnanimous people. Let the people look at your exemplary behaviour and evaluate your character son! Your thoughts will determine what words will come out from your mouth; your words will state your actions; your actions will determine your habits; your habits will portray your character; your character will mold your destiny. You have already heard the wonderful comments Krishna made about you. That should be an important signal that you are walking on the correct pathways that will lead only to success."

*****

On my return to school the following Monday, I calmly entered my classroom. Krishna anxiously greeted me in the presence of the other students and our history teacher, Mr. Jackson, who was seated at his desk evaluating test papers.

"Mitra, what did your parents tell you about your class? Are you a low class East Indian or a high class East Indian?"

His poignant question caught the attention of Mr. Jackson, who smiled. And before I could respond to Krishna's question he interjected by saying, "What kind of high class and low class discussions are you having Mitra?"

"Mr. Jackson, Krishna wants to know whether I am a low class East Indian or a high class East Indian," I politely answered. Mr. Jackson smiled and said, "Very interesting question! We should all explore our family history."

As soon as the regular class started, Mr. Jackson spent most of the class time asking questions about the ancestral background of the students. Most of the students did not have any significant information about their backgrounds.

In my class there were students from various ethnic origins. There were some boys whose forefathers either were African slaves, indentured Portuguese, indentured Chinese or indentured East Indians. This open discussion revealed the blatant ignorance of our own ancestry. Mr. Jackson, after realizing that we did not know much of our family's genealogy, immediately created a class assignment.

He outlined a detailed plan of it on the blackboard. But some of the students objected. However, when he indicated that the project would be due at the beginning of the next term, and would be worth twenty percent of our term mark, most of the boys became very co-operative. Mr. Jackson said that we should consult with our parents, grandparents and the elders in the family, and the extended family, to find out more details of our family history. In short, we had to excavate the secrets of our ancestors.

*****

In order to learn more about my lineage and to complete the history assignment, I decided to spend a part of my holidays with my maternal grandfather, who I addressed as Nana. He lived in Palmetto Bay by the seaside. He was very excited to see his eldest grandson who, while attending college, had come to spend some of his holiday time with him. He hugged and kissed me. Nanee did the same. Nana had no idea that I had a hidden agenda.

On the following day, Nana took me to visit some of his friends who knew me when I was a little boy. He proudly told them that I was attending college and playing cricket for the college team. After we visited all his friends, I was tired. We returned home, had dinner and we both went to bed. We slept on the very same bed that we slept on when I was an infant. Before falling asleep, Nana talked about his business and how he spent his time. He was extremely happy being with me. We wished each other a very good night and went to sleep.

*****

The next day, I told Nana that my history teacher gave me an assignment which I had to submit to him on the first day college classes resumed. The project was worth twenty percent of the term's history mark and it would be very crucial in determining my final grade.

Nana said that he was happy that I was studying history because it was one of his favourite subjects at school. He wanted to know how he could help with my assignment and promised to do his best.

"Nana, it is about my family ancestry."

"What do you mean by your family ancestry?"

"I have to write about where you and Nanee (maternal grandmother) were born, your early childhood, adolescence, and adult life. How did you meet Nanee? What kind of living conditions did you and Nanee experience and enjoy while you were in India? What made you and Nanee come to Trinidad? How did you become a businessman? I want to know all the fine details. The more information you give me, the more marks I will get."

Upon hearing my request, he became silent and looked very apprehensive. He looked at me pensively and with his eyes beginning to tear up, he said softly while hugging me, "Do you really want to listen to your Nanee's and my life stories? Have you got a few days?"

"Nana, I have all the time in the world to spend with you. I am on holidays. I really want to know as much as possible about the origin of my mother's family background. This is invaluable information. You may have stifled it within you for a very long time. But, should you reveal it to me, so that in the future I will be able to tell my children and my friends about the origins of my family. Mama did not tell me anything about her family's background. Papa told me that you are the only source of original information concerning my mother's family roots. You will be telling your eldest grandson about his maternal parents and grandparents. Don't you think that I should learn about my family's background? Don't you think it is important, Nana?"

Over several bitter sweet days that followed, Nana related this incredible story to me. I must honestly confess that each session was filled with lots of tears and crying from both of us. Seated on the chairs facing the large window overlooking the waters of the Gulf of Paria in Palmetto Bay, we talked in the dining room at different times. One day, the tide would be coming in; on another day, it would be receding. Nana kept looking at the ocean as he spoke slowly but purposefully. The sounds of the rushing and ebbing tides which permeated the room provided a soothing and peaceful ambiance for the revelation and recollections of my Nana.

*****

I waited patiently for Nana to begin his life story. Two days after my arrival at Nana's, after breakfast, finally, Nana told me that he was ready to start. Nana said a short prayer, made himself very comfortable in his chair and began to relate his story.

He was born in Hyderabad in the Indian state of Andhra Pradesh. His parents named him Premchand. They were cloth merchants. He was their only surviving child and lived with them in a small village on the outskirts of the city of Hyderabad. His family lived in a very simple and modest home and enjoyed a very quiet life. They were not very wealthy but were very happy and comfortable with their lot in life. His humble father and his loving mother worked together in their own small clothing business, not that different from what he was now doing, but on a smaller scale.

They earned enough to send him to the private school which was located not too far away. He either took a buggy or walked to school with a few of the neighbourhood children. Those parents who could afford to send their children to the private school willingly did so. They were aware of the fact that an excellent education and a British schooling would be invaluable.

His parents were heavy smokers. They were consumptive, old and frequently very ill. After school, he usually assisted them in the business. Sometimes, his mother would take him to buy merchandise in the city. There, she would frequently introduce him to some of the big merchants. His mother would tell the prominent merchants that when her son had finished his education, he would like to work in the clothing business in a managerial position.

A few of the merchants told him that, after graduating he should contact them, but only if he was seriously interested to start work. His mother was a very beautiful, talented, intelligent, and a shrewd business woman.

After successfully completing the courses in his school, his father told him that he should look for a job in the city with one of the big clothing stores. His father commented that in the big city, he would meet very interesting and helpful people, and could become wiser and, no doubt, he would prefer the urban way of living to the rural way.

*****

Mr. Singh, who owned one of the biggest clothing stores in the city, soon employed Nana as a control manager and book keeper. Nana's village was about one hour from where he worked. And he travelled to and from work on his neighbour's buggy taxi. After working in Hyderabad for only one year tragedy struck his family. Both his father and mother died. After their cremations, the ashes were scattered into a nearby river. Nana, on observing how smoking affected his parents lives, never smoked or chewed any tobacco products in his entire life.

At this point, Nana could not continue his story. He stopped and started to cry loudly. I embraced him and wept with him. After our catharses, I told him that he could continue his story when he felt better. I could not sleep that night. Nana was also restless.

The next day, he returned to his clothing business as usual. He was very busy with his customers, and I helped him serve them as I did when I was much younger. He was very pleased with my efforts. I was doing everything possible to please Nana because he was the only source of any essential information about my maternal grandparents. I needed to be patient and cooperative with him so that I could get as many details for my history project. After lunch he left the clerks in charge of the store and I accompanied him to George's rum shop which was located five buildings away.

While walking, he said that he needed to buy a bottle of Hennessy cognac to help him control his emotional outbursts and calm his nerves. It was not easy for him to recall vividly his life as he wandered down memory lane, and it was not very palatable for him to reveal and relive the trials, tribulations and temptations that he had to endure as a young man. After he bought the bottle of Hennessy cognac we walked back slowly to our home. We reminisced about the days when, I was a little boy and we walked that same road. But most of the landscape had changed. There were new homes, a wider variety of flora and reduced fauna, a different demographic and more traffic congestions. After dinner we retreated to the living room. We sat down in relaxing chairs and quietly listened to melodious and lilting East Indian songs and music from the latest Bollywood movies. Nana loved to sing and sang some of his village love songs which he blended with some of the latest hits from the Bollywood movies. Most of the time, when he was alone, he appeared happy, constantly humming and singing.

*****

His parents' deaths, although expected, greatly affected him emotionally and physically. He was allowed to stay away from work until he felt well enough to return.

Nana was alone. Although he inherited all his parents wealth he was aware that it would not last him a life time. He needed to return to work as soon as possible. He continued to live in the same house where he was born.

Nana returned to work much to the delight of Mr. Singh.

After two weeks Mr. Singh and his wife called him into the office. They stated that they were very pleased with his performance, and gave him a much deserved promotion. They also offered him additional responsibilities and an increase in salary. He graciously accepted and thanked them for the generous offer. In addition, they advised him to sell the property that his parents left for him, and to move closer to his work place. They volunteered to find a place where boarding and lodging were offered at a very reasonable cost. Also, they promised that they would purchase all the stocks that were left in his parents business. Nana took their advice and willingly exercised the options. They found a very lovely landlady who adopted him as a son. The Singhs bought all the stocks that were left in his parents' shop at a very generous price. He never regretted his decisions.

Nana's new responsibilities were to keep a close check on the sales, repurchase merchandise that was frequently in demand, monitor the sale prices of equivalent merchandise in the other stores located in the immediate vicinity and determine the working schedule of the other employees. He was now considered part of the management team.

The Singhs were planning to open a new store in another part of the city, and were training him to be the manager. Nana felt very fortunate that quite soon he would become his own boss. They concluded the meeting by informing him that it would be at least one year before the new store would be opened for business. This was refreshing and hopeful news for him. His parents would have been very proud of him.

In a very short time, under Nana's leadership, business sales greatly increased. The business was growing very rapidly and needed more staff. Mr. Singh told his fellow business associates and friends that he needed two new employees. Mr. Singh wanted to hire a young woman who could add some flair and feminine panache to his already successful and lucrative clothing business. She would encourage customers to make more purchases from their large collection of women's clothing, accessories, and cosmetics.

*****

One week later and still with no applicant for the job, Khanna visited the store and asked to speak with Mr. Singh. Khanna was a very wealthy land owner and business man who lived in the city of Hyderabad. He was looking for a position in a reputable business for his wife's niece, Nirmala. Khanna informed them that Nirmala was an educated, beautiful and ambitious young lady who was very much interested in working in a large store with lots of people. Mr. Singh asked Khanna to send her in for an interview as soon as possible. At that point in the story, Nana yawned and looked exhausted.

I said, "Nana, let us call it a day."

Nana got up and went to the washroom, and then retired to bed. I followed Nana's example. I thanked him for the interesting stories and I impatiently waited to hear the remainder of his trip down memory lane.

*****

The next day, Nana got up late. He apologized and said that he was experiencing mixed and stressful emotions reliving his early years and his life with Nanee. He asked me to be patient with him whenever he succumbed to his passionate memories with tears and loud cries. He had buried them for such a long time that he needed lots of energy, time and courage to unearth and relive them.

I calmly and understandingly answered, "Nana, you are doing fantastic. I am greatly indebted to you for opening up the channels of my maternal gene pool. You take as much time as you need to relate your story. I need to have this information which will become my own memories."

Nana continued by singing this song, "Ye Zindagi Ke Mele."

He would then explain the meaning of the lyrics of the song.

Nana continued his very interesting story. Nirmala was coming in for an interview, and Mrs. Singh remarked that if the young lady possessed the suitable qualities necessary for the advertised position then she would be employed.

Mrs. Singh did not know what to expect. She was hoping that Nirmala was beautiful, pleasant, and would be able to encourage the potential customers to increase their purchases. Nana said that he became extremely curious to see and to meet this young woman.

Within the hour, the most beautiful woman Nana had ever seen appeared. Slowly and intentionally, she walked into the store so that everyone present had to look at her twice. She approached the counter with a broad, charming smile. As soon as Nana saw her, his hormones kicked into overdrive causing goose bumps. His heart quickened its pace as the young woman softly, and slowly said to him, "My name is Nirmala. Are you, Mr. Singh, my employer?"

"No I am Premchand, I am an employee. I will fetch Mr. Singh."

Upon hearing the woman's gentle and friendly voice the Singhs came out of their office.

It was love at first sight for Nana. He knew that he would love to get to know her intimately and hoped to befriend her as soon as possible.

The Singhs interviewed Nirmala and employed her immediately. Nana was called into the office and was told to arrange her work schedule.

Nana congratulated her and immediately introduced her to the other staff members. She smiled at him and acknowledged the other fellow workers.

Nana said that he was very encouraged by her enthusiasm and vibrancy. He kept looking at her slim body from every possible angle. Whenever he was not occupied with business affairs he kept staring at her every moment. He made every excuse to be near her and to find a reason to begin a conversation with her. Nana had this glowing smile on his face as he related to me his feelings for her. I dared not interject for fear he might lose his train of thought.

Nirmala seemed reluctant to converse with him regardless of his sincere advances. Within a few weeks, her dynamic personality and superb rapport with the customers resulted in a significant increase in sales. The Singhs were ecstatic and more than pleased with her performance. This, however, did not deter Nana from actively seeking her friendship and possibly her love and respect. He continuously showered her with praise and complimentary remarks. For over two months, she was not receptive to any of his private advances. She would smile but gave no indication that she was interested in having a relationship with him.

*****

Nana decided to seek the advice of his best friend, Govind, and not from his other friends for fear of any competition. He asked Mr. Singh to allow him to leave early from work. Nana took a rickshaw to where Govind was working. He told him that he had to talk with him about something very important. They agreed to meet on Sunday morning.

The next Sunday, they met at Nana's home. Nana told his good friend, Govind, about his experiences with Nirmala. He told him that he was in love with Nirmala. Govind said that he knew her and her family very well and assured Nana that he would do anything in his power to help.

*****

With a big smile on his face followed by a big yawn, Nana got up, stretched, and said, "Mitra, it is time for some chai and some Indian sweets. Let us go outside and sit on the bench under the mango tree." I agreed.

The maid prepared the chai for us. I took out some of the Indian sweets from the glass container, placed them in a colourful enamel bowl and took them to where we were going to have tea.

Nana went ahead of me and walked along the seashore. I listened to the sounds of the crashing waves and inhaled the salty air. He stood and pensively watched the raging ocean waters through the mangroves. I looked at the blue crabs as they left the safety of their burrows in search of food. This setting brought back memories of my childhood days when I used to set traps to catch them.

We sat down on the small painted wooden benches beneath the mango tree. The maid brought the chai. We ate, drank and dabbled in a bit of business and school talk. Nana kept on smiling, looking up at the cloudless sky as though he was in a dreamland. He smiled mischievously at me and continued his story.

He confessed that his love for Nirmala was inexplicable. However, he wondered whether or not she was aware that he was madly in love with her! He wanted her to be his wife. Somehow he had to let her know how he felt about her.

Nana had a very responsible position in the business so he could not make open advances to her in the store. He told the female employees that he was in love with Nirmala and that she was not responding. They told him that he was young, educated and handsome, and that he would finally conquer her heart with patience and determination. Nana continued to woo her in his own special way. His gut feeling was that she secretly loved him but she was too proud to express it. She was on his mind all the time. He was breathing, eating, sleeping and dreaming only about her.

He looked at me and commented, "Mitra, one day you too will understand what can happen when the love bugs enter your blood stream and start to gnaw at the love strings of your heart."

"Nana, it seems that you were madly in love with her!"

"I was absolutely and passionately in love with her. I needed her as much as I needed to breathe oxygen to stay alive."

"Nana it is getting dark and the sand flies and mosquitoes are biting. We should go inside and have dinner."

Nana nodded in agreement and we went inside. We washed up and had a very simple dinner. After dinner, I looked at Nana's face. He was animated and smiling as he asked for some cognac. I immediately fetched him some. He drank it slowly and lots of water. We went to bed as soon as the raindrops started to beat upon the corrugated galvanised sheets on the roof of the house.

*****

Nana did not have any time the next day to continue his story. A day later, he told me that he was ready to start again. Nana had to sing another song before he could begin. He had some cognac, and passionately and emotionally, sang, "Tu Pyaar ka sagar Hai."

At the conclusion of his melody, he cried, refocused, wiped away his tears. He closed his eyes as though he was about to meditate and remained very silent for several minutes.

Finally, he opened his eyes, smiled and resumed his narration. He said that one very busy day, at the end of work he decided to follow Nirmala to her home. He walked slowly behind her, keeping a safe distance. His gut feeling was he had to tell her how much he loved her. He called out loud and deliberately, "Nirmi." There was no response from her. She did not turn around or flinch. He repeated louder, "Nirmi", as he quickened his pace to get closer to her. She stopped, turned around and came toward him and said, "I love how you addressed me, Prem. I love the name, Nirmi."

He responded, "I love you very much Nirmi."

She held his outstretched hands and he hugged her. She beamed with joy and happiness. He looked into her eyes and he kissed her cheek while holding her closely.

"Would you like to have some chai with me Nirmi?"

She responded in the affirmative. They walked side-by-side to one of the chai shops in the back streets. They spoke for about thirty minutes about how they were going to continue their newly formed relationship.

After drinking chai, Nana walked with her to the corner where the buggies stopped. He waited with her until her buggy came. She got on and they waved goodbye. He went home energized, ecstatic and on top of the world. His hunger was satisfied with the newly discovered love of Nirmala. Life was no longer the same. He had broken through her love shield. Under any and all conditions he wanted to be with her for the rest of his life.

Nana soon fell asleep and started to snore.

*****

On the following day, Nana asked me to accompany him to the city of San Fernando to purchase merchandise for the store. We had a fantastic bonding day, sharing and eating katchorie, bara with chutney and drinking Solo soft drinks in the big city. When we returned home, the maid had prepared a late lunch for both of us. We ate and took a siesta. We awoke around four o'clock. We remained indoors and he continued his story by saying when he returned to work at the store the following morning he felt very happy and refreshed. He felt as though he was re-born. When she arrived he noticed a drastic change in her attitude and her emotions towards him. She was happy and very discreet and wore a constant smile throughout the morning.

In order not to arouse any suspicion amongst the other staff members and the owners, Nana deliberately stayed away from Nirmala's operational space until late afternoon. However, he did slip her a written note at an opportune moment. The note read, "Meet me after work at the same chai shop, Nirmi, I love you, Prem." The day slowly passed until it was time to quit.

They arrived at the chai shop within a few minutes of each other. He embraced her and kissed her on her cheeks. They agreed that they should not meet too frequently at the same chai shop. Although they were budding lovers, she had to protect herself from the public eye because after all, she was a Bramhin. She was not supposed to associate with the lower caste. Nana was of a much lower caste. They decided to change their rendezvous as frequently as possible. In the event that her uncle and aunt would get wind of her love affair, there would be serious problems.

*****

I was very anxious to hear what happened next. Nirmala and Nana were happy and peaceful in each other's embraces. However, Nirmala was not aware that they were being watched. Apparently, whenever they went for chai, which was at least twice a week, she used to arrive home late. The Khanna's maid noticed her lateness, and inquired about it. She told the maid that she went for chai with the girls with whom she worked.

The maid reported her lateness to her aunt, who then told her husband. Unknown to her, Khanna sent out his hired helpers to follow Nirmala after she left work. She told Nana that the maid was asking too many questions about her lateness. He told her not to worry about the maid. Nirmala looked at him and said that she did not feel good in her body, mind, and spirit about the maid's questioning, although neither her aunt nor her uncle had directly asked her any question.

*****

After several chai meetings and feeling very comfortable with Nana, Nirmala told him that she was ready to reveal the 'Pandora's Box' of her life to him. He was told not to interrupt and to listen attentively.

She became an orphan when her father was murdered by burglars in their mansion in the suburbs of Madras two years previous. Her aunt, Mrs. Khanna, was the only surviving sibling of her father, Sharma. During the two years that she lived with her uncle and her aunt, they acted as her surrogate parents. Her mother died three days after she was born. For fifteen years she lived with her father. She was brought up from birth by two wonderful, caring, nurturing, and loving women who worked and lived with them until her father's untimely death. One of the women was her mentor and tutor. The other looked after all of her personal needs. Her father gave her the best education possible. She attended an English private school in Madras. Her family was well respected in all social circles. They were Brahmins and according to the social norms, she was not allowed to mingle with the lower castes. However, her father did not honour the caste system. He associated with everyone because he was a wealthy, well respected and prominent businessman in the city of Madras. Her father was murdered in their home. With her father's unexpected death, she was then forced to live with her aunt because her father had written it in his will. He had given her aunt, Mrs. Khanna, the power of attorney over all of her inheritance and her future schooling, and education until she reached the age of eighteen.

The Khanna's liquidated all her properties in Madras. They pledged to keep all the funds in safe keeping for her until she became eighteen. For one year, Nirmala deeply mourned her father's death. She had no one to turn to but to rely on the goodness, kindness and compassion of her uncle and her aunt. They took her everywhere and tried to marry her to their old friends. Her refusals of all offers resulted in grave bitterness towards her. Nirmala wanted to continue her education which she had begun at the English private school in Madras. They were very compliant and told her to make all the necessary arrangements with any private school, and they would provide whatever funds were needed.

Nirmala went to one of the private schools in Hyderabad and told them that she was a student in another private school in Madras, and after showing them her academic record, was accepted. She attended classes for approximately four weeks. On the fifth week the principal called her to her office and informed her that the Khanna's had not paid the term fees in spite of several reminders. She was then asked to leave the school but was guaranteed re-admission when all fees and dues were fully paid.

Nirmala questioned her aunt about her inheritance. The aunt claimed that most of it was spent on her boarding and lodging. She realized that her aunt and uncle had spent most of her inheritance, not on her, but on lavish parties. Nirmala was very disappointed, disillusioned and hurt. She had to start looking after her own future. Since she had no other family who could give her some assistance, she then had to look for a job. The Khanna's had no further use for her, having squandered her inheritance. They were still trying to marry her off to any interested Brahmin.

At this stage of Nirmala's story Nana started to cry and told her not to worry because everything would turn out well. Nana looked emotionally and physically drained. He got up and told me it was time to adjourn the story telling. We went to bed after Nana had some hot cocoa with some cognac and I had warm milk and cookies.

*****

The following day, Nana decided to resume his story. Nana sang another one of his life questioning songs:
"O Duur ke Musaafir, hum ko bhi saath le le re."

After he stopped crying, he continued.

There was going to be a commotion in the store. Khanna came into the store very quietly but asked for Mr. Singh aggressively. The Singhs recognized his voice and immediately came out of the office. Khanna shouted at Mr. Singh and asked him why did he permit this low caste, poor, homeless, starving clerk to escort his niece from chai shop to chai shop.

Nirmala overheard her uncle's loud, sarcastic piercing voice. She left what she was doing and came and stood behind him.

"Where is Nirmala?" her angry uncle shouted.

"She is standing behind you," Mr. Singh answered. Khanna called her a little whore and wondered why she would associate with such a low class person. He accused her of not only demeaning herself but also defaming his entire family.

Khanna looked at Nana and shouted, "You untouchable bastard, stay away from Nirmala. If you don't, I will have my people silence you forever. Stay away. Under no circumstance should you have any relationship with her. Do you hear me, you idiot?"

He was terrified and extremely embarrassed. As Khanna was leaving the store, Mr. Singh hugged Nana and softly said, "Premchand, don't worry about what he said to you. He and his entire family are too arrogant and rude. He claims to be a Brahmin but his behaviour is contradictory."

Nana sadly watched as Khanna tightly held and squeezed Nirmala's arm, as he forcefully pulled her out of the store.

She was unwilling to leave. The other staff members looked pitifully at Nana. He remained rather quiet and docile for the rest of the working day.

How strange it was that a few hours earlier he was walking calmly in the gardens of Elysium with Nirmala; now, he was confronted by this sad reality. That evening he returned home very unhappy and could not eat. Being restless, he did not know what to do and had a sleepless night. The following morning, he returned to work, full of despair and a sense of inner emptiness. He felt as though someone very special and dear to him had died. Two weeks elapsed. Nirmala did not return to work.

Nana asked Mr. Singh whether she would be returning to work and he responded negatively. Another week passed and still there was no news about Nirmala. One night as Nana was trying to relax in his home, it dawned on him that maybe he should contact his very good friend Govind.

At that juncture of the narration, Nana started to cry aloud. I got up and held him closely. I too started to cry. He freed himself and went to the bathroom.

After a few minutes, he returned and continued crying. I just sat looking at Nana with tears running down my cheeks, as he continued to relate the agony and ecstasy of his earlier life.

*****

The next morning Nana told me that he wanted to finish his story. He said that the narration was causing him a lot of grief and stress. But, he felt obliged to continue. I assured him that his life story was very important for my history assignment.

Nana smiled, laughed, and sang one of his favourite songs from an old Bollywood movie. If Khanna believed that he would stay away from his niece, he was wrong; he did not know that Nirmala and he had exchanged their life stories during their chai meetings. He was madly in love with Nirmala, was determined to make her his wife and was willing to do anything to achieve that goal.

*****

One evening after work Nana went to Govind's office and told him that he had some very urgent and important matters to discuss. Govind told him that he would come to his home on the weekend.

Early Sunday morning Govind arrived. Govind excitedly asked "What is happening? You look so confused and distraught. Please speak to me."

"I have told you only the good part, Govind that I am in love with Nirmala - now listen to the flip side of the story." Nana told him about Khanna's behavior at Mr. Singh's clothing shop, and the threats he made. Govind was speechless and turned pale. They remained silent for a while. Then, he asked Govind whether he could help him. Govind replied that he did not foresee any problem. Nana inquired about the plan of action.

Govind told him that he was a frequent visitor to the Khanna's home. He was well known and loved by the entire family. On several occasions, he had accompanied them to bazaars, weddings and other social functions. Immediately, Govind planned an emergency visit to the Khanna's later that day.

*****

One week later Govind visited Nana's workplace, and invited him for chai. Over chai Govind revealed the following wonderful story. He told Nana that he met Nirmala and they had a long private conversation about their relationship. She confessed that she was in love with Nana. She promised that she would do anything possible to escape from the Khannas'. Nirmala asked Govind for any assistance he could provide. He told her that he would ask her aunt to take her out and during that time he would escort her to Nana's home. She became very excited and elated.

Govind got her aunt's consent and was told that he could take her (Nirmala) out anytime. Govind's plan was to bring her to Nana's home every Sunday. Nana was more than excited and thanked him profusely. They left the chai shop, and on parting Nana remarked, "I will see you on Sunday Govind with my Nirmi!"

Nirmala arrived on Sunday with Govind. He told Nana that he would return in two hours to get her. Finally, after one month, they had some private time together. Gradually they became more trusting and confident that they were going to be lifelong partners.

I looked at Nana. He was smiling but appeared to be physically and mentally exhausted. I told Nana that we should continue the story at another convenient time. He protested and we went outside for some fresh air. We walked around for about one hour. We returned home and went to bed.

*****

The next morning, Nana was up very early, waiting for me in the back yard. I had a quick bite and joined him under the shade of one of the orange trees where he continued his story. Surprisingly, on one of these secret meetings, Nirmi said, "Prem, let us elope, let us leave Hyderabad, this is no way to continue to live. We have to start looking towards the future. I am very grateful to Govind for what he is doing for us. The Khannas think that Govind and I are in love. They are expecting us to get married. In a year or so, Govind will be a full-fledged Lawyer. They will try to force us to get married. I do not love Govind. I want only you to be my husband."

"Nirmi, are you saying that we should run away?"

"Yes, Prem, let us start planning immediately. We will get our funds together and buy two one-way tickets to Madras, a city with which I am a bit familiar. From there, we can travel to any other place in India."

"Nirmi, are you serious? What about Govind?"

She told Nana that they should not divulge their plans to either Govind or anyone else. Everything must be done secretly. They would find out the departure times for the trains from Hyderabad to Madras and, at the most opportune time after Govind has left them alone in the house, they would take a buggy to the train station and board the first train leaving for Madras.

Nana was quite amazed at Nirmi's wild and wonderful ideas. "But Nirmi, why are we not telling Govind?"

"If Govind knows, he may tell others because he still loves me. He does not hesitate to express his dying love for me at every opportunity he gets. I know it. I do not know if he is setting us up or genuinely trying to help us. I cannot trust anyone except you. The Khannas continue to hurt me emotionally, financially and socially. We cannot wait to find out the true intentions of Govind. We must get away as soon as possible."

Nana agreed with her and decided that on the last Sunday of the month they would escape to Madras. That last Sunday, as soon as Govind had dropped her off, they left on a buggy for the train station. The train was scheduled to leave in fifteen minutes. They hid amongst the other passengers. They boarded the train and left Hyderabad forever. They never looked back at the sights of the city as the train chugged out of the station.

It was a long, boring and tiresome journey that took almost four days.

Finally, the train arrived in Madras. They took their simple belongings and staggered out of the carriage into the crowded concrete platform. They used the public bathrooms. Then they went to the nearest chai shop where they bought some foods and drinks. While sitting they looked at each other and said they hoped they had made a prudent and wise decision by eloping. They hugged each other and prayed silently that the Hindu gods would shower them with good health, prosperity, good luck and rewarding opportunities for the rest of their lives.

They searched for a place for boarding and lodging and found one in the area where Nirmala went to school.

After a couple of days in the boarding and lodging facilities, they searched for work in the nearby clothing stores. Every morning, while they were unemployed, they went to the Hindu temple to prayer.

At this stage of the story, Nana suddenly became silent. He looked at me and started to cry and scream in agony. He walked around, looked outside and finally resumed his sitting position where he remained silent as he reminisced. He cleared his throat and sang: "In-saaf kaa mandir hai yeh, Bhagwaan kaa ghar hai."

*****

Nana continued that they landed jobs in two different clothing stores. They were on the job for just a couple of weeks when Nirmala heard from one of the staff members that there was an opportunity to go overseas to work on the sugarcane plantations on a tropical island.

"Nirmi, can you get some more details about the opportunity to work overseas?"

She said that she would when she returned to work.

Nirmala returned to the boarding house after work. They had dinner and he asked for more details about the opportunity to work overseas. Nirmala said that the staff member told her about her elder brother, who went to the recruiter's office and learned that they are still looking for workers to travel to British Guiana and Trinidad to work in the sugarcane estates. They decided to visit the recruiting depot and get all the information directly from the officers. They went on the weekend but, unfortunately the office was closed. At the same time they met other people who were also interested in going to work overseas in the sugar estates.

They discussed the risks and rewards of leaving India and travelling to a foreign land to begin a new life. On the Monday they returned to the recruiting depot very early. They were first in line when the office opened. The man in charge was very polite and inviting. He asked them if they were married. They responded in the affirmative. He slowly read the clauses of the indentureship contract to them. They asked him for some time to think about it before making any decision.

Later they returned to the officer to secure more information. They wanted to know when the ship would set sail. It would sail for British Guiana and Trinidad in ten days. Also, they wanted to know what kind of work they would be doing on the island of Trinidad. He told them that when they arrive in Trinidad representatives from different estates would take them to the sugarcane plantations where they would live in barracks. Then they would be assessed as to their physical and mental abilities. Some could work either in the fields or the weighing scales or in the factories, or in the offices, or even for the owners. Those who had formal education and could impress the representatives might not have to work in the fields. They told the officer that they were interested in enlisting and were advised to return the following day for the medical examinations.

*****

Two days later, they learned they had successfully passed their medical examinations and were asked for their marriage certificate. Nirmala, as usual, was always thinking about the next important decision that they were about to make. She suggested that they change their names on the marriage certificate and all official documents. Their marriage certificate was obtained from the nearby government registry.

Nana's original name was Premchand Kumar which became Prem Bhatia. Nirmala's name was changed from Nirmala Sharma to Nirmi Bhatia. They registered their marriage with these new names. From that moment, he called her Nirmi and she called him Prem.

Nana got up, and with teary eyes came towards me with opened arms. I got up and hugged him and we sang our way into our bedroom.

*****

The following evening, Nana continued his narration.

They asked for permission from the recruiters to go to their boarding room to get their belongings. Permission was granted with the advisory warning that if they were not back in time for the sailing of the ship, they would be replaced by other successful applicants.

They went home very excited. First, they paid their bill to the owner of the boarding and lodging facility and then told their employers about their decision. They returned to the facilities of the shipping company two days before the ship set sail. During those two days prior to departure the accommodations were very uncomfortable. On the departure date, they slowly walked onto the ship. There were hundreds of indentured Indian workers, from different castes, different religious and ethnic backgrounds, who spoke a wide range of dialects. It was a dynamic mix of cultures, customs and ideologies. They were given a very small tent located in the middle of the deck which was reserved only for married couples.

*****

They stood on the deck of the boat and looked at the mainland of Madras as the boat departed. Hugging each other, they looked at Madras as it gradually disappeared.

At first, the sailing was smooth but it became rough as the ship left the friendly waters of the Bay of Bengal in its wake. They sailed towards the Cape of Good Hope. The seas behaved as though they had gone mad. Most of the passengers suffered from sea sickness. The vessel survived the rough seas and headed northwards along the western coast of South Africa.

It took many weeks of sailing across the Atlantic Ocean to reach the mainland of South America. Finally, after several weeks the vessel arrived in the waters of British Guiana, located on the mainland of northeastern

South America.

The captain announced that those who were bound for the estates in British Guiana should get all their personal belongings, gather their family members and be ready to get into the small boats which would take them to their new homes. They bade farewell to those with whom they had bonded over the past months. They wished them best of luck and all success in their new homeland.

*****

At last, the ship headed towards the Island of Trinidad and dropped anchor outside Nelson Island in the Gulf of Paria. They were taken ashore with all their possessions where they were quarantined for the final medical examinations. Only those who failed to satisfy the doctor's medical examination were left on Nelson Island for medical care. Those who successfully passed the medical examination were taken to the mainland of Trinidad. The estate representatives received them and took them to the Forest Park Estate barracks in central Trinidad with horse drawn wagons.

"Mitra, I feel very tired. I will finish the story tomorrow."

*****

At lunch time the following day Nana spoke positively about their lives on the Forest Park estate. He said that when they arrived at the estate, they were taken to the barracks which housed many families. Already they had made acquaintances with a few of the families while they were on the ship and they shared a genuine camaraderie. After few days of rest the plantation manager interviewed the married couples privately. They were asked about their education and their working experiences. They were fluent in both Hindi and English.

Nana was assigned to the main weighing scales at the sugar mills. He had to weigh the loads of farmers' sugarcane, record the weights in tons, hundred weights, and quarters, and issue receipts to each farmer who had brought in sugarcane. He had a very responsible job. Accurate record keeping of these weights were essential. These slips, with the recorded tonnage, were used by the accounting department to pay the farmers. These were his responsibilities during the sugarcane harvesting season. However, during the growing season, he was assigned as wagon driver for Mr. Statham one of the overseers at the estate. Nana's education and work experiences in India gave him better working opportunities and living conditions.

Nirmi was very fortunate also. The wife of Mr. Statham interviewed her and was very impressed with her personality and command of the English language. Consequently, she employed her to tutor her daughters.

The five years went by very quickly. They successfully and happily fulfilled their contracts. After a few years, having saved sufficient funds, they bought a few pieces of land. Some years later they built the clothing business place where I was interviewing Nana.

I told Nana that his stories were very enlightening and invaluable for me. Nana hugged, kissed and thanked me for listening to his saga and helping him relive his love life.

Nana said that he thought that no one in the family would ever ask about his life story. He thanked me and told me to tell everyone in the family about his life.

"I love you Nana, thank you again."

I was confident that I had recorded all the essential information that I would need to write a comprehensive report about my maternal grandparents ancestry. I assured Nana that I would get the whole family to visit him and Nanee frequently. I asked Nanee why she did not join Nana when he was talking about her. She smiled and did not answer. Nana hugged me tightly, smiled and bade me farewell. I felt very sad to leave him. I told the maid, the store employees, and outside helpers to continue to take good care of him. They all smiled as I walked away to the train station.

*****

On returning to my parents home at Chauhan Junction, my eldest sister, Ushi, informed me that many of my school mates were looking for me to discuss the history assignment. I asked my sister if she told them where I went. She told them that I was spending some of my holidays with my aunt in St. Helena. It pleased me because I did not want my class mates to know that I was doing research for my history project. My aim was to obtain one of the highest marks in the class.

My father asked me about my learning experiences with Nana. I told him that Nana had fantastic stories and he started asking questions about Nana's background. I told him that I would tell him everything, after hearing Ajah's stories. Papa was very understanding.

*****

One Sunday afternoon, Ajah (my paternal grandfather) and I were sitting quietly in our living room. He began to sing his customary Hindi folklore songs, which he sang in Uttar Pradesh as a youth. He sang those songs with me when we were working in the sugarcane fields in the village of Chauhan. The songs and chants were soothing and melodious. When Ajah was satisfied with his meditative singing, he went to fetch a cup of water to quench his dry throat. I joined him in the kitchen for a glass of milk.

Ajah looked at me and said, "Gwalvanse [his pet name for me]. Where yu went for over two weeks?"

I told him that I was at Nana's home.

"What was yu doin by yu Nana?"

"Ajah, I went to find out from Nana about his life in India before he came to Trinidad and what he and Nanee did while they were in India."

"Why yu want to know about yu Nana's life story?"

"Well Ajah, my history teacher gave the class an assignment to find out the life story of my parents and my grandparents. He told us that it was very important that I know about my family background."

"Wat do yu mean?"

"Ajah, I need honest answers to the following questions."

"What kinda questions?"

"I want to know what kind of family life you had in (Uttar Pradesh) in India. What made you and Ajee leave India and come to Trinidad? Who encouraged you to leave your family? How did you get here? How did you meet Ajee? What did you do when you arrived in Trinidad? These are some of the questions for which I need answers. There are many more questions which I will ask as you give me your family information."

"Yu Nana answered all dem questions?"

"Yes Ajah."

"Is dis schoolwok very important?"

"Yes Ajah. The homework is for marks and the more information I collect the more marks I could earn. Nana has already told me his life story."

Ajah replied, "For marks! OK. Yu think that yu have enough time?"

"Yes Ajah. I have lots of time."

Ajah said that he had lots of very interesting stories to tell. Some stories were nice, others very sad, and still some not so good. He needed a drink to relate his life story. After he had his drink, said that Ajah would first he (Papa) would interpret I agreed and told them that in my notebook. We all soft and soothing singing

nilingly and slowly, he
ly and his life. He re-
il sittings.
evout Hindu. She was
dian mythological gods
tter life for everyone in
gods and goddesses that she
would follow her. However, his
of Lord Buddha. Ajah was giv-
tors left Tibet several generations
the politics and the way the people
s forefathers left Tibet, crossed the
valley in Nepal for a couple of gen-
erat... ted to Uttar Pradesh, the state south of Nepal in India.

He had three brothers and three sisters. There were too many people living together in a tiny house in a small village. They were farmers and did not have any formal education. However, they spoke Hindi and some English. Ajah and his friends would travel for many days over great distances in search of work. Being uneducated and young, their attempts were futile.

They were all poor and were always hungry, and barely survived on the harvest of home grown vegetables, peas and ground provisions. The few cows that they owned did provide milk for his household. But they were able to barter some of their products that they harvested. Life was extremely difficult

They lived in the countryside surrounding Basti; the young boys and girls in the district played simple games (Gulli Danda), and spent most of their free time singing and dancing. They would travel, in small groups, to the homes of wealthy people, who would give them some money for their singing and dancing performances (something similar to trick or treat at Halloween).

The majority of them were Ahirs, a pastoral class. They sang Birahas and danced to the rhythms of the Nagara drum beats. They also told stories to one another which they learned from their parents and grandparents. The stories were taken from the Bhagavad Gita, the Mahabharata and the other Hindu religious books. Many of the teenagers in the village would leave the village and travel by foot or carts to other towns, cities and states. Sometimes, they were gone for weeks but their parents never worried because they always returned, with either some money, food, or a companion. Their absences eased the burden of their parents who had to feed them and provide places for them to sleep.

*****

I then asked Ajah, why and what made him decide to come to Trinidad. Ajah related the following story.

One sunny afternoon, the village boys and he were playing Gulli Danda in one of the cleared and weeded open grounds. Three male strangers came and stood quietly on the sidelines watching them. Some of the boys became concerned about these three unfamiliar faces in the village and started to point and talk about the three men. They stopped their game, approached the strangers and asked them what they wanted. They said that they were recruiting (the recruiters were called arkatis) young, healthy and capable men and women from the village who were interested in making lots of paysaa (money). The men asked the boys whether they would like to work for a lot of money.

Most of the boys and a few girls responded, "Yes, Sahib."

Every teenager in the group became very excited at the mention of lots of money. They were very anxious to know what they had to do. Finally, amidst their positive reactions to such a heaven sent offer, one of them bravely exclaimed, "Sahib, what we have to do to get all this paysaa"?

The spokesman for the three men said that they were in search of people to plant, to nurture and to harvest sugarcane.

One of the teenagers shouted, "Where are the sugarcane fields? Are they far away?"

The spokesman answered that the sugarcane fields were on a warm tropical island called 'Chinidad' (Trinidad). The recruiters promised that they would be safely taken there by ships and would be brought back safely to their village on the completion of a six month contract.

At this point Papa interjected with the following quotation:

"A person who never made a mistake never tried anything new."

- Albert Einstein

The boys got together and started to discuss the golden opportunity offered to them by the Arkatis. The girls listened to the boys' debates but were not interested in leaving their families. Out of about twenty boys, five of them decided to accept the offer to travel and work on the sugarcane fields in Trinidad for lots of money.

A few days later two of the men returned. Ajah and four other boys decided to accept the Arkatis' offer. They were told to meet the men the following day at a predetermined time and location. Ajah did not mention his decision to leave the village and travel to another country, either to his parents or siblings. He wanted to surprise them with the large sum of money that he hoped he would bring back home in six months.

He and his four teenage friends met the men and they were transported safely by wagon to Benares, a city located a little more than one hundred miles south of Basti. Most of the boys had been to Benares before in search of employment. In Benares, they met many more people who were very excited to go to Trinidad to work on the sugarcane plantations. Some of the recruited indentured workers said that they were going to work in 'Chinidad' instead of Trinidad. Since they were leaving to work on the sugarcane plantations in Trin idad, the name 'Chinidad' seemed most appropriate.

In Benares, his friends and he were medically examined by both Indian and British doctors. Ajah passed all the medical examinations. However, none of his companions passed the examinations. The recruiters did not care about the health of the people they recruited because they were paid according to the number of potential labourers they brought into the coolie collecting depots.

I asked Ajah what were his feelings and reactions when all four of his companions did not get accepted to go to work in Trinidad. He said that he was disappointed. However, he was very happy and excited that he had passed all the medical examinations and was selected. Ajah was looking forward to travelling to the new land where he would make lots of money in just six months, and return to help his family live a better life.

His village friends tried to dissuade him from accepting this new opportunity. Ajah said that he was faced with two choices while his friends had only one choice. His friends' only choice was to return to Basti and continue to live in poverty, starvation, hardship, and possibly in misery for the rest of their lives. Carefully considering that option, and being brave, Ajah rejected it. Given such a rare opportunity, although unknown to him, but one which may lead to a pot of gold, he said goodbye to his friends in a bittersweet way and reminded them not to tell his family that he was leaving the country.

As his friends departed, he was shocked to learn that the contract that he was about to accept was not for six months but for five years as an indentured labourer on the sugarcane plantations. He spoke to other recruits to get their opinion. After considering his dismal living conditions and the prospect of a bleak future in his village, he willingly accepted the contract.

He may have had some hesitations about leaving the small village of Basti, but he was also confident that his decision was the only intelligent one.

At this stage of the story, I told Ajah that I believed that he made the correct decision by leaving India.

I quoted these famous lines from Shakespeare's *Julius Caesar* Act 4, scene3. Brutus' speech to Cassius:

There is a tide in the affairs of men.
Which, taken at the flood, leads on to fortune;
Omitted, all the voyage of their life
Is bound in shallows and in miseries.

On such a full sea are we now afloat.
And we must take the current when it serves,
Or lose our ventures.

Ajah wanted to know what those words meant. In Hindi, Papa briefly explained the meaning of Brutus's speech to Ajah. He smiled after Papa simplified the meaning for him.

At this stage of Ajah's narration, I became very sleepy.

Ajah noticed my tired eyes, and said, "Gwalvanse, yu sleepin. We go continue de story tomorrow."

I hugged and thanked him and Papa. We all retired to bed very exhausted.

*****

The following evening, Ajah, with his large white enamel cup filled with dark rum diluted with hot Hong Wing coffee, continued his Hindi and English hybrid stories in the presence of Papa and me. I must declare that, without the benefit of Papa's excellent translations and interpretations, I would not be able to completely understand all the details and nuances of Ajah's stories.

He said that the main clauses of the contract were read to him very quickly in Hindi by an official who spoke with an accent he could not understand clearly. There was an Indian recruiter who tried to translate and to explain the fine prints of the clauses but most of the meanings were distorted by poor translations and explanations. Most of what they said did not make any sense to him but he was determined to seek a better life.

After he signed his indentured worker's contract, he was led to the coolie depot. He was given a spot to sleep in an open area with many more successfully recruited labourers. They were given food and drinks which kept them healthy so that they would remain alive and fit for their mysterious journey.

Ajah said that he slept next to people from different parts of India. They were people of different castes, religious beliefs and different opinions about the unknown voyage to Trinidad. He remained in the coolie depot for many days with all the new recruits. He developed close friendships and relationships which later lasted many years.

He was transported by train from Benares to Calcutta with hundreds of indentured labourers. In Calcutta, he met a new group of recruits from Bihar and Uttar Pradesh. They were kept in the coolie depot until it was time to board the ship. All these new experiences filled him with strange and mixed emotions. He started to wonder whether he had made a mistake by leaving his family to seek greener pastures. He was in a world of complete strangers. With sheer courage, positive attitude and steel endurance, he was able to withstand all the new challenges, discomforting experiences and unpalatable living conditions in the depot.

*****

All the indentured workers were taken from the depots by small boats to the ship which was anchored in the Bay of Bengal. They finally boarded the ship which would take them on the long voyage to Trinidad. All unmarried men slept on the deck, in the open air, at the front part of the ship. There was hardly any space to move and definitely no privacy. It was similar to the scenes that you see in warehouses, arenas and sports gymnasiums where the homeless are accommodated after a hurricane, earthquakes or any natural disasters. It was unhealthy, disgusting, and inhumane. What could he do? He had already signed the indentured worker's contract for five years. There was no turning back for either him or anyone else on the ship.

*****

Then a big turning point in Ajah's life occurred. One night, as he was going to join the single men to sleep in the front deck, he noticed that there were people who had very small tents in the middle deck of the ship. They had some privacy and protection from the elements. He wondered how they managed such private accommodations.

Next morning, when the sun was above the horizon, Ajah went and met the captain. He inquired about the possibility of getting a tent. The captain informed him that the tents were only for married couples. All single indentured workers slept on the open deck regardless of gender. Single women slept in the rear of the ship, single men in the front and married couples in the middle deck of the ship.

Ajah was an adolescent and was unmarried. He walked around the deck looking for any single woman who would be interested in getting married. He asked the first female he encountered whether she was married. She said she was not. He asked her whether she was interested in getting married. She replied in the affirmative with a broad smile. Ajah then held her hands and when she did not resist his advances, he asked her to accompany him to the captain's quarters. He did not even know her name, her age, her caste, her religion or her origin. Those details were not important for his purpose. He really did not want a wife. He wanted some sleeping privacy. In order to get sleeping privacy, he needed to get married.

It was during the official marriage ceremony performed by the captain that Ajah learned the woman he married was about nineteen years old. Also her name was Ambina and she was from Bihar. Later he realized that she was well educated and was able to speak English, Hindi and Bhojpuri. What a way to tie the marriage knot! He was very lucky to find a beautiful and educated woman.

Ajah mentioned that the ship, its crew and all the indentured workers were always blessed by the prayers offered throughout the day by many people of religious denominations. The followers of Islam prayed five times a day, the Hindus offered prayers during the early morning and at sundown and the few Buddhists chanted mantras. Many of the fellow travelers, who brought along their favourite musical instruments, performed daily on the ship's deck. Both male and female, regardless of their cultural differences sang their favourite folk songs, told stories, played their melodious musical instruments and danced their folk dances. They created their own happiness regardless of the stormy weather. They did not despair. The journey was extremely long, uncomfortable and rough. Most of the recruits were a special breed of people who could quickly adapt to any adverse situation.

*****

Three months after leaving Calcutta, India, they arrived in the waters of the Gulf of Paria in the Bocas on the north western tip of Trinidad. They disembarked onto small boats which took them to Nelson Island. The indentured workers were examined by qualified medical doctors before they were allowed to go ashore on the mainland. Those who passed the medical examination were taken by small boats and those who failed were kept back for appropriate medical treatments and care.

*****

Choates and Ambina had finally landed on the shores of Trinidad. After they were claimed by the representatives of the estate to which they were indentured, they were taken by wagons to the barracks of Woodford Lodge Estate in Chanagar Village.

Ajah said that he was tired and promised to continue his life story the following evening after he returned from the sugarcane fields around Chauhan Village.

The following night, I could not find Ajah in his room or anywhere in the house. I asked Papa for him. Papa told me that Ajah had to look after one of his friend's cows which was giving birth and was experiencing some difficulties with the delivery. Ajah was the local village veterinarian. He had no official certification. However, by applying his intuitive knowledge and practical experiences which he acquired from personally tending to his parents' bulls and cows very early in his boyhood in Basti, he was regarded as the most competent 'professional' to care for the many needs of his friends' animals. In short, he was known as 'vet' to his friends.

*****

The following evening, Ajah was ready to continue his story. As usual, he had his rum and hot coffee while he narrated. Ajee and Ajah lived very modestly in the poor conditions in the barracks in Chanagar village. The room was small and each barrack building housed many families. The crowded conditions reminded him of his own home in India. There was an upper floor where they slept in very close quarters. The kitchen and eating areas were at the ground level. Whenever it rained, the kitchen became a real mud room.

There were many disagreements and fights amongst the different families. Disparities in religious beliefs, caste segregation, misunderstandings, charges of marital infidelities, robberies of valuables, and the dissemination of unsubstantiated rumours and scandals were daily social events. It was an insane living environment. Ajee prayed for the five years to go by quickly so that they would be free to buy land, to build their own home and to start a family.

First, Ajah and Ajee worked on the fields as laborers. Ajah earned one shilling per day while Ajee earned less for the same work. Ajah believed the wage inequity was unfair, but he was in no position to challenge any clause of his contract.

Fortunately, Ajah was made a driver for a team of workers. He was given this added responsibility because the overseer, who was in charge of his area, was impressed with his work ethic and diligence. This added responsibility resulted in a larger pay packet. He got his regular pay for his regular daily gardening duties and earned extra shillings for his leadership role as team motivator and task master.

At this point, I asked Ajah whether he had considered going back to Basti to rejoin and help his family. He said that he had left his family as 'a thief in the night' and that he was very ashamed to return. He was not sure whether he would be welcomed back as a 'prodigal' son or be considered a 'black swan.'

When the five years of their indentured worker contract elapsed, Ajee and Ajah left the barracks. They had sufficient funds to buy land and construct a modest home. Ajah built his first home on the left bank of the Piparo River. They bought other plots of vacant land in Chauhan Village and Chauhan Junction. On these vacant properties, they constructed buildings for doing business and houses to rent to those who were not able to purchase anything after they completed their indentured workers' contracts. They always embarked on many more ambitious projects as soon as they accumulated sufficient funds. They did not believe in borrowing money from anyone for any purpose.

*****

Ajah was a budding entrepreneur endowed with common sense. He was a risk taker and a devout and diligent worker. From the owners of the Woodford Lodge Estates, he leased several acres of land in different areas of Montrose, Chauhan Village and Edinburgh. On these leased lands, he continued doing what he knew best - planting, growing, and harvesting sugarcane. He made arrangements with other sugarcane farmers to buy young sugarcane suckers (young plants). With the help of hired workers, he cultivated and harvested bountiful crops of sugarcane every year.

As Ajah and Ajee accumulated more money, they leased more lands from the Woodford Lodge Estates. At first, they ventured into growing edible vegetables, ground provisions (plants that grow in the ground) and fruit trees on a small scale. They harvested tomatoes, egg-plants, yard beans (bodi), pigeon peas, peppers, cucumbers, pumpkin, and several other vegetables. They also grew ground provisions such as sweet-potatoes, cassava, eddoes, yams, and dasheen, just to name a few.

On Thursdays and Fridays, with the help of hired hands, Ajah would harvest whatever vegetables were ready.

Very early Saturday morning, he would take his produce to the Benevolence Market on his own ox-driven carts to the vendor spots, which he had reserved and had paid for the entire year. He spent most of the morning selling his produce and only returned home after all or most of his stocks were sold. Any unsold produce were given away to the less fortunate. Ajah was an excellent merchant with lots of gumption.

As Ajah's cash flow increased, he continued investing in various other promising ventures. He bought more properties in Chauhan Village, Palmetto Bay and St. Helena. In St. Helena, he grew rice on many acres of paddy fields.

Ajah also built small houses on the properties in Chauhan Village and Chauhan Junction. He rented his buildings to tenants who paid their rents at the end of each month. At the Chauhan Junction site, he constructed a commercial building. He anticipated and hoped that someone would rent it, open a rum shop and a grocery store. He rented the vacant building to a Hakka Chinese merchant, named Massa, who did open a rum shop and grocery business, just as Ajah wished.

As Ajah's business ventures grew, his wife, Ajee was also having babies. Over a period of fifteen years, they were blessed with four off-spring. The first and the last were girls. The eldest daughter, Runala, was only sixteen years old when she was married. The third child was a boy. They named him Nanda. He died unexpectedly when he was only eight years old. Their last child was a girl, named Omeera. His only surviving son was Roshan (Papa).

*****

Ajee was from a middle class family from western Bihar. Her aspirations to further her education to a higher level were interrupted when her mother died suddenly. Her father almost immediately took another wife. Ajee was disliked by her stepmother because she was more beautiful, better educated, more stylish, smarter and younger than her father's new wife. Her stepmother wanted Ajee to marry her older deformed cousin from another village, who was uneducated, poor and quite primitive. Her stepmother finally cajoled her husband to discontinue his daughter's formal private education. She believed that too much education was very detrimental to a girl's married life. Girls should be housewives, look pretty and satisfy their husbands' needs. Her stepmother requested that Ajee be kept at home and get married to one of her cousins as soon as possible so that she could have her father and his estate all to herself. Her father was so in love with his much younger wife that he obeyed her completely. Ajee was forced to stay at home by her father in spite of her brother's disapproval. Finally the decrepit cousin was brought to the home to finalize marriage arrangements for Ajee.

Ajee had two brothers who were very successful businessmen. Her father was very proud of them and frequently boasted about their accolades. When his wife was alive, they were all proud of Ajee's natural beauty, excellence in the arts and her academic progress.

After Ajee's marriage arrangements were finalised, she realised that as long as her stepmother was with her father, her dreams of a glorious, harmonious and successful future was not going to happen. She decided, unknown to her parents, to secretly join a group of 'freedom seeking' girlfriends who were also rebelling against the strict discipline and restrictions of their parents. Their parents were trying to marry them to anyone who would take them regardless of caste, class, academic achievements and socio-economic standing. There were many offers but the girls refused all dowry seekers. Ajee and her friends also believed that their future happiness and successes could only be realised through higher education.

Soon Ajee and her friends learned from a reliable male friend about the working opportunities in Trinidad. Ajee was a young, intrepid and restless adventure seeker. She finally decided to run away from home. She met a few other girls all of whom were escaping from the tyranny of their parents and were also heading for Calcutta. They travelled by foot, hitch-hiked and did whatever was necessary to get to the recruiting depots in Calcutta. Finally they arrived in Calcutta and scouted for the recruiting offices. They got to the correct destination and were welcomed by the Arkatis. They completed all the indenture ship forms and took all the necessary medical examinations which they passed. They were accepted as indentured workers bound for Trinidad. Like Ajee, they all married indentured workers on the boat.

At this point in the storytelling, Ajah got up, yawned and came towards me and said that he was tired and needed a drink. Immediately, I fetched him a drink of Vat.19 Rum which he gulped down. He wiped his mouth with the back of his hand and with rum on his breath said, "Gwalvense, yu go do yor homework now. I hav no mor to say. Yor Papa go tel yu the rest. I goin to sleep now."

I hugged and thanked him as he was about to leave for his bedroom. Papa was quiet. Also, I thanked Papa for his translations and interpretations. He did not answer. I wished him good night, I went to bed. I could not fall asleep. Ajah's and Nana's stories kept replaying in my brain. What fabulous courage, fortitude, perseverance, and ambition that my grandparents exhibited as adolescents and young adults!

What should I emulate from their experiences? I analyzed the behaviour patterns of all four grandparents and decided to adopt as many of their marvelous qualities into my own life's pursuits. They had given me a sense of resilience, tenacity, the invaluable instinct for survival and the quest for a better life. I have been left with a legacy that is inspiring, audacious and enriching which is more precious than gold.

For the next few days, no mention was made of the contents of Ajah's story. Then, Papa asked me to relate to him Nana's story. I told him that I had to finish my history assignment first. He understood.

*****

A week later I asked Papa if he was ready to hear Nana's story and he responded positively. We decided to talk in my room. I sat at my study desk, with my note book which contained all the information on Nana's story, and gave him a detailed account. Papa was very startled to learn about the adventures of Nirmi and Prem. He commented that a movie should be made about their plight and flight. After relating Nana's story I told him that I had a few questions about Ajah's and Nana's stories. He encouraged me to ask them.

According to Ajah, Nanda was Papa's only brother but he had died. Then, who are Uncle Ganga and Uncle Vishu I asked.

Papa said they were not his blood brothers. They were his playmates when they were kids. Unfortunately, when their parents died in a sugarcane field fire, they became orphans. Since their parents had travelled on the same ship as indentured workers, had worked together and had become very good friends of Ajah and Ajee, they adopted the boys. However, Papa told me that I was never to repeat this fact to anyone and that I should continue to respect them as my true uncles.

Papa asked me whether I had any more questions. I told him that I found it rather strange that when Nana was relating his stories, he never encouraged Nanee to participate.

"Did you ask him why Nanee was not sharing her stories with you?"

"I did not think about it. But I asked Nanee. She smiled and did not answer."

"Well, Mitra. Your Nana did not tell you everything. I learned a bit of Nana's family history from your Mama."

"What do you mean? Are there family secrets?"

At this juncture, Papa said, that before he could sincerely answer my question, he would have to tell me a very interesting story.

I sat quietly, taking notes as I listened to Papa relate the following stories.

*****

Mama (Aruna) was the only child for Prem (Nana) and Nirmi (Nanee). On hearing rumours that her husband (Prem) had a son with another man's wife, Nirmi decided to secretly make investigations. She learned that her husband definitely had a son with one of the women from another village. Immediately, she contacted her daughter (Aruna) who was attending St. Mildred's Convent and told her to come home. On her return, her mother related the story of her father's outside child. The marriage was no longer held by sacred vows. The harmony and happiness that existed within the family disappeared. Aruna and her mother were faced with a dilemma. They had to find ways to prevent the outside son from sharing in their inheritance.

There were continuous squabbles and fights within the family. Nana realized that his main opponent was his daughter, so he tried to get her married as soon as possible. He invited several suitors to visit Aruna. She was educated and attractive, but had no intentions of getting married at that stage of her life. Her father became extremely annoyed and decided unilaterally to get her married far away from home into any interested family. He thought that marriage was the only way to get her out of their home and business. Aruna was about seventeen, and seeing the unhappiness, and deteriorating health of her mother, she decided to drop out of school and take care of her. Also, she started to take a very active part in the business so that her father could not bring his son into it.

*****

By chance, Nana was attending a wedding in which Ajah and his entertainment troupe were performing. At the end of the wedding ceremony, Ajah was asked by the bride's father if he knew any one in Chauhan Village who had a son who wanted to get married. Ajah made some more enquiries and was introduced to Prem (Nana).

Ajah and Nana discussed and decided to get their children married, without consulting their families. According to the East Indian tradition at that time, fathers' promises were binding. Any attempt not to fulfill their pledges would bring only disgrace to the family that first defaulted.

Nana returned home, and for a couple of days did not say anything to either Nirmi or Aruna. Finally, they were extremely shocked to learn about the arrangements he had made. Immediately, both mother and daughter flew into a fiery rage. Aruna cried for many days, had sleepless nights and lost her appetite. For days she did not speak to her father. She could not believe that her father had arranged her marriage without first consulting her. Her mother became extremely ill, suffered a nervous breakdown and had to be hospitalized.

*****

Meanwhile, when Ajah returned home he proudly told Ajee that he had found a beautiful young lady for Papa (Roshan). She asked him to explain. He then told her that he met a business man, named Prem, who was in search of a husband for his well educated and charming daughter. Ajee then asked what happened. Ajah replied that he had agreed to get Roshan married to the man's daughter as soon as possible.

Ajee went berserk and almost killed him. For days they argued and quarreled, without revealing the family dissension to Roshan. Finally, Papa was told that he would be married within six months to a girl named Aruna. Papa and his mother both cried and screamed at Ajah and continued to harass and quarrel with Ajah, who completely ignored their complaints. At fifteen Papa was too young to be a husband. Neither he nor his mother had ever considered his marriage while he was still attending school. He was doing extremely well academically and was looking forward to being a professional, in either the legal or engineering fields. He definitely had to be a Houdini to escape from this trap. According to the East Indian custom, father was king of his castle. All children had to obey their father's commands. If they refused they were disinherited and then had to leave the family's home. I recalled hearing my friends' fathers saying, to them, whenever they were rude or disobedient, that as long as they live under their roof, they must obey and do whatever they said. Such was the common speeches that echoed throughout many East Indian homes in my village. Papa told his classmates and teachers that he had to leave school to get married. They were all very surprised but dared not interfered in the family's affairs.

While marriage arrangements were being made, Papa's mother became extremely unhappy, depressed and very ill.

She was greatly disappointed to see her dreams for her son's future as a professional disappear. She had wished that her son would have an opportunity to enjoy a higher standard of living and a better quality of life which she believed would result only from an excellent education and a well-paying job. Ajee endured the marriage ceremonies with the help of her fellow Jahajins and close friends.

*****

Meanwhile at the Palmetto household, Aruna's and Nirmi's friends assisted in the marriage ceremonies. Despite the dissensions within both the bride's and the bridegroom's families, the wedding took place. However, for at least one month the marriage was not consummated, because according to East Indian customs a chaperon was assigned to the newly wed to prevent any romance between the married couple.

Finally, Papa and Mama spoke to each other. Initially, Mama was resentful, but on realizing that they got married under duress and despite their personal objections, they agreed to make the marriage successful.

Mama told Papa she had to return to her parents' home as often as possible to look after her mother, who had a nervous breakdown, and also to protect her inheritance from being usurped by her stepbrother. Papa understood the situation and decided to cooperate with her. The loving relationship between Nirmi and Prem never returned.

*****

Meanwhile, at Papa's home, the constant quarrels and fights between Ajee and Ajah continued and consequently Ajee's health deteriorated significantly.

Finally, Papa and Mama had a baby boy, who lived for a short time and died from an unknown disease. Mama miscarried two other babies. She then had another baby boy, who lived for a few months. Papa and Mama thought that their marriage was cursed because they were forced into it. These four deaths in the fledging marriage was disheartening.

Then Mama's, mother (Nirmi) died. Her death brought extreme pain and sorrow to Mama and Nana. She shuttled between Palmetto Bay and Chauhan Village to take care of her father and the business. Fortunately for her, the stepbrother did not show any interest in the business. One year later Papa's mother died.

After the death of Nanee, Nana became very lonely and needed a companion. One of his friends, who was a widow and lived in the village, visited Nana frequently. Within a few months she moved in to live with him. That woman became my new Nanee. That took place before I was born. So the woman whom I was calling Nanee was not my biological Nanee.

CHILDHOOD

CHILDHOOD

Mama became pregnant again for the fifth time. She labored for a long time with excruciating pains. The doctors did their best to comfort her during her delivery. As Papa, looked at the tiny, anemic, colicky, and unhealthy body of the baby boy, he remarked, "I do not think this baby will survive."

With constant prayers from the immediate families, and their loving caring and devoted friends, the baby survived and thrived. The baby boy had a fighting spirit, passion and desire to live. They called the baby boy, Mitra. My mother, (Aruna), changed dramatically into a loving, responsible and full-fledged wife. My birth was a blessing for both families.

*****

Papa continued by telling me that when I was a baby, and toddler, I was greatly loved by my mother, my aunts and my grandfathers. I was the only baby in the Choates' family at that time. I spent most of my early childhood between Papa's and Nana's home. What a blessing! My two grandfathers were from different parts of India, but from them I learned to appreciate their religious beliefs, morals, customs, cultures, and many more attributes of life. They had entirely different backgrounds, ways of living, vocations and perspectives on any and every issue in life.

Ajah was reasonably well off, but he was always frugal. By contrast, Nana had established a standard of living that his wife, Nirmi, had adopted from her Bramhin family in Madras. I was also growing up in a fascinating and enlightening world of various types of farming culture, business people and the people of the small villages. My Papa spent many years of his married life working in the sugarcane plantations, planting and managing the vegetable and provision gardens, looking after the dairy cows, the working bulls and the poultry stocks. For performing these activities, his father gave him whatever finances he needed. He used those finances to purchase the things he and Mama wanted and needed. She got whatever she wished for at her father's home, and expected the same at the Choates. She was a spendthrift, and bought whatever she wanted in order to be in vogue with the wealthy people. Papa was also a stylish dresser who wore fine clothing and drove nice cars.

At the end of the Second World War Papa was still employed by the Americans who had bases in Trinidad. He was employed as a chauffeur for a military transport truck. He made a good wage and Mama was very proud of him. One of my earliest recollections was terrifying. One evening, my Papa came home dressed in his American uniform, which he wore on his job. Papa looked like one of the American soldiers that I had seen on the military transport trucks as they travelled on the main road in front of our home. I was always afraid of those men in their uniform. They looked quite different from the ordinary people in the village. When I saw this uniformed person coming into our living room, I screamed out loudly and ran to my mother for protection. Mama picked me up and said, "That is Papa. Don't be afraid, he will not hurt you. He loves you."

Papa came slowly towards me with a loving smile, picked me up and told me not to be afraid. After he hugged and kissed me he gave me candies and chicklets. I got accustomed to seeing Papa in his working uniform and was no longer afraid at the sight of the American soldiers.

*****

Ajah bought me a red tricycle. At first he placed me on the saddle and held me as he pushed the tricycle in our yard. I cannot recall any initial feelings or reactions but soon I was on my own peddling across the yard. I wanted to go on the road but they were very protective and tied the tricycle with a rope to a tree so that I was limited only to the open spaces in the yard.

As I matured and after observing how Ajah loosened the rope on sev eral occasions, I realized that I could also loosen the rope. One day when I was alone at home, I fiddled with the knot on the rope and it came loose. I untied my tricycle and boldly ventured into the back streets. I peddled slowly, then quickly along the paved back street until I arrived at the corner of two streets. I stopped, looked around and wondered. As I was sitting on the tricycle, a big lady who lived in the house with lots of flowers in her yard, came out and asked me if I knew where I was going. I became afraid and started to peddle quickly back to my home looking back to see if she was following me. When I arrived at the back gate of my home and realizing that I was not followed, I decided to ride in the opposite direction to the other street corners. That was the first time I was on my own.

When I returned home, I re-tied my tricycle as best I could. My neighbor called my Mama when she returned home from shopping and told her what I had done in her absence. Mama called me into the kitchen and gave me milk and cookies. Then she asked me what I did after she had left me in the yard riding my tricycle. I was quiet and did not know how to answer. She smiled and said that she would take me on the next day to ride in the back roads to meet her friends and acquaintances. Mama even introduced me to the lady with the large flower garden.

I soon became a confident rider and decided to go beyond the last crossroad. One day, as soon as I crossed the last crossroad, a little boy saw me and ran towards me. He asked me to allow him to ride my tricycle. I was happy to share my tricycle with him. As he peddled, I walked as fast as I could behind him. He was very happy and invited me to his home. It was the first boy I met on the street after I started to ride on the backroads. I peddled to his home which was situated on the corner of the main road and the backstreet on which I lived. His home was much larger than our home. I was led into the kitchen and kindly asked to sit around a clean table. He poured milk in two small bowls. There were small boxes on the kitchen table. He opened one of the boxes and poured some small flakes like biscuits from one of the boxes into each of the bowls of milk. I asked him what was it. He said they were corn flakes. He gave me a spoon and told me to eat. It was very tasty and I liked it. After eating the corn flakes, he asked me where I lived. I told him. Then I said goodbye and peddled away to my home.

At first, I was afraid to tell my mama about my experience. But the corn flakes were so delicious, I had to confess to my parents of my experience with the little boy. Papa and Mama looked at each other, smiled and said nothing. From that day, there was always corn flakes in our kitchen. My parents also enjoyed eating it.

*****

The perimeter of our home was completely bordered by thick hibiscus plant hedges. Throughout the year, there was a spectrum of colors of hibiscus flowers and several varieties of flowering plants in bloom all around our property. In between the flowers were patches of vegetables. I was in charge of cleaning, watering and nurturing the garden. Sometimes Mama and Papa would help. My sisters were always picking the colourful flowers and putting them in glass containers to decorate the living and dining rooms.

Ajah made use of most of the land surrounding our home. Coconut trees were planted along the hibiscus fences. A variety of matured fruit trees was planted all around the back yard; they bore luscious fruits in abundance at different seasons of the year. I remembered climbing the mango, the orange, pomerac, golden apple, cimite, breadfruit, and many other trees to pick ripened fruits. There were always fresh fruits on some of the trees which ensured that I should never be hungry.

Many of the coconuts were sold to the coconut vendors from time to time. As soon as my Ajah realised that I could count correctly, he allowed me to sell any fruits on the property that our family could not consume. We also had chickens which climbed the ladders to the top of many of the trees in the backyard when it was about nightfall. There were boxes around the trees in which some of the hens laid their eggs. I milked the cows in the mornings while Ajah or Papa did it in the evenings. We had a large supply of fresh milk every day. Any extra eggs and milk were sold to our neighbours.

*****

At a very early age, I became aware that there were other smaller people around in the house, either on the bed or crawling on the floor. Apparently, according to my only surviving aunt, I was always beating and hurting those smaller infants. I was told and always reminded that I was a bad little boy. These two little people were my two sisters.

My first baby sister was named Ushi and the second baby sister was named Elyana. Elyana looked like an oriental baby and was always very quiet. Mama was always breast feeding her.

I was told that when I was a baby, I was also breastfed just as both my sisters were. Elyana eventually started to drink boiled cow's milk to which granulated sugar was added. Ushi and I shared Elyana's milk occasionally. Even as a small child, according to Mama, I was able to boil milk very carefully on a coal pot. I used to re-fill the baby's nursing bottle whenever she started to cry.

*****

Papa bought another new Chevrolet car which he drove as a taxi between Port of Spain and San Fernando. He used the other older car to rent to one of his friends who wanted to ply it as a taxi. Papa had no fixed working hours. He would be there at one moment and then would disappear for hours before returning home with lots of coins – (six cents, twelve cents, shillings, florins and crowns). Papa always would bring back chewing gum, candies, cakes and ice cream for Mama and his three little angels. When Papa went to work, Mama was very busy washing, cleaning and taking care of us. Papa and Ajah did most of the cooking, shopping and yard work while Mama looked after the little children. Life for me was just playing, laughing, eating, sleeping, and according to my family members, being very mischievous. As a result, Mama was always disciplining me.

*****

Papa did not forget the values of an excellent education. He taught me how to read, count and how to be clean, be responsible, punctual and very respectful to elders. He enrolled me in a private school in the village. My teacher was a little fat lady named Miss Marple. At the little private school, I learned to sing many songs, to write properly, read aloud in front of the other students, play organized games and listen carefully and follow instructions. I met other students from the wealthy and prominent families of the village of Chauhan and Montrose. My classmates remained my friends for a long time. One morning, just after Papa took me to class, Miss Marple had a meeting with him. In the evening of the same day, Papa told me that the school would be moved to a new location about a mile away. Papa promised to drop me off to school. I asked Papa if my friends would be going to the school and he gave me a positive response.

At the new location, which was newer, cleaner and bigger, I met many children. I clearly recalled that some of them were bigger and older than me, but were also very kind and friendly. They often shared their snacks, sweets and drinks with me. Within a few days, I made more friends. The little boy who had given me corn flakes was now in the same school. Most of the children enquired about my family and where I lived. A few of them became very friendly and invited me to their homes. Some of them lived on the way to school. I told Papa that he did not have to drop me off to school and I would walk to my friends home, meet them and go to school. At first, he was not in favour, but after I told Mama how good my friends were to me, she persuaded Papa to allow me to meet them.

*****

I recalled distinctly walking the same roads I used to peddle my tricycle. Now I had to cross the main road. Before attempting to cross the street I practiced what Papa and Miss Marple taught me. First, I stopped, then looked in both directions and when safe, carefully crossed the street.

My favourite friends lived in a large house on the other side of the main road. A big grocery store and rum shop were on the lower level of their house. My friends, their parents, and their extended family lived on the upper floor. Whenever I went in the shop to wait for them, the father and uncle of my friends, who operated the business, would always tell me to go upstairs to meet them. I would walk up the long narrow staircase which ended in the kitchen. Usually they would be having breakfast. The mother would welcome me and would invite me to join them at the breakfast table. She would offer me a cup of hot chocolate and something to eat. Although I had breakfast with my family, I did not refuse her hospitality. I had an open invitation to visit their home at anytime to play, study, or socialize with her children, nephew and nieces. I told my Mama about the hospitality of the Sitalal's family. She was happy and asked me to get the recipes for the dishes that I enjoyed as they were different from what she made at our home.

One day my friends' mother invited me for lunch. I was introduced to salt fish buljol and cassava pone. My friends' mother asked me if I ever had salt fish buljol. I looked at her with a blank face and told her that I did not know. She asked me to join her children at the lunch table and served us the following delicious foods. She told me the name of every piece of food she placed on my plate. First, she poured me a cup of hot chocolate and a glass of water. On my plate she placed a piece of "Johnny Bake", saltfish buljol, fried plantain, boiled and fried cassava, and sweet potatoes. I ate everything on my plate, and she was pleased to see me enjoying her cooking.

I told my Mama about that delicious lunch. She said that she could cook the same dishes for me. I was excited, and looked forward to eating those dishes. Mama did not hesitate to change her dinner recipes as I gradually informed her of my new culinary experiences. When my days at the little private school ended, I continued to be friends with those children, whose parents appreciated me.

*****

I can recall the first day when I was taken to the Canadian Mission School in Benevolence Village. I was only five years old. On that memorable day, my mother dressed me and handed me my khaki school bag. Inside that bag were my first primer book, my wooden framed slate, a slate-pencil, my lunch (sada roti with curried cabbage and allo), wrapped in brown shop paper, and re-wrapped in a not too large piece of cotton cloth, a small bottle filled with boiled and cooled cow's milk. Mama held my tiny hand and led me to the front gate of our home. A group of young girls were passing in front of our home on their way to the same school that I was about to attend for the first time. Mama knew their families and a few of the girls. She asked them to take me to school. They were more than happy to take care of me. Mama was very happy to say goodbye to me as I left to go to a public school. One of the girls was always holding my hand and made sure that I was protected from the cars. As I walked along with them, there were many different buildings, lots of people and every thing looked so different from what I was accustomed to. Finally, after walking for quite a long time we arrived at the school. The school was not a little house like Miss Marples'. The school had several rooms and a large park with lots of cars. The girls took me to a man who was wearing a suit and tie. They spoke to him and answered his questions. He thanked them for bringing me to school. Then he took me to the teacher of the class to which I was assigned.

My teacher was beautiful, well dressed and friendly. She asked me for my name and some other things which I cannot remember.

On the very first morning at school, I was asked to read. After my reading performance, my teacher left the class and spoke to two other teachers in the adjoining classrooms. Recess time arrived. I went with my new classmates into the neighbouring yard across the street to buy a sugar cake. I passed through the gates like everyone else to get to the sugar cake vendors. I had just eaten my sugar cake when the school bell rang, signaling the end of recess so that all the students knew they had to return to their classes.

I realized that it was a long way to go back to my class through the school gate. All the other students quickly headed for the gate. I decided to take a shortcut by trying to jump over the drain into the open area which was much nearer to my class. Unfortunately, I fell into the drain and struck my chin on a protruding concrete slab. I climbed out of the drain covered with mud and my chin was bleeding profusely. Some of the students saw what happened and hurried to report my accident to the nearest teacher.

I got out of the drain and started to walk towards my class when a teacher, Mr. Yadav, came to my assistance. He was kind, gentle and immediately took care of me. I still bear the scar from my first day of school

Mr. Yadav cleaned my wound as best as he could. He spoke to my teacher and told me to wait for him at the main gate. He got his bicycle and having placed me on the crossbar of his green coloured Raleigh bicycle, he rode a few miles to the nurse's office which was adjacent to the doctor's office. Mr. Yadav spoke to me while he was slowly cycling to the nurse's office. He mentioned that my chin had suffered a rather large wound and it would need to be stitched. I wondered how the nurse was going to use a Singer sewing machine to stitch my chin. The only kind of stitching that I knew was done on my Mama's sewing machine. I started to think what Mama would do to me for not following the other students to my class after recess.

At the clinic, the nurse cleaned my wound with alcohol and iodine, put some yellow liquid (flavin) on a piece of cotton, placed it on my wound beneath my chin and bandaged it.

Mr. Yadav said that I was extremely fortunate. The cut was not too deep but would leave a lifetime scar. There was no need for any stitches. He smiled and thanked the nurse. Mr. Yadav brought me back to my class. He smiled when I thanked him. He was a caring and compassionate teacher.

When I returned to my class, my teacher smiled, hugged me and kissed my bandage. I took my seat and joined in the class activity. The class was doing simple arithmetic. I answered all the questions she asked me. At the end of the last class, she called me and told me that my wound would heal and that I should always take good care of myself.

When I returned home, my parents were very concerned. My Mama was not annoyed. Ajah was laughing and said that I was looking like a little man with a white beard. The next day, Papa took me to school. We went to the principal, Mr. Harrold, who called Mr. Yadav. Papa asked many questions about my accident. He left very satisfied with whatever story they told him. I went to my classroom.

After singing the national anthem of England and reciting the morning prayers, the regular classes commenced. My teacher asked me to take my book bag and to accompany her to another class. The new teacher told me that I was promoted to her class because of my advanced reading and arithmetic skills. My new teacher was also young, beautiful and wore lovely clothes. She showed me the resource reading books in the cupboard and told me that I could borrow any of the books that I wished to read at home. This lending privilege was offered to all students who were interested in extra reading.

When I was in this class, I sat next to a creole boy named Jamboolay. He was always disrupting the class by throwing paper balls across the classroom laughing aloud and talking to other students while the teacher was teaching. He was frequently ordered to kneel down with his hands raised above his head in front of the class. Many times he was beaten with a leather belt. When I witnessed the punishment handed to him because of his unacceptable behaviour, I was more than ready to listen to my teacher and refrain from talking with him. Jamboolay had a nasty habit of peeing in his empty milk bottle whenever the teacher refused to give him permission to go to the washroom. He was denied washroom privileges because whenever he was permitted to go to the washroom he used to walk around the school and disrupt other classes by calling on his friends. I learnt a lot about respecting the teacher and school rules by just observing the penalties Jamboolay paid for disobeying them.

The next year, I was promoted to Miss Farhan's class. I became the teacher's pet. She also granted me the special privilege to borrow any book from the resource books from the classroom cupboard. She advised me to read the *Royal Readers* and the *Happy Ventures* books. I was also entrusted with the responsibility to look after collecting her lunch bag from her home every school day morning and to take it back to her home after school. I was also placed in charge of the 'rod of correction.' It was a big thick bamboo rod which I proudly held in my hand as I carried it to and from her home to the classroom every school day.

One day, Miss Farhan gave one of the boys a severe beating with the bamboo rod. The boy got very annoyed at me and claimed that I was responsible for his punishment. After school, the boy waited for me, and took away the bamboo rod and gave me a severe beating. Next day, I reported the beating to my teacher. Miss Farhan sent the boy to the Dean of Discipline who dealt with him severely. No student ever interfered with my responsibilities again.

*****

I noticed that there were many unusual social privileges that were given to certain children during lunchtime. My school accepted and accommodated students from all religious and socio-economic backgrounds. However, during lunch time, I noticed that students from wealthy and prominent families were allowed to have their lunch in their classrooms. Those of us whose parents were neither prominent nor wealthy had to eat our lunch outside the classroom. My sisters and I had to eat our lunch either standing up or walking around the playground or sitting on a rare vacant spot on the steps outside the school. Many times, we had our lunch and pocket money taken away by a few of the bigger boys. A chilling fear always ran through my body and mind whenever I saw the big bad boys coming towards us. Being quite aware that we would be roughed up by the school bullies, who would take away our pocket money and our lunches, I would advise my sisters to take as many bites as they could before the boys could catch us and to put their pocket money in their socks.

We complained to our Papa about the 'lunch bandits.' Papa made arrangements with some of his friends to allow us to have our lunch in their homes. It was then I realised why the wealthy and prominent peoples' children were allowed to have their lunch behind closed doors in the safety of their classrooms.

*****

I lived in a very rural part of Chauhan. At the rear of the row of houses across the main road in front of our home were large tropical forests, sugarcane plantations, cocoa, coffee, grapefruit, oranges, guavas and coconut fields. In fact, within half a mile from our home in any direction, the landscape was like the landscapes that you see in the Edgar Rice Burroughs jungle movies.

The children of the village used the natural landscape as their frontier playground to re-enact the cowboy, bandit, and Indian tales depicted in the western movies. Frequently, unknown to my parents, a few boys and I would boldly venture into the thick pastures and forest until we would reach the banks of the Piparo River. We saw many large poisonous snakes and black tarantulas as we made our way through the bushy and fully treed areas. Being forest wise, we always returned home untouched. I was, however, accident prone. One morning, when I was attempting to climb the steep bank of the river, I had an accident. I was almost at the top of the river bank when the wet dirt below my feet loosened and I slipped down the side of the river bank into the silt-laden waters of the river. On my way down the bank, a broken cider bottle, which had been abandoned on the river bank, ripped into the lower part of the shank of my right leg. When I returned home and told my parents about my accident they became very annoyed. However, on seeing how awful the cut was, they became very concerned. I had to remain at home for weeks before the wound healed. The neighbours thought that it was turning gangrenous. They often frightened me by telling me that the doctor was coming to cut off my leg. I cried and begged all the gods and goddesses to which my Mama had introduced me to please have mercy and heal me. I promised to be an obedient boy.

My absence from school hampered my academic progress. I missed many valuable lessons and all the remaining important tests and examinations of the academic year. At the end of the year, I was promoted from standard 2A to standard 3B on the recommendation of my teacher, Miss Patel. My younger sister, Ushi, came first in her standard 1A class. She topped her class in every subject. She was promoted from standard 1A to standard 3B. This was very embarrassing for me. My friends, who had been promoted to standard 3A, laughed at me every time they saw me. I tried to avoid them as much as possible. My younger sister and I were in the same class.

*****

A very profound and memorable life lesson was taught to me when I was in standard 3B. One sunny school day, one of my friends, Errol from another class, asked me to accompany him to the tamarind tree. This tamarind tree was on private property two streets away from my school. I had not visited the tamarind tree for more than a year. When we arrived at the site of the tamarind tree, there was a sign that read, 'Trespassers will be prosecuted.' I told Errol that we were not supposed to go on the private property.

Errol said, "Look, there are boys on the tree. You see. We can climb the tree and also have fun."

Although I pledged to obey rules, the temptation to perform some of

Tarzan's gymnastics got the better of me. The boys who were on the tamarind tree clearly saw both of us. Two of them were senior prefects. I was afraid that the prefects would report us to the Dean of Discipline. We exchanged hellos and started climbing the tamarind tree.

Errol climbed to the side of the tree where the senior boys were and I climbed to the less crowded part of the tree to avoid the direct eye contact of the prefects. After a few minutes, all the boys left. Errol and I were the only two left on the tree. A few minutes after the prefects left the area, the school bell rang to signal the beginning of the afternoon session. Errol, in his haste to get down from the very top branch of the tree, missed his footing and fell to the ground. He screamed, yelled and cried as though he was going to die. I came down gingerly to the ground which was not my normal style. I went quickly to Errol's aid. He was writhing in pain as he clutched his left arm. I told him that we should go to the nurse's office. He said that he would be fine. We left and ran to our separate classroom.

Shortly after class started I could hear Errol's loud cries and groans penetrating throughout all the classrooms in the school. The silence of the school was unprecedented. I could hear Errol's cries and groans fade as the nurse took him away to the doctor. The school resumed its normal academic hum and I breathed a sigh of relief. I hoped that Errol did not mention my name to his teacher and that the two prefects would not point their fingers at me. I remained silent in my seat and feigned ignorance of what was transpiring.

Some ten minutes after Errol's departure, Mr. Norton, who was talking to Errol's teacher, called me. He told me that the headmaster wanted to see me immediately. I had to walk along the corridor in front of all the senior classes before I could get to the raised platform of Mr. Harrold. The prefects and some boys were looking at me as I passed in front of their separate classrooms to get to the headmaster's office.

Mr. Harrold was very welcoming, and asked me to kindly sit down. "Do you know why your teacher sent you to me?"

"No, Sir."

"Do you know Errol John?"

"Yes Sir."

"Did you hear the groans of Errol?"

"Yes Sir."

"Do you know why he was groaning?"

I remained very silent. He repeated the question. I continued to remain silent with my eyes looking down at the wooden floor. He got up and looked at his rack of straps, took out the thickest one and forcefully hit the back of his chair. He was not looking at me as he struck the chair again. The menacing sound that reverberated throughout the left wing of the school would have awakened the dead and send shivers through the nervous system of the living.

Mr. Harrold turned towards me, looked me in the eyes with the menacing strap proudly hanging from his broad shoulder and softly said, "Errol, in his pain as he left for the doctor's office, told me to call you for more details about the tamarind tree accident."

I realized the very precarious situation I was in and I had to tell the truth. After replacing the strap on the rack,

Mr. Harrold sat down. He repeated the question, "Do you know why Errol was groaning and screaming?"

I told him the story only about Errol and myself.

He continued his interrogation by asking whether there were other boys on the tree or on the ground around the tamarind tree. I remained very silent and very scared.

Mr. Harrold repeated the question more sternly. I told him that there were other senior boys on top of the tamarind tree when we arrived at the site of the tree.

"There were senior boys!" he exclaimed.

"Can you give me just one name?" Mr. Harrold softly asked. I gave him the name of one of the prefects. He got up smiled and said, "You have done very well, now go back to your class."

I returned to my classroom. It was very quiet as everyone looked at me disdainfully. Mr. Norton had many straps displayed on his table. He knew about the accident from the teacher next door but did not have any details. Mr. Norton asked me to relate what happened to Errol. I repeated the story that I had narrated to Mr. Harrold. The class became very noisy. Mr. Norton looked at me and was very angry.

He gave me six lashes with his black leather strap on my buttocks in front of my classmates and my sister. The lashings burnt and stung me as I cried walking back to my seat.

Later, I could hear the severe beatings that were taking place in the headmaster's office. I became very worried as I rubbed my burning buttocks. I started to wonder whether the headmaster was beating the prefects. If so, they might be looking for me after school. They had seen me at the headmaster's desk. They saw me with Errol at the tamarind tree. It was after my meeting with Mr. Harrold that they were beaten.

After school was over, just as I feared, the senior boys and the prefect ran me down, caught me and gave me a severe beating. They cuffed, kicked, slapped and threw me into the dirty concrete drain. My lips and nose were bleeding. My body felt broken. Many students noticed but no one came to my assistance. I cried with pain all over my body. Then, I went to the road side stand pipe and washed my face, hands and feet.

I had received severe punishment twice that same day for something that I did not wish to do. By not respecting the trespassing sign and by telling the truth I was beaten twice. I was told by my teachers that the truth would set me free. My body was paying a high price for telling the truth. I was certainly not free of pain.

On my way home, I learnt that my sister Ushi had already told everyone that she met on the road about my disobedience and the punishment that I received from the teacher. She ran home and informed our parents about the beatings that I got for climbing the tamarind tree.

As soon as I arrived home, Papa started to beat me with the belt he pulled off from his waist. My Ajah intervened and stopped the flogging. My sister had no pity for me.

The following day, I returned to school and did not report the beating the senior boys gave me for fear of getting more beatings. I believed that discretion was the better part of valor in that situation. Errol met me during the morning's recess at the water tap. I told Errol about the beatings I got from Mr. Norton, the blows the senior boys and prefects dealt me, and the belting from my Papa. Errol said that he was sorry and showed me his broken hand wrapped in plaster of Paris.

*****

In my Standard 3B class, Mr. Norton was very instrumental in enriching and enlarging my knowledge and he taught me as a judicious parent. Also, he imparted to me some very profound and invaluable skills. He told us that we should pay very careful attention and write down any information that we deemed to be valuable, whenever we were present at any place where useful and important information was disseminated. In any classroom, listen attentively to the instructor, note everything that was repeated or casually emphasized because most of the time, those emphasized concepts would reappear on tests and examinations. As a result of Mr. Norton's counseling, I spent class time listening, learning, questioning, clarifying and I made doubly sure that I understood the lesson fully before leaving the classroom. By the middle of the year, my very good and trusted friend Zuban and I had learnt the names and the capitals of the major countries of the world. We could locate on any detailed map, the capital of the major countries of the world, the major islands, famous mountain ranges, famous deserts, famous rivers, all the oceans, famous lakes and many more geographical features. We were very familiar with the information in the Student's Companion, and had mastered using the dictionary to learn the meaning of many new and foreign words.

Every Friday, during the last hour of class, Mr. Norton held a knowledge battling session. The class was divided into two groups. Two captains were selected based on the performance of the students in the class. Two of the top students were appointed captains. One captain stood on one side of the class and the other on the other side. Zuban was a captain of one of the teams and Sandy was captain of the other team. They tossed a coin to see who would be the first captain to select the students to be on their team. Sandy's team won the majority of the 'mental gymnastics' battles. The 'mental gymnastics' battles did wonders for my knowledge base and self-esteem.

The end of the academic year was fast approaching and in a few days, final tests in all subjects were about to begin. I studied very diligently because I had to catch up with my former classmates from standard 2A. On the last day of school, Mr. Norton read out the final results for the academic year. I came first in the class and won a few awards.

Mr. Norton gave me the following books as prizes for scoring ninety nine percent in the following subjects: English, geography, and history. In front of the class, as he shook my little hand and patted me on the head and shoulder, he presented me with an *Oxford English Dictionary*, a *Student's Companion* and a *World Atlas*.

I was then promoted from Standard 3B to Standard 4A Special, where I rejoined my friends from Standard 2A. That was the first and last time that my younger sister Ushi and I were ever in the same academic class.

*****

After school on Thursdays and Fridays, I often went to the vegetable plantations to help Ajah harvest some of the crops. Very early on Saturday mornings, Ajah and I would take these products to the retail Benevolence market. We transported our stocks on our own carts drawn by our own oxen. Whenever we had lots of stocks, Ajah would drive one of the carts and I would drive the other. We always had two leased stalls in the market. Ajah's friends in the market place often helped us unload the products, and carry them to the selling stalls. We had a hand weighing scale with several pound weights.

I collected the money, gave change and kept the rest of the cash in a khaki bag which had a draw string which I kept wrapped around my waist with a piece of rope. We believed that the money bag should always have a few garlic pods and a white cowrie with the money. This was done for protection from evil eyes, jealousies and especially, for great accumulation of wealth and constant good luck. I was able to manage the market business carefully. We marketed tomatoes, eggplants, peppers, pigeon peas, eddoes, sweet potatoes, cassava, carille, and husked coconuts.

We always took between ten and twelve different types of produce to market. I wore a hat to cover my head from the hot morning sun. Whenever it rained, I used a large green banana leaf as an umbrella to keep the rain from wetting me.

While I was selling our produce, Ajah would leave me in charge of merchandising and sales and would scout the market for scarce commodities. He would buy them with the money we had already made from selling our products. He would bargain with other vendors and buy out their stock at at a low wholesale price. Periodically he would bring back bags of this produce and put it for sale at a higher price in our stalls. I was very lucky, in that most of our home grown produce, being cleaner and better priced, were sold out very quickly.

I would often get annoyed with him. I frequently reminded him that it was Saturday and I wanted to play with my friends. I wanted either to fly my kite and enter the kite fighting games, or dance the wooden spinning top that I made, or pitch marbles for buttons with the boys. I had so many choices but I needed free time.

Ajah would smile and softly said to me that we had a chance to make more money by selling those new stocks, and that in a few hours, we could either double or even triple our cash flow. I must have a little more patience. I would always agree with his decision which I trusted. He was my best friend. At that time, I did not realize the valuable financial discipline he was inculcating in me. Ajah would bring me sandwiches, pop, mauby, peanut punch, rice cakes, rye and bhalley, and many more delicacies to comfort me as I diligently and dedicatedly looked after the marketing and selling business.

*****

One Thursday after school, I met Ajah in the vegetable plantation, as he was reaping vegetables to take to market on Saturday. We had finished reaping the tomatoes, peppers and were picking the pigeon peas when it started to rain heavily. There were loud thunder claps and enormous lightning displays. I became very scared. The canals between the vegetable beds were filled with fast-flowing water. Centipedes, water snakes and spiders were crawling around the water and the wet dirt.

I held on to Ajah and cried, "Ajah, why doesn't God help us? Why is God frightening me?"

Ajah replied, "Mitra, the day yu see God tell Him that I want to talk to Him."

"Why Ajah, isn't there a God?"

"Yes, there is a God but he is in every part of yu, he goes with yu everywhere, and he looks after yu all the time, because he is inside yu. Yu are made from God's energie and juice. God is inside yu. If yu do not get up and apply yuself, nothing go get done, so start depending on yuself and the God inside yu will help yu to succeed in anything yu do."

I listened to Ajah's statement and remained very confused and frightened. I did not understand his explanation.

After the thunderstorm and blinding lightning display, as we were returning home on the bull cart, Ajah held me closely and uttered these everlasting and life-changing statements to me, "Next week, yu go be on holidays and two ah we go go to Benevolence. We go dress up nicely and visit some very important people and places. Is that okay with yu? Yu don't have to be afraid. I will take care of yu".

I continued hugging Ajah for his body warmth and garlic aroma and said," Ajah, whatever you want me to do, I will do".

As agreed, Ajah and I left for Benevolence just after breakfast. He took me to the doctor's office, the nurse's quarters, and Mr. Sampath's drug store. They were located adjacent to each other. As we left these professional buildings, Ajah said, "Did yu see how clean and neat the doctor's, nurse's and druggist's places were? How nicely dressed they looked? The doctor and the druggist had on jacket and tie. The nurse had on a white clean uniform with a small cap. Did yu see all that, Gwalvanse?"

"Yes Ajah."

Ajah then took me to the court house to observe the court in session. I saw the judge, the lawyers for the defence, and the prosecution, the jurors, the spectators. I carefully scrutinized the beautiful architecture and furniture of the court house.

"Ajah, this is a nice place, I like it," I commented.

Ajah smiled and said, "Mitra, yu like this place," to which I replied, "Yes Ajah!"

We left the courthouse and visited the library, the bookstore, the Benevolence Railway station, the large department store, the large Chinese rum shops, groceries and restaurants. I became very tired after all the walking and talking. We stopped and had lunch at one of the vendors in the market. Many of the vendors knew us very well. Some of them wanted to know what we were doing on a weekday in the Benevolence Market. Ajah spoke to them privately. I did not ask him any questions.

We returned home in the late afternoon. I got into my home clothes. I saw my friends playing cowboys and bandits, but I was too tired to join them in their games.

The following morning Ajah told me that after lunch, we would be going back to Benevolence to visit a few more people and places. I was ready and eagerly waiting for Ajah to come home from the sugarcane fields. He came, had a shower and got dressed. We had lunch at home. Ajah held my hands as we walked along the shoulder of the road. He took me to the Barclays bank, Mrs. Keshwar's pawnshop, Ishwar's jewellery shop, Mr. Singe's photographic studio, the Bombay stores, the private high school, the travel agency and many other important and interesting buildings. By speaking and listening to the owners and the professionals in each of the different buildings, he thought that their words of wisdom would convince me of the immeasurable value and importance of an excellent schooling, and education, from an early age. After another exhausting but informative few hours, we returned home.

I was sitting at home quietly with Ajah and Papa in the living room when Ajah told Papa that he had taken me over a period of two days to see the important offices and people of the town. Also, he had shown me where they worked and how they performed their daily responsibilities. Then, Ajah looked at me and made these life-changing offers. He said that I had to decide whether I wanted to work in the sugarcane plantations, the rice fields or sell in the market or become as as one of those well respected, prominent and successful business people he had introduced to me. He added that if I wanted to be like anyone of those successful people, I would have to study very hard, and at the appropriate time and place, I should be able to recall and apply any of the valuable information that I had learnt. I must read all the books in my teacher's cupboard and do all my home work. I must always stay around people who are smart and are willing to help me climb to the top of the ladder of success. He always reminded me to be careful with whom I associate. "Show me your friends and I will tell you who you are," he always quoted to me. Ajah was correct in his assertion.

In order to obtain my certificates I should study diligently and continuously. He reminded me that I was in charge of my destiny. Furthermore,

I should always look upwards and onwards. He promised to give me the funds to purchase any book that I would need in my studies. If I should become interested in any hobbies or anything that would give me an academic advantage, I just had to ask him for the necessary funds. What a wonderful offer from my Ajah!

Papa added, "Mitra, knowledge is power only when you make use of it at the appropriate time, place and with the right people."

They both said to me, "Good luck and all our blessings to you. We will love you forever."

I got up, hugged and kissed Ajah and Papa several times without saying a word.

As Ajah got up to go to the washroom, I said, "Thank you Ajah. I will do the best I can."

He looked at me and said that since I did not like selling in the market and working in the fields, I had the choice to stop doing them immediately and start taking my studies seriously.

Ajah said that he would miss me in the fields and the market place but my formal schooling and education were most important. He added that I should always look at the very successful people in Benevolence and try to learn from them.

Ajah returned and continued by saying people on the whole were always looking at my behaviour everywhere. Whenever I did something good, some people will smile and praise me. If people are not happy with what I did or what I was doing, they would dislike me. I had to be honest not only to myself but to everyone else.

"Ajah what does that mean?" I inquired.

Papa interjected and elaborated with some of his words of wisdom.

"Let me explain it, Baph!"

Papa said, that I should always try to do my best at everything; should not do things that would make people get annoyed and unhappy with me; should always be fair when playing with my friends; always respect the elders; always ask questions whenever I was not certain about anything; should always try to avoid anyone who had been unfair and unjust to me; avoid anyone who insults or tries to disgrace me, either publicly or privately and finally, avoid negative people or anyone with negative thoughts, ideas or intentions. I should clearly remember my signature is on all of my actions.

*****

After leaving Mr. Norton's class, I was promoted to Mr. Narad's class, in which my educational journey became more interesting and enlightening. My new class had many brilliant, talented and sociable students. Fortunately, I was able to befriend many of them, who were gifted, open-minded and cooperative.

There was a budding tenor singer, name Trevor Kahn. I saw him perform many times both on the school stage and on the public square. He was one of my classsmates in Mr. Narad's class. Trevor was a very friendly, easy going and entertaining person. Sometimes at recess he would sing a few verses from any one of his opera repertoire. His favorite renditions were: "La Donna e mobile" from Verdi's opera, *Rigoletto*, "Lucia de Lammermoor" written by Donizetti, "O Sole Mio" and "Ave Maria." He knew several more arias and opera pieces but these were his common renditions to his classmates. We were all very proud to be associated with him.

I called Trevor, 'the barefoot' Enrico Caruso. He was blessed with a powerful and impressive voice, and was able to not only to imitate the voice of the great Enrico Caruso, but also that of Gigli and many others. He could remember the Italian lyrics as though it was his mother tongue. He even knew the stories of all the operas from which he sang, and the meaning of the Italian words.

Trevor became one of my best friends. On several occasions, he took me to his uncle's home to listen to the arias from various operas and the voices of these great tenors he admired and imitated. He showed me how he practiced and learnt the lyrics and their meanings.

With his book opened, and as the song started, Trevor would synchronize his voices with that of the singer. He came alive and energetic as though he was performing in front of an audience. I saw how he was transformed just by listening to these great voices. I was encouraged to become more outgoing and expressive.

*****

One day, after lunch Mr. Narad asked the students of our class about their hobbies and what exciting things each did after regular school day was ended. Since this was an impromptu class session, a couple of the students had nothing to say or did not know what to say. A few of the brilliant and eloquent students stood up and spoke about their hobbies, their sporting activities and how they spent their free time. I listened attentively to some exciting and interesting stories.

One of the smart girls, Helena, volunteered to speak first. She said that she collected coins – not only from Trinidad and Tobago, but also from other countries. Her dad, a banker, was very instrumental in encouraging her to start and maintain her coin collection. Helena elaborated the reasons for collecting the coins, and hinted that her hobby was the 'hobby of kings' and that it was the 'king of hobbies.' No one asked any questions or challenged her statements.

Another student, Ramesh, said that after school, when he arrived at home his mother had a glass of cold Ovaltine and Arrowroot biscuits for him. When they were finished snacking they would either play chess or checkers before dinner. After dinner, with the help of his elder siblings, he would do unfinished homework and some extra questions and then go to bed.

Another boy said that he lived in the countryside and that his parents were farmers. On arriving at home, after changing into his home clothes, he would go into the fields and untie the animals so that they could return, before dusk, to their pens at his homestead. He also said that his job was easy because the animals were conditioned like Pavlovian dogs. As soon as the animals saw him they knew it was time to go home. They would stop grazing and wait for him to set them loose. As soon as they were untied they walked in indian file across the fields to their pens. When he arrived at home he would water and feed them. He would then have a simple dinner with his parents. Then he would either do his homework or some quiet reading before going to bed.

The class ended and Mr. Narad said that over the next few weeks, he would give each student an opportunity to describe their hobbies, special interest and their after school activities. The girl who sat next to me inquired about my hobbies. I told her that I collected the photos of movie actors and actresses of the period. The photos, included in every bubble gum package, were either black and white passport size or similar to baseball players cards. She told me that she also collected the photos of the actors and actresses. I always kept my collection with me in my book bag and they were held together with rubber bands. She had hers in an album which had extra pockets in which she placed her duplicates. She asked me whether I would like to trade cards. I was more than excited to get the photos of some of the actors and actresses I did not have. After a week she presented me with albums in which I started to keep my photos.

She told me that she also collected coins and if I knew anyone except the rich girl in our class, who collected coins.

I responded I would talk to my eldest sister, Ushi. At home, I told Ushi about the girl who sat with me and she wanted to start collecting coins. Ushi wanted to know why I was telling her about collecting coins. I replied that both of us could start a coin collection with all the silver coins that Papa and Ajah have in the tins and jars, and also Nana had lots of coins. Ushi smiled and agreed to begin our coin collecting immediately. I asked the girl in my class about purchasing an album for my sister. She met my sister and gave her one.

Also, in my class were twin brothers who lived further away from me in Chauhan village. One evening, as we walked home after school, the twins stopped at the Lum Lee and Lum Shue shopping centre. They asked me to join them as they wanted to find out whether Hardeo had received his delivery of new comic books. I had no idea, at that time of my life, what was a comic book. Under the large protruding gallery of the shops, hundreds of multicoloured books were hung on several wire lines which stretched across an open area. I became curious and asked my friends about the books. Before they could answer, Hardeo responded that they were books containing a collection of some of the comic strips that were in the daily newspaper.

After their conversation with Hardeo, we continued our walk home. As we walked, I asked them to tell me more about these comic books. They informed me that they had been reading comic books since they were in the lower standards, and that they found them to be informative, interesting and entertaining. They offered to loan me a few of their comic books. I accompanied them to their home where they loaned me four western comic books.

My father, on seeing them became very interested. He wanted to know where I got them. I told him. He took the books, smiled gleefully and said that he wanted to read them too. Papa was a fanatic for Western movies. He spent a lot of his spare time reading books written by Zane Grey, Max Brand and many more writers who wrote Westerns.

He took me to see not only westerns but also war dramas and detective movies. Most of the Western movies at that time were mainly in black and white. When Papa read his Westerns he had to imagine the scenarios. The drawings and the sketches in the comic books were in beautiful colours: landscapes, small villages and towns came alive.

After reading about a dozen of the Western genre, Papa decided to buy comic books in different genres. He bought the cowboys, gangsters, heroes, war stories, the *Tarzan* series, crime stoppers comics and many others. I was allowed to read Papa's collection. I bought the classics and the masked heroes: *Dick Tracy, Mandrake* and the *Zorro* series, with the money I got from Ajah. I became very familiar with the famous cowboys, gunslingers and outlaws, especially the Frank and Jesse James gang, Billy the Kid, Doc Holliday and Pat Garret. I also bought a few of the *Nyoka* and *Wonder Woman* comics for my sister, Ushi. I was greatly fascinated by the roar of the iron horse (the train) and dreamt of travelling in them some day. Papa and I were able to animatedly narrate different genres of comic books, movies and pulp fiction stories to each other in the presence of my sisters and friends. The twins and I spent a lot of time discussing the comic books stories. I was very grateful to them for introducing me to comic books. My exposure to comic books not only enriched my knowledge about literature, geography, history, fictitious and real crime fighters, but also helped me to build a strong 'covalent' bond with my father, my sisters and a few of my classmates.

I was introduced to the world of science fiction when I saw the *Buck Rogers* serials, the *Flash Gordon* serials and the movie, *The Day the Earth*

Stood Still. I loved and greatly appreciated going to the movies. By paying very close attention to the background sceneries in the movies, I was able to learn a great deal about the physical geography of the landscapes in which the movie was filmed. Also, I waited until the end of the credits to see the location or locations where the movie was filmed. I learned much about how the people lived, the natural wonders and the man-made wonders of other countries of the world just by making these observations. I hoped to visit and appreciate these places in the future when I would have the money and the time. My life did not just belong to the place where I was born, where I went to school or where I lived. This world belongs to all of us. We should all see it before we leave it. Other thrilling and exciting serials that greatly impressed me were: *The Drums of Fu Manchu, Daredevils of the Red Circle, Spy Smasher, Captain Marvel, Captain America, Phantom* and many others.

*****

During the academic year, when I was in standard 4A special, our teacher, Mr. Narad, organized a field trip to the Woodford Lodge Sugar Refinery to see how sugar was made. The school was located less than a mile away from the sugar refinery. When we arrived at the factory, there was an English overseer who told us that he would be our tour guide. Our teacher joined the students and listened attentively to him. There were many trailers lined up to deliver their load of freshly harvested sugarcane in the factory's large parking area. They dumped their loads into a long rectangular concrete trench. At the bottom of the trench, there was a slowly moving metal platform on which the sugarcanes fell. As the platform moved forward the sugarcanes were washed. Then they were chopped and shredded by revolving razor sharp knives. Water was continuously added to the shredded cane before it was crushed between large steel rollers. The juice was collected in large stainless steel tanks. The remaining fibrous materials, called bagasse, were taken away by trucks to another site. The sugarcane juice was mixed with calcium carbonate to neutralise it. This mixture was allowed to settle and the clarified juice was concentrated by evaporation. This process formed syrup which contained about sixty percent sucrose.

The syrup was supersaturated and seeded with crystalline sugar. After cooling, sugar crystallised out of the syrup. The end of the tour which was followed by a question and answer session in the warehouse where the brown crystalline sugar was stored.

"What happens to the bagasse"? I asked.

The bagasse was burned to generate electricity, and to manufacture paper. My teacher asked about the formation of molasses. The guide said that after the crystallization process, and all the sugar was centrifuged out of the syrup, the remaining liquid was molasses. We returned to school and had to write a report on our trip to the sugar factory.

*****

After the birth of my sister, Elyana, my Mama was always tired, sickly and lethargic. She became very anemic and weak and as a result, was constantly hospitalized. She was either in the San Fernando General Hospital, Couva District Hospital or the Port of Spain General Hospital. My two younger sisters and I did not miss her presence at home because Ajah and Papa took care of us in her absence. We got used to being left alone at home, but we visited her two or three times a week. We did not like the medicinal scents that permeated throughout the hospital wards. However, we always loved the ice cream, cookies, cakes, biscuits, soft drinks and other delicious treats that we got after visiting our Mama.

Whenever Mama, Papa, and Ajah would be away from home and leave us unsupervised for many hours, they would warn my sisters and me not to leave the house and wander in the streets. They told us that should we leave our home and roam the streets evil men would kidnap us, kill us and then feed our livers to thoroughbred horses. Of course, we stayed inside the house most of the time and read our school books. Sometimes, we played hopscotch with the other children in the large back yards of the adjoining homes without any adult supervision.

Occasionally, I would leave my sisters with the other children and sneak away with a couple of boys. We would walk in the nearby fields, away from the main road, catching butterflies or birds or bathing nude in the muddy waters of the Piparo River. We often caught crayfish and catfish which were roasted and then eaten.

My friends' fathers or the elder kids regularly took us to the movies at the Sunset Cinema in Benevolence, one of the main forms of entertainment for most of the village people. After seeing any movie of either the western or jungle genres, many boys could describe them in vivid details with sound tracks and actions. They not only had photographic memories but they were also natural actors. It helped that we lived in a village surrounded with dense tropical forests, sugarcane, cocoa, coffee, coconut, and citrus plantations, so that we had natural movie sets on which to re-enact the exploits of Tarzan, cowboys, sheriff and Indians.

*****

On one such occasion, my playmates and I were re-enacting a cowboy scene in which the sheriff and his posse were in search of the bandits who robbed the village bank of all its money. The 'make believe' sheriff had a group of boys on whom he could call to form a posse at very short notice. The sheriff formed a posse to hunt down and apprehend both me and my gang as we roamed through the forest and fields. The boys rode imaginary stick horses. As they rode, they made the sounds of galloping horses with their mouths, accompanied by the sounds of the background musical score from the western movies they had seen. It was a fantastic display of imitation, imagination, creativity, acting talent and colorful dreams.

One evening as my gang and I were setting up an ambush for the sheriff and any member of his posse, we unwittingly captured the sheriff as he got separated from the main body of his posse.

Two members of my gang took him deep into the forest. They blind-folded and tied him to the trunk of a cocoa tree with the lianas they ripped off from nearby trees. Then we heard the galloping sounds of horses made by the advancing posse. We rode away in another direction towards the sugarcane plantations where we hid until it started to get dark. All the cowboys, the posse and my gang returned to our respective homesteads.

It was very dark, when the voice of the mother of the captured sheriff pierced through the village evening silence.

"ANYBODY KNOW WHERE CISKO GONE?"

She rephrased the question loudly.

"ANYBODY SEE CISKO, MY SON?"

The village immediately came alive. Most of the parents came out of their homes. They were carrying flashlights, flambeaux, and gas lamps. The fathers came back into their homes and got their sons out of bed and repeated Cisko's mother's question.

A few of the boys who played the role of bank robbers confessed quickly to what they had done to Cisko. The men ordered the boys to lead the way into the dark, snake infested forest. I was very frightened and imagined snakes and tarantulas on the branches of the tree and in the bushes. We found the sheriff tied to the tree and his entire body was covered  ts. He was alive, exhausted, and ntied him, took him down very . The village doctor and nurse, immediately. None of the boys ooperative and responsible for sko, who acted as sheriff, was

another baby girl after Elyana. home. Ajah was the only per- l that morning. I would like to ght and Papa had taken her to nknown to me and my sisters. Ajah told me that I had to stay chool that day and not leave the house because he had something important for me to do. My two sisters were sent to school with the from the village. I did not know why I had to remain at home. made me breakfast and told me that my baby sister had died that had to be buried later that day. I had to stay with the dead baby until returned from his appointment. He did his business transaction and came home about noon.

When Ajah left, I went into my parents' bedroom where my little sister's body was resting. I had to babysit the dead baby, who was very pretty and dressed in a pink dress and pink booties. She had a blue tikka on her forehead. I lay beside her until Ajah returned.

Ajah brought with him two friends, Jagro and Sukhu. One of them had a shovel in his hand the other one had a garden fork. Ajah said a few mantras over the dead baby. He wrapped her body with a piece of white cotton and gently placed her tiny body in a small empty smoked herring box which was lined with white sheets of tissue paper. We left on foot for the cemetery located in St. Aquinas village. Ajah carried the little box under his arm. At the cemetery, his friends dug a grave of about two feet deep. They said some more prayers and then covered the box with dirt to form a small mound. This grave site was located just obliquely across from the village mortuary. This baby's burial was my initiation to the first death in our family.

Surprisingly, no body in the family cried or showed any sign of sadness or unhappiness. No one ever spoke about the dead child. Life continued as usual.

*****

Besides playing cowboys, sheriff and bandits, we also acted as Tarzan, howling like him and using lianas to swing over the narrow river to the other side, as there were large trees on both sides of the river in the densely forested areas. One day, we decided to make sugarcane syrup. We rode our imaginary horses through the sugarcane plantations and through the canals that separated the sugarcane beds. We headed for the derrick which was located outside the weighing scale station. I was quite aware of its location because occasionally, I would accompany Ajah when he took his loads of sugarcane to the weigh scales. After tying our imaginary horses to the tall mature sugarcane plants, so that no passerby could see them, we went to the derrick. No one was around. We used the gears in the motor to grind the sugarcane that we had stolen from the surrounding fields.

Two boys brought the stolen sugarcane and gave them to me. I broke them into smaller pieces which I pushed slowly between the teeth of the gears of the pulley system. Two other boys pushed the wooden lever bar clockwise to get the gears moving. When the lever was pushed around, the cables in the pulley system moved upwards. Attached to the end of the hoisting cable was a large metal hook which was used to hoist loads of sugarcanes into train carriages. We decided to accomplish two tasks with our energetic efforts. We used the turning gears to grind the sugarcane for its juice, and as the hook moved up, one of us sat around the top of the hook and acted as a lookout for anyone coming. When the hook was about twenty feet into the air, we stopped the clockwise motion and reversed it so that the hook could come down. As the cable was lowered to almost most ground level, another boy would climb on the hook to take a ride to the top. This action was repeated until all our tins were filled with freshly squeezed sugarcane juice, and most of the boys had acted as lookouts. We had successfully done this activity several times before. However, on that particular evening, as one of the boys was at the highest point on the derrick, he began to yell, "Get me down guys, the overseer is speeding very fast in his Land Rover coming in our direction."

We instantly stopped the forward motion and reversed the direction of the pushing so that we could get Sudeen down to the ground before the overseer could trap us. Unfortunately, when we heard the roaring engine of the Land Rover coming through the dirt traces between the fields, we all ran into the sugarcane plantations leaving Sudeen stranded about fifteen feet above the ground.

From our hiding places, we saw the overseer with his gun and a big German shepherd dog hurriedly alighting from his stopped green Land Rover. He shouted to Sudeen to hold on tightly, and patiently and slowly, pushed the lever bar to lower the hook. We watched quietly as he took Sudeen away. The dog never stopped barking. We were all confused and scared.

We were quite aware that if our parents ever heard about that poaching incident, we would be punished very severely, and possibly be grounded for a long period. We decided to keep quiet. We hoped that Sudeen would not be jailed. After drinking the juice, we vowed never to do that activity again.

We untied our imaginary horses and galloped to our homes retracing our tracks. I left my horse in the back yard corral. I briskly walked to my homestead and nervously remained on my bed. Soon after I could hear Sudeen's mother asking about him, because she had seen all of the other boys returning home.

At the same time, the police car arrived with Sudeen. He was not crying but was annoyed. He told his mother what had happened and mentioned the names of all of us who were involved. We all got belted by our fathers.

*****

The neighbours' older sons and daughters structured games for the children almost every evening for about one hour. We sang, danced and played village running games – lohar, rope skipping and top dancing. There were two older, pretty girls who took a special interest in me. Since these girls were much older, I addressed them as tanties, as a mark of respect. One in particular, Tanty Tina, hugged and kissed me almost every time she met me. She made me feel very special and loved. She always brought me sweetie (candy). She knew my weakness for sweetie.

One Sunday morning at about lunch time, after playing games with the children, Tanty Tina asked me to accompany her to her bedroom upstairs. Being wealthy, their house had five bed rooms, a living room, a family room, and a balcony and their kitchen and dining area were in a separate building. They had beautiful furniture and several trucks and cars. The bottom ground floor was used for family and friends discussions and conversations.

Tanty Tina's bedroom was in the front part of the house. She closed the door. She told me that she liked me very much. There were lots of sweetie on the table. She said, "All these sweets are for you, but before I give them to you, I have something very special and nice to show you first. Would you like to see it?"

I was very curious and nodded my head. She told me to close my eyes and do not open them until I was told to do so. I closed my eyes and waited for her to talk. After a short time, she told me to open them. When I opened my eyes, Tanty Tina did not have any clothes on. She was lying across the bed. She told me to come between her legs so that she could show me the nice thing. I did what she said. She sat up as I approached her. She held my head and told me to look at the nice thing that was between her opened legs. I did not know what she had hiding. What I saw looked like a black hairy spider. I thought that it was one of the small tarantulas that I had seen many times in the forest. It had a pink open mouth down the centre. Tanty Tina's Tarantula was not exactly like the one in the forest, as she pulled my head close to it. I was about to scream when she held her hand over my tiny mouth. She sternly told me not to scream and as she held me closer and said that she was not going to hurt me. She took my face and rubbed it several times in her Tarantula. It was very wet and felt sticky. It had a very stinky smell. My face started to burn as I pulled away and started to wipe my face with my shirt sleeves. I thought that the tarantula bit me and peed on my face.

At the same time, I could hear Tanty Tina's brothers calling her to come for lunch in the kitchen. She quickly put on her clothes and told me that I must not tell anyone about what happened. If I did then she would personally cut off my little pee pee and kill me when I was alone. After opening the door she told me to go and wash my face at the standpipe. I really believed that it was a tarantula or a special spider with a pink mouth. I dared not tell anyone about what she did to me and what threats she made. From that day onward, I tried to stay away from Tanty Tina but she continued to ask me to go upstairs with her, but I always ran away. I had become afraid of my once favourite tanty.

*****

Mama was pregnant again. I was too young to know whether my parents knew anything about birth control. According to Ajah, Papa and Mama loved to have babies. There were already four children in the family. Mama spent more time at her father's home than at our home in Chauhan Village. Unfortunately, Mama had to have a blood transfusion after the baby was delivered. She was sickly, and I had to rub her feet, back, legs and shoulders with warm coconut oil mixed with brandy. Mama was not able to do much physical activity. Much of the household chores like laundry, ironing and general house cleaning were done by hired helpers.

*****

Once again, the angel of death visited our home. My little baby brother, who was beginning to stand up and take a few steps, got very ill, and died. This was another horrible and traumatic experience for my family. Nana, Nanee, my aunts, uncles, cousins and friends and their parents came to pay their respects and express their sincerest condolences to our family. During the wake for the little baby, Papa and his friend played "all fours" (a card game), drank lots of coffee, and ate Crix biscuits with cheddar cheese. There was no sign of sadness during the wake.

The following morning, one of the village carpenters, Mr. Gazong, came to our home. He spoke to Papa who told him to construct a coffin for the baby boy. Gazong measured the baby and built the coffin. I stood around watching him build the box and cover it with cedar wood. He lined it with satin cloth and then stained it with mahogany vanish, a scent which still reminds me of my little baby brother.

The funeral took place on the evening of the same day that the coffin was built. There was neither a hearse nor any Hindu or Buddhist funerary. After placing the small coffin on his shoulders, Ajah, accompanied by a few friends and relatives, went to St. Aquinas cemetery.

*****

Mama was very disappointed to see so many of her babies die. She had nine pregnancies, endured extreme labour pains during each child's birth and had only three children alive. She vowed not to have any more children. Mama continued making her regular visits to her father's home and paying visits to all her friends and relatives in Palmetto Bay. I spent a lot of my life with my Nana and Nanee whenever Mama went to visit them. Papa did not visit very often. Papa stayed with Ajah at our home in Chauhan Village.

Nana had a very beautiful home. There were three bedrooms, a dining room, living and family rooms, a spacious kitchen and a large clothing shop in the very front of the building. He had a stable at the rear of the home for his horses and a garage for his buggy and cart. Also, there were many fruit trees and vegetable gardens on the property. Nana had a large piece of land which occupied an area between the sea and the Southern Main Road. The concrete walls that Nana had constructed to protect property were gradually eroded by the forces of the rushing waves. The mangrove trees lined not only the back of his property, but also all the properties that were along the waters of Palmetto Bay.

*****

During the time I spent with Nana and Nanee, I experienced a completely different way of life and standard of living. I mingled and interacted with different groups of people and met and stayed with several of Mama's adopted aunts, uncles, cousins and friends in Sum Sum Hill and Forest Park.

There the young boys and I used to go hiking in the hills next to the Forrest Park Estate. There was a large pond with lots of water lilies and fish. We used to catch fish with homemade fishing rods and earthworms as bait. No one ever interfered with us as we relaxed fishing. The only sounds we heard came from the spinning windmill which was on the lawn of one of the overseers of the estate. We bought our catch home and either the boys' mother or elder sister cooked them for dinner. Besides fishing, we went with nets to catch butterflies, and set traps to catch birds. The few times that I was there were very memorable and exciting.

*****

At other times, Nana would take me, on either his buggy or horsedrawn carts, to do business in the countryside. He was very proud to introduce me to his customers and friends. He enjoyed leaving the store and travelling the countryside. Fortunately, we were never ambushed or attacked. We always returned home unharmed with every penny we collected. But when we arrived back home, very exhausted and very hungry, Nanee and the maids always had warm food and hot drinks for us.

*****

Sometimes I had to attend the school at Palmetto Bay. This happened whenever Mama was staying away at Nana's home, because she was ill. From time to time, the headmaster would visit my class and would ask me to read.

My teacher, in my defense, would tell him that I had already read for the day. Nevertheless he would ask her to send me to his office so that I could read. One day, while I was in his office reading, he came and stood next to me. He held me closely and told me that I was a very nice smart boy. As he was talking, he slid one of his hands up my short pants and held on to my pee pee and started to squeeze it. Instinctively, I got scared and tried to pull away from him. I could not. He kept on squeezing my pee pee with his fingers and tried to kiss my face. I started to cry.

He released his hold on my pee pee and I said, "I am going to tell Mama and Nana what you did." He said nothing as I ran out of his office. I told Mama about the incident and her response was, "Don't you see the headmaster likes you very much. He was just playing with you."

*****

Most mornings Mama used to take us to the beach to bathe and to ride the incoming big waves. She believed that the sea water contained lots of good minerals for our skin. I did not like the salt water because it irritated my eyes and burnt my skin.

Sometime, Mama and Nana would take me to the jetty where all the fishermen sold their catches. They purchased either fresh fish or fresh shrimps. Because of my frequent visits to the seafood vendors and by constantly asking questions about their catches, I was able to identify most of the fish and seafood. Mama, and Nana were very proud of me when I told them the names of the seafood.

*****

Nana's family had great respect for breaking bread with family and close friends. My family, for the most part, sat together to have breakfast and dinners. Prayers were said before we were allowed to eat or drink. We loved to eat the hot and spicy food that Nana's maid cooked. Nana never ate left over food. When I asked why he did not eat left over food, he said that stale food was dead and decaying and was not good for the mind, body and spirit.

Nana was a very proud and successful businessman. He was always well dressed and groomed. The shoes that Nana wore were always polished and shining. He believed that the condition of a person's shoes spoke volumes about their character and personality. "Always wear clean shining shoes," he preached to me.

*****

Papa visited us daily when we were staying at Nana's home. He would bring us cakes and ice-cream. But he seldom stayed overnight because he did not want to leave Ajah alone at home; and also most of his friends resided in Chauhan Village. As soon as Mama felt healthy we returned to Chauhan Village. I really loved living there because with my friends I was able to do many exciting and interesting activities. There were more open spaces in the forest where we could play games and roam without any interference from our parents and their friend. I was back in adventure land in the forested areas with bananas, sugarcane, cocoa, citrus, coffee plantations and rice fields.

*****

Ajah usually got up very early every morning to go to work in any one of his many fields which were located a few miles from our home. He always walked to the fields regardless of the weather conditions. This daily walking to and from the fields kept him physically fit. I cannot recall ever seeing him ill.

Before Ajah left for work, since he was always the first person to get out of bed, he would make a pot of Hong Wing Coffee. Coffee was one of the staple drinks of village people. In fact, the village had a coffee aroma. For breakfast we ate home-made roti, talkarie made either with green eggplants, tomatoes, bodi, cabbage, potatoes, okras, or green mangoes. Allo (Irish potato) was also one of the staple foods for the village people who were predominantly East Indians.

Sometimes when I was off on school vacation, I would ask Ajah to take me to the sugarcane plantations. Although he had told me that I did not have to work in the fields but rather to take my studies seriously, I still wanted to be with him. I loved him and he always told me stories about life. What memorable experiences he left me.

We either walked to the fields or rode on carts drawn by bulls. For lunch, he prepared roti wraps with left-over cooked vegetables, or cheese or fried eggs. Raw garlic and kuchela were always added to the food in large quantities as flavouring condiments. Our lunch drink was water which was kept in boolies (calabash container). The lunch was wrapped in a clean dry cloth. We would sit in the field and eat our lunch in the shade of the sugarcane plants or below the carts. After lunch, whenever I felt hungry, I would go to the vegetable garden patches within the plantation and pick cucumbers, tomatoes, beans or any other edibles that were in season, and munch on them.

*****

When I was still a young boy, Ajah would frequently take me to the shops at Chauhan Junction. He bought me treats from the vendors who sold their home-cooked savouries in front of the shops and on the street corners. He bought bara, phoolarie, katchorie, and soft drinks like Solo, Wynola and Juicy. We would eat some of the savouries and we took the rest home to share with the family.

On one of those days Ajah took me to Massa's shop which was at the junction of three main roads. There, Massa told Ajah that I was growing up very quickly and maybe I could help him do simple chores in the shop on weekends for a little pocket change. Ajah was excited but could not give him an answer. Ajah told Massa that he would have to speak to my Papa for his permission.

Later that day, Ajah told Papa that Massa would like to teach me some shop-keeping skills on weekends. Papa said that it was a great idea and that he would take me to the shop at Massa's request. I reminded Papa constantly about the offer Massa made. After a few days Papa brought very encouraging and exciting news. He told me that Massa asked him to bring me on Friday evening after school to the shop. I had to bring clothing for the Friday night and possibly Saturday night. I was bursting with joy, excitement, and great expectations.

The following day, I told my friends at school that a Chinese business man invited me to spend the weekend with him working in his shop. They were happy, and wished they were given the same opportunity. One of my friends questioned the motives of Massa, who originally came from China. Massa's motives did not concern me. I wanted to learn anything different from what I already known.

The evening finally arrived and Massa warmly and laughingly welcomed me behind the shop's counter.

He said, "Mitra, I teach you all bout my bijness. You jus watch me, I teach you how to weigh and wrap goods. You see. Don't worry a ting." I listened to Massa attentively. I was in a new learning environment.

Massa took me to the back area of the shop and introduced me to a very beautiful young lady who had yellow hair, blue eyes and skin colour like a movie actress. Also, this young lady looked like one of my sister's toy dolls. She was shorter than Massa and very slim. He told me that she was from Venezuela and that her name was Carmalitta.

"Ola," she said.

I did not know what she had said nor did I know what to say.

She repeated the word and followed it with the word: "Hello."

"Hello," I replied.

She told me to say "Ola not hello."

From that day on I would greet Carmalitta with the word "Ola."

Carmalitta was Massa's girlfriend, according to my Papa. She was a very excellent house-keeper and a fantastic cook. She baked, stewed, broiled and curried chicken, pork, beef, fish, and other foods.

One day, Carmalitta welcomed me to her home with some Spanish snacks and orange juice, and told me that they would have dinner after the shop was closed. I told her "Thank you," for the snacks.

She said, "No say thank you, you say Gracias."

I attempted to repeat what she said by saying "grass yu ass."

She started to laugh loudly and said, "No. No grass you ass." She continued laughing and repeated, "You say slowly Gra-ci-as."

I said, "Gracias."

She was delighted. She said that she would teach me to speak her native language, Spanish. I said "Gracias."

She smiled and said, "You learn quickly."

Massa came into the kitchen and asked if I was ready to work. "Yes Massa," I said. He led me to one of the two pan scales. Massa showed me the different parts of the scale and described the function of each part; he also showed me how to use the calibrations on the scale to weigh small items ranging in weights from half an ounce to one pound or sixteen ounces. Then Massa took different pound weights and illustrated with various provisions how to weigh any item heavier than one pound and up to ten pounds. He also showed me how to use the scoops in the flour, sugar, and rice barrels to fill the brown paper bags. I was doing a fine job according to Massa. At dinner, he confirmed that I would be spending the night with them. After dinner he told me that he would need my help on the following morning. I was very intrigued by his statement.

After dinner, Carmalitta tucked me into bed. She hugged and kissed me and said "Buenas Noches."

I said something sounding like "Bwayna nochay."

She laughed and left the room. She repeated it as she was closing the door. I repeated it to her satisfaction.

I was always an early riser from bed. I cleaned up and was greeted by the sweet voice of Carmalitta saying, "Ola Mitra, Buenos Dias."

I responded with a smile, "Ola, Bonos de ass."

She smiled and said, "You will soon learn, my little sweetheart."

For breakfast I had corn flakes and hot cow's milk. This was followed by a cup of hot chocolate drink, toasted sliced bread with pineapple jam, small fried sausages and eggs.

After breakfast Massa told me that he would like me to weigh out a few goods. I was excited, and impatiently waited for his orders. He asked me to weigh and to parcel out sugar, flour and rice, and to stack them below the counter next to the barrel containing the commodity being weighed. I scooped the sugar, flour, and rice into brown paper bags. There were bags that could hold two pounds, five pounds or ten pounds of these commodities. I weighed and folded the bags of each commodity at the different weights he requested. Initially, these tasks were exciting and challenging but

but gradually it became very labour intensive, exhausting and time consuming. The following weekend, Massa showed me how to knit and fold brown paper sheets with my fingers to form parcels. I mastered this skill after wrapping numerous quarter and half pound packages of baking powder, cooking salt and soda powder.

*****

Massa had the most lucrative business in Chauhan Junction. He was the envy of the other businessmen in the neighbourhood. He had a great advantage over the other businesses because of the prime location of his shop on the Southern Main road. There were lots of parking spaces available in and around his place of business. Because of his convenient location, his business became the most popular "watering hole" for most of the alcohol consuming travellers between the main cities of Port of Spain and San Fernando.

One Sunday at lunchtime, I was at home with Papa, Mama, my two sisters, Ushi and Elyana. Ajah came home with tears running down his face, and yelled out loudly, "Dey kill Massa! Dey kill Massa! Dey kill him ded!"

Papa heard him yelling and ran quickly into the front yard of our home.

"What happened? Who kill Massa? Baph," Papa questioned loudly.

Ajah continued repeating his message with loud cries of lamentation. Our yard was quickly filled with inquisitive neighbours, who kept asking many questions about what happened. Ajah wiped his face with a damp towel which Mama provided and asked for hot coffee with rum. After having a few gulps of the rum and coffee he sat down on one of the benches and slowly related his very intriguing and puzzling story to the gathered neighbours and the roadside water-carriers. Ajah said that on that particular Sunday morning, he was awakened by a very strange dream. The dream was more like a nightmare. In the dream, a very powerful voice told him that many serious life-changing events were about to happen to him and to his family. He said that he could not understand the dream but he did not feel good about it and was afraid to say anything to anyone about the

the dream. The dream, he said, greatly affected him. He had his breakfast very early and sat down in the hammock for a much longer time than usual. He was very confused what his dream could be saying to him. Some little voice in his head told him to go to the shop and to ask Massa for the monthly rent which was overdue.

He left home very puzzled and slowly walked the short distance to Massa's shop at Chauhan Junction. As it was Sunday, the shop was closed for business. There was no one around except Ajah. He knocked on the galvanized gate several times. No one answered.

He called out, "Massa! Massa! Massa! Are you sleepin?"

There was still no answer. He knocked on the galvanized gate and called several times again. He became worried. Where did Massa go? he wondered.

The morning was unusually quiet. A very eerie, fearful and uncertain feeling crept over him. Since there was no response, he decided to return home thinking Massa probably went out to visit with his brother in nearby Kalcutta village. On his way home, his dream re-entered his mind. He was almost home when his gut feeling compelled him to return to the shop. He went back, repeated his knockings on the galvanised gate and continued shouting, "Massa! Massa! Massa!" There was still no answer. He scratched his head and thought. "Weh is Massa? How could me get inside the building without a key?"

Ajah decided to use the passage way that lead to the urinal at the rear of the shop's outer walls. The urinal was located at the back of a ten foot brick wall, which enclosed the living area and the rear of the business part of the building. Massa and Carmalitta ate their meals there, relaxed in the hammock, cooked their meals, showered and entertained their friends.

Ajah carefully climbed the wall with the help of a wooden ladder which was already leaning on it. He climbed to the top of the ladder from where he was able to see into the living area. Massa was lying on the concrete floor next to the hammock and in front of the doorway leading into the bedrooms. He was wearing a white vest which appeared to be covered with blood. His sliders were also covered in blood and his sapat (wooden shoes) were partly off his feet. Ajah looked and looked again, in utter despair, as he stood on the ladder, not knowing what to do next. After coming down the ladder very carefully he walked away from the back of the building and said nothing to anyone on his way home.

Papa took him with his car to the Benevolence Police Station.

The sergeant, two policemen and a detective came to the business place and cordoned off the building. They repeated the investigative steps that Ajah told them he had taken. One of the policemen climbed over the wall and opened the galvanized gate. Papa and Ajah were allowed to be at the scene of the crime, while specialized members of the forensic department did preliminary questioning, and collected all relevant data. Papa said the following statement was painted with white paint on the brick wall facing the living area. The painted message read, "KILLROY WAS HERE."

The police did not arrest anyone. No charges were laid against Ajah. Massa was shot by someone with a firearm loaded with a scattershot bullet. There were ten little pellet marks on the concrete wall immediately behind Massa's dead body. The murder of Massa remained one of the unsolved cases in Chauhan. Was Massa robbed? No one knows what really happened.

The motives of the killer or killers may have been robbery, because people knew Massa had a very successful and lucrative business. On Saturdays, Massa would have lots of cash in his home. Maybe the other business men in the vicinity wanted Massa gone. One of them might have hired an assassin. Who knows?

Ajah's dream had turned into a real nightmare. He did not collect the rent. Fortunately, Ajah owned the property outright. He had to find a new tenant. It was difficult for him. Papa was a taxi driver and had a taxi business, and showed no interest whatsoever in the rum shop or grocery. Ajah thought about many potential options as the building remained unoccupied for months.

*****

While Ajah considered his options, Mama was preparing for the arrival of another baby in a few weeks. She was very ill and was unable to do any household chores. Two village women were employed to do all household work and to take care of my sisters and me.

Mama's pregnancy was causing her much stress and anguish. I heard Mama shouting to Papa, "Why you give me belly again Roshan? I told you that Bhagwan (God) took away the last two babies. That was a message from God not to have any more children. The baby is kicking so damn much. The baby wants to kill me before it even born."

"You can't blame me, if you did not want to have more babies you could have stopped."

A few days after their blaming each other about the apparently unwanted pregnancy, Mama sighed and told Papa, "The baby is going to come out today. I am beginning to feel contractions. We should pack a bag with the things the doctor told us to bring to the hospital."

Papa calmly said "Aruna, the bag is packed and is already in the car. As soon as you think we should go to the hospital in Couva Village, just let me know."

It was night time on a Friday. Papa and Mama went to sleep in their room, my sisters went to their room and I went to sleep with Ajah in his bed.

Mama's screaming voice broke the silence of the early morning, "Roshan, we have to go right now to the hospital. The baby is coming out, I can feel it. Hurry up. Get the car."

"Ajah! Ajah!" I shouted as I shook him awake.

"O Buddha! Help us," Ajah exclaimed. He got up briskly and headed directly to the kitchen. He was quite aware of what was happening.

I got up, sat on the bed and waited quietly to see what would happen.

Mama continued to groan loudly with a mixture of loud painful cries and shouts of "O God! O God! Roshan, hospital time! Hospital quick!"

My sister, Ushi got up and joined me in Ajah's bed, slowly wiping away the sleep from her eyes. We quietly walked towards Mama's bedroom.

Papa was dressed to leave for the hospital holding Mama in his arms. As he was about to step into the living room, Mama, terrified, cried out, "Roshan! My water just broke."

Papa steupsed (sucked his teeth) and said, "Your water buss (burst) already? My Lord it is too late to go to the hospital."

Papa slowly and carefully put Mama down on the bedroom flooring. Papa left hurriedly and said, "Aruna, just relax, I am going for Mrs. Ramjee, the local mid-wife. Keep on breathing and relaxing. You children stay and look after your Mama. I will be back in a flash."

Mrs. Ramjee lived not too far away from our home. Papa must have been gone for just a few minutes but for my sisters and me it felt like a very long time. We just stood and looked at Mama's half naked body. She remained lying on the floor writhing in pain, with her legs wide opened with the soles of her feet on the floor. As I looked at Mama, groaning in pain on the floor, the bright light of the kerosene lamp revealed a very strange, but frightful scene to me and my sister, Ushi. Something was pushing its way out from Mama's belly between her legs.

Ushi started to scream. She ran to the front door and shouted loudly, "Papa! Papa! Hurry! Hurry! Mama belly buss, come Quick! Quick! Papa! Hurry! Mama belly buss. It bleedin plenty. Hurry Papa hurry. Mama deadin."

No sooner had Ushi finished her screaming, Mrs. Ramjee and Papa appeared at the doorway.

Mrs. Ramjee's first orders, "Roshan, get some hot water. Quick! Quick!"

Ajah had already prepared boiling water.

"Mitra, you hold the light so I can see clearly what I am doing," ordered Mrs. Ramjee.

I saw the baby's head almost out of Mama's belly. The baby's head was covered with black hairs. Mrs. Ramjee continued to tell Mama, "Push, push, continue to push hard Aruna, the baby is coming out nicely."

Papa was sitting on the floor beside Aruna, with the basin with hot water on the floor and a towel over his shoulder.

Mrs. Ramjee carefully welcomed the blood covered baby. She announced with a great smile, "Roshan, you have another son!"

Papa proudly said, "Yes, my prayers are answered. Aruna, did you hear what she said? We have another son!"

Mama quietly said, "Bhagwan, I hope that he is healthy and good looking".

Mrs. Ramjee slapped the baby boy on his buttocks. He cried out loudly. She cut the navel string, washed the blood and slimy fluids from the baby's body with the hot water. Some Dettol was added to the water to keep everything sterile. Papa took the baby in his arms, touched the baby's little head, tiny arms and legs and kissed his head. He had bright eyes and a nice face.

Mrs. Ramjee cleaned up Mama. Papa gave Mrs. Ramjee the baby to hold. He lifted up Mama from the flooring and carried her to her bed.

Papa kissed Mama and said, "Aruna, you have done it again. God bless you and the baby."

Papa called Ajah who was in the kitchen drinking coffee and rum to see his new grandson. He started to sing one of his happy Bihara songs. Before he entered Mama's bedroom, he asked, "Is Aruna cover up"?

"Baph come, come she have on clothes. Come and see for yourself your beautiful grandson."

Ajah kissed Mama and touched the baby's head. Ajah told Mrs. Ramjee that she was a very good midwife and thanked her. He gave her some money, and she said, "Thank you Choates." She left them in the bedroom.

While Ajah was in the bedroom, Papa had made Mama a cup of hot Ovaltine with a few teaspoons of Courvoisier cognac and honey. Mama told us to leave the room. She fell asleep.

The rest of us went into the kitchen and had breakfast, hot sadha roti, and pumpkin talkarie. Ajah had already made a pot of Hong Wing coffee. After breakfast, the news had seeped into the neighbours' homes.

Mrs. Ramjee was proudly and loudly shouting the good news to the neighbours as she went to her home. Expecting many well-wishers to drop by at any time, Ajah and Papa started to clean and tidy up the house, and the yard.

"Papa, what the baby's name?" I asked.

Papa replied that the Pundit (Hindu priest) would come in a few days to tell us what should be the best name for the baby. The Pundit will read the Patra (holy book), and by using the time of the birth, the day, and the month, when the baby was born to come up with the best name.

For the next few days, there were lots of friends, acquaintances and families visiting. They bought gifts, money, jewellery, and goodwill to Mama and the baby.

Finally, the Pundit arrived dressed in his kurta and dhoti. He wore his Nehru cap and an Indian designed sandal. He sat with Ajah, Papa, and

Mama with the baby in her arms and spoke with them about the selection of the baby's name. The pundit read the Patra several times, played with his whiskers, scratched his sideburns, closed his eyes and declared, "The baby's name will be SHARMA." He closed his book, said a short prayer and blessed everyone present.

Papa conservatively and respectfully gave him gifts of food, money and clothing. He thanked him for his good services, and took him to the Kutiya (Temple).

Mama smiled and turned to us and proudly said, "Children, you know something, your little brother got the name of my mother's father. Sharma! Sharma is back in my life. Is this boy a reincarnation of my maternal grandfather?"

We did not understand what she was saying to us. My sisters and I were very happy to have a little baby to play with. For a while, Mama was very weak, sickly and tired. Papa took Mama regularly to the doctor. Mama's feet, arms, hand and back were always hurting, and every morning and evening, I had to massage her with bay rum, limacol and puncheon rum.

Papa and Ajah had a talk about the need for daily care for Mama. They asked one of the employed women to look after Mama and the baby for a few more dollars. She prepared lunches and dinners and cleaned the house and took personal care of Mama. We were able to look after our own personal care. Elyana, our youngest sister, had to be monitored by Ushi and me.

Every morning, Papa made breakfast for Mama, my sisters and himself. Ajah, who left very early in the morning, made his own breakfast. We took the lunches, prepared by the village woman, to school. Sometimes Papa drove us to school in his taxi, especially when it was raining.

He drove his taxi sporadically during the day. But he spent his free time with Mama and the baby at home, serving them whatever they needed. He loved all of us.

After two months, Papa decided to take Mama and the baby to her father's home. Nana and Nanee promised to take care of the baby and Mama while they were staying with them. They also had other helpers who cooked and performed other domestic chores. Mama was more than happy to return to her father's home.

My sisters and I paid frequent visits to see Mama when she was at Palmetto Bay with her father. Whenever we visited Mama, Nana gave us anything that we asked for because he loved us very much. At Nana we did our homework and read stories to Mama and the baby from the books we had borrowed from our teachers. We were always willing to help do anything around the house. There were no other children living around Nana's home, so we spend the little free time we had helping in the store and meeting the customers and answering their questions as best as possible. Sometimes Nana would take us in his buggy to the railway station to see the train when it was arriving. He would talk to some of the people and would proudly introduce us to his friends and customers who were returning from work.

After visiting Mama, Papa would come for us in the night to take us back to our home in Chauhan Village. Whenever I was at Ajah's home and had free time, Ajah would frequently ask me to accompany him to his sugarcane plantations and vegetable fields. I was always very happy to be with him because he was always answering my questions and teaching me new things. Also, he took me to his many properties to collect the rental income. He showed me how to market and sell the vegetables, ground provisions, coconuts and dairy products that we had at our home. We used our home as a mini market for the neighbours.

*****

With the unexpected murder of Massa, Ajah needed to find some replacement income. The business was closed for more than two months according to Ajah with no income coming from that property. Fortunately, he did not have a mortgage on the property. However, Ajah never gave up hope of finding a new tenant. According to Papa, Ajah preached that people should always look upwards and onwards. Also they should not look back at their failures because with courage, positive intentions, genuine effort, strategic actions, commitment and concentrated mindfulness, success would finally result. Only be patient. He did not graduate from any business institution. However, in all his business ventures, he succeeded admirably with his common sense.

*****

After the police investigations, court proceeding and probating of Massa's will, Ajah was free to enter his business property at Chauhan Junction. He suffered great financial losses. When the police investigations were in progress, the building was looted many times by the villagers. Much physical damage was done to both windows, doors, and the building. Ajah was very disappointed in the performance of the police. He complained but to no avail.

Ajah realized that many of the people to whom he had been generous and to whom he had loaned money were gloating at his misfortune. Even the less fortunate people of the village remained very envious of his success. He knew that the property was strategically located and was an oasis for those who were frequent travellers on the main roads between Port-of-Spain and San Fernando. He gave away Massa's remaining furniture, cleared and refitted the business building so that he could rent it again. He advertised for a tenant who would be interested in renting his commercial property. After two months, no one showed any interest. Ajah had already lost rental income for over six months. On realizing that he could not rent his commercial property he decided to ask Papa to re-open the business.

He summoned Papa to an in-house meeting. I sat quietly listening to the business proposal Ajah presented to Papa.

Ajah said that he was caught between a rock and a hard place. Although he had advertised for tenants who would like to operate a liquor business, a grocery business, or any other business in the Chauhan Junction property, no one had shown any interest. He did not know whether the monthly rent was too steep, or whether the murder of Massa had frightened any interested party.

Papa asked, "What do you want to do with the property Baph? Are you going to sell it and buy another property? Baph, what are your plans?"

Ajah told Papa that he would like him (Papa) to re-open the rum shop and grocery store, and that he would provide all the initial capital to stock and equip the business, and that he would not have to repay the initial capital investment. Ajah emphasized that Massa's shop was the busiest in the Chauhan district, and since he was making lots of money, then Papa should not have any problems being more successful than Massa.

Papa countered, "If Massa made good money, how come he owed you the last month's rent when he was murdered!"

Ajah responded by saying Massa owed him rent because his Venezuelan girlfriend stole his money and went back to her country. During the previous six years Massa always paid his rent on time.

Papa looked at Ajah and said that he appreciated being given the first opportunity to re-open the business, but was afraid that he would be shot like Massa. He pointed out that most of the people in the village were looking at them with large green eyes, and that the person or persons who shot Massa did not enter the inner part of the business. Both gates were closed and all the cash Massa had in the shop was not stolen. Papa believed that Massa was killed by a hired gunman. He enjoyed driving his taxi and collecting the rental fees from the other drivers. He did not have his own home as yet, but as soon as Aruna would get better, he would start looking either to purchase or build a beautiful home in the village.

Ajah was not happy with Papa's answers. He got up walked into the kitchen and got some hot coffee. He added some rum to the coffee. He re-entered the living room. Papa was about to leave the room when Ajah calmly said, "Roshan, yu refuse my golden offer. Dis offer will take yu away from the daily deathtrap of the highways. Well, I have no choice but to make the same offer to my youngest daughta, Omeera and her husband, Shiv."

Papa said, "I am sorry that I can't accept your great offer, Baph. Good luck to whoever wants to take it. I have to make some money. See you both later."

*****

After a few days, Ajah asked Papa to take him to Kakandy Road where his youngest daughter, Aunty Omeera lived with her husband in a two bedroom brick house. Ajah asked me to accompany them. Omeera was married to one of the brothers of the Seebarran clan, who included six brothers and three sisters. They all lived side by side along the stream that flowed parallel to Kakandy Road in front of their homes. All the brothers and sisters lived like one big happy family. They were mainly rice farmers, fishermen and hunters. Their homes were a few miles away from the Caroni swamp, the Wyma River, the Caroni Flamingo Birds Sanctuary and the Gulf Of Paria. Each family had their own guns, fishing equipment, boats, dairy cows and working bulls. They sold their fish and cascadura as well as all their milled rice, and their ground provisions in the local market in Charlieville. They were not wealthy but enjoyed a very adventurous, and rustic life. My Aunty Omeera was a seamstress and an excellent cook. Her sewing skills and culinary talents brought her some extra money from her clients in the village.

We arrived at Aunty Omeera's home late in the afternoon. On seeing her brother's car in the yard, she came running out of the house, very happy to see her father, brother and nephew. She hugged and kissed all of us. She led us directly to the kitchen which was in a separate building behind the main house. As soon as we got in the kitchen she offered us food and drinks. Papa asked for a beer, Ajah had some rum, my aunt had a Solo soft drink and I drank orange juice. She laughed, talked, asked about her bhowgie (brother's wife), the baby, Ushi and Elyana. When we arrived, Aunty Omeera was about to complete the sewing of a wedding dress for one of her clients. About half an hour later, Aunty Omeera popped these questions, "Baph, Dada (big brother), why this sudden visit? Everybody you said were all right. What is happening?"

Papa said, "Baph wants to talk to you and Shiv about some important business."

Aunty's countenance paled and she became very quiet.

"Way is Shiv?" Ajah inquired.

"He gone to play all fours [a card game] with his brothers in a house next to the Kutiya [a Hindu temple] on the other side of the railway tracks," answered Aunty Omeera.

Papa said that he would go and look for him. Ajah and I stayed with Aunty Omeera.

Papa returned with Uncle Shiv about half an hour later. Uncle Shiv was drunk and was smelling of alcohol.

"What de hell is going on? What do yu want from we?" Uncle Shiv shouted.

Ajah looked at his daughter and Shiv, and in a very calm but friendly tone told them, "I have a bijness offer for two ah yu."

Uncle Shiv immediately abandoned his drunken stupor. "Bijness deal! What kind of bijness yu talkin bout?"

Ajah looked at his daughter and son-in-law and said that he wanted both of them to come to the shop at Chauhan Junction tomorrow morning. But Uncle Shiv must be sober before they could talk business. Uncle Shiv and Aunty Omeera had no idea of the nature of Ajah's deal. They looked very confused and dumbfounded and Uncle Shiv, in his drunken stupor, said that they were not available the next day but they could in two weeks.

Papa, Ajah and I left Aunty Omeera's home in Papa's car and headed for our home.

*****

Two weeks later, Uncle Shiv and Aunty Omeera came very early to our home instead of the shop in the junction. They were clean and casually dressed. Uncle Shiv was sober but very apprehensive. My aunt hugged and kissed me. Ajah invited them to breakfast. They went into the kitchen and got what they wanted to eat. Papa came out of the bedroom and greeted them. He had a quick bite and left to drive his taxi. After they had their breakfast, Uncle Shiv wanted to discuss the business proposal.

Ajah said, "Shiv, we do not talk about serious bijness at my home. We have to go to de shop and when we get dere, I go show yu de entire rum shop and the grocery. Then we go talk about money and serious bijness. Lay we go. I have many other important tings to do today."

We went to the Chauhan Junction property. I was afraid to enter the gate when Ajah opened it. I asked Ajah to show me where Massa's body was found but he ignored my request. We sat on wooden benches around a small table. No refreshments were offered. Ajah kept the meeting very businesslike.

Aunty Omeera asked, "Where is Dada (big brother)?"

Ajah responded, "He is busy making money with his taxi business. He is not interested in selling in a shop."

No sooner had Ajah replied to Aunty Omeera's question, than Papa arrived and joined the meeting.

Ajah addressed Uncle Shiv and Aunty Omeera in a very serious tone, "I wana make yu an offer today. I want to give yu a chance to own and run a rum shop and grocery bijness."

My aunt interrupted immediately, "Baph, we don't have any money to open any kind of business. The little money we get from sewing and selling a few fish, bird meat, rice and provision is adequate to buy groceries, Ely cartridges for hunting, and seines for fishing. Whenever we have some money left, we use it to go to the movies and to travel around Cunupia, Perseverance and Warren to visit relatives, attend prayers, weddings, and funerals."

Ajah was an active listener. According to Papa, Ajah asked them some probing questions dealing with their life's intention, commitment to success and quest for a better quality of life and standard of living.

Ajah said, "Listen Beti, I have a good plan for both ah yu. Listen, I will give yu de money to stock the shop. Both of yu could buy and sell alcohol and groceries. As you make a profit, yu can keep it for yuself for de first three months. After dat, yu will pay me a monthly rent. Consider this money as a father's gift to he small daughta and she husban. Yu can rent out de house yu have in Kakandy Road and keep de rent. Sell all de animals, and hire people to seed, plant and harvest yur small rice business. Come into dis building as soon as possible. Bring all you things. Start making some good money, Shiv."

Uncle Shiv commented, "There got to be some trickery here. This offer is too good to believe. Why are you not asking Roshan to re-open the rum shop and the grocery shop? He is your own son, your own flesh and blood."

"Shiv, do yu want it or don't yu? I go give yu two weeks to make up yur mind. Go back to yur brothers, sisters, friends and family and tell them what I tell yu. Yu hear what dem have to say."

I sat, observed and remained quiet. I guessed that Ajah needed me as a witness to the offer, in the event, that later my uncle and aunt should deny that they were ever given an opportunity to change their way of living and careers.

Two weeks later, they still had not communicated with Ajah. He was worried sick. He asked a few of the men in the local council whether they had any family or friends who would be interested in renting his business property. He got no positive response.

*****

Surprisingly, one of Uncle Shiv's brothers and his wife came to our home in Chauhan Village in search of Ajah. I told them that he had gone to the bank and the lawyer's office.

"We will wait for him at the roadside," the woman said.

Ajah returned home after doing his financial and legal business. The couple returned to our home. Ajah was very puzzled to see these people. He did not recognize them. They were strangers as far as he was concerned. The man, whose name was Sahadeo, told Ajah that he heard that he was looking for someone to re-open the rum shop and grocery business at the Chauhan Junction property.

Ajah replied, "Who tell yu so?"

"One of my brothers told me that you desperately wanted to re-open the business. Also, you would stock the business and would collect monthly rent only after the business is in operation for three months," replied Sahadeo.

"What yu sayin, Sahadeo is true, but dat is only for my daughta and her husban. Anybody else will have to buy their own goods, sign a legal rental contract, and pay monthly rent, with two months rental fee up front as security before dey could do any bijness in my property."

Sahadeo became restless and started to speak loudly at Ajah. At the same time Papa, and his best friend, Uncle Deo from next door, and other neighbours heard the raucous behaviour of Sahadeo and came to the rescue of Ajah. The Sahadeos quickly assessed the situation. The couple, realising that they were outnumbered, quickly vacated our property.

Papa, on seeing the harassment and unnecessary stress his father was experiencing to get the business place rented and get back into full operation, decided to help. He asked his best friend Uncle Deo whether he would like to go into business with him. He immediately declined. He was a barber and he enjoyed that career. And it was a very comfortable way of making a livelihood for his family.

The following morning, Papa hugged Ajah and softly said, "Baph, we are going to Kakandy Road to talk to Omeera and Shiv. We will have to let them know that one of his brothers has seen the pot of gold at the end of the business rainbow and is trying to get the business property for himself. We would not mention the brother's name to them. This would surely make them become aware of the great value one of his brothers saw in the opportunity to have a business place; instead of having to search for food every day in different places."

Ajah told me to get dressed and go to school. I obeyed. He promised that he would tell me the whole story in the evening.

Ajah and Papa reported that when Uncle Shiv and Aunty Omeera heard what one of his brothers did, they decided to accept the offer without hesitation. They took Ajah's advice, rented their house, sold the animals, hired people to work the fields and opened the liquor and grocery business at Chauhan Junction.

*****

Once again, the junction became vibrant, busy and alive, and Ajah was very happy with the results of his negotiations. The business began to grow under the new ownership and management. It became very profitable for my uncle and my aunt. I helped them do the simple shop work that I had performed when Massa was the proprietor. But I also watched, listened and learned how to order for groceries from my uncle and his friends.

My Aunty Omeera treated me with great love and included me in most of her daily activities. We ate, prayed, and worked together. I now had a choice of living and attending school with my mother in Palmetto Bay or to remain in Chauhan Junction. I chose to stay with Uncle Shiv and Aunty Omeera in Chauhan Junction.

While living with my uncle and my aunt, I was exposed to a new exciting and interesting way of living. Uncle Shiv was a part-time fisherman, a part-time hunter, a part-time farmer and also a very skilled craftsman. He repaired his guns, fixed his fishing equipment, and sewed fishing seines. He and his die-hard friends met on Thursday afternoons, when the rumshop business was closed, to cast lead weights for the seines and clean their Winchester and Remington double barrel guns. They also sold and traded firearms. Littered around the house were cartridges for their guns, fish knives, parts for outboard motor engines, and many other tools and instruments which they used in their hunting, boating and fishing outings.

Whenever my uncle and his friends invited me on hunting, or fishing trips, I would become very excited to participate in these new learning experiences. As his medium size motorized boat coursed its way through the blackish water of the narrow channels of the lagoons and water ways of the Caroni swamp, I witnessed my uncle aiming and shooting flamingos, snowy egrets, plovers, doves and ducks. As he shot into the flock of flying birds, some fell from the sky and landed either in the murky waters of the swamp or the mangrove. His friends, who were in another boat, would release the dogs to fetch the wounded or dead birds.

The waterways and lagoons were endowed with many snappers, snooks and groupers. On many occasions snakes were visible on the branches of the mangrove.

*****

As the liquor and grocery business blossomed, more help was required during the weekend to serve the growing number of customers. My uncle brought one of his teenage nephews, Roop, to help him in the business. Roop owned a bicycle on which he took me to many new places, including movies, prayers and school. Frequently, he would take me along to his girl-friend who lived in the village.

After visiting her, he would buy me cake and ice cream, and would tell me that I should not tell his uncle or aunt about his girl-friend. I promised to keep quiet and I did.

One week day, early in the morning, I was cleaning the ice box in the presence of my Aunty Omeera when Uncle Kedar entered the shop and shouted, "I want to see Roop. Where is the fucker? The mudass fuck me lil datta, Sumita! Now the gyal have belly. Where is the bitch? I go kick he ass."

Aunty Omeera was confused. "What the hell you talkin bout? Roop don't have time to do that to your Sumita. You daughter must be carrying baby for somebody else."

Kedar became silent.

Roop's aunt, in his defence, got annoyed with Uncle Kedar, "How the hell can you say such nasty thing about my nephew, Roop? He is a good, decent boy. Everybody say that your daughter, Sumita, is always having all kinda man in de house when you and Dulcie go to the sugarcane plantation. So you be very careful how you woking your mouth about Roop. You giving the boy a bad name without any evidence."

Uncle Kedar, in a softer tone than before, continued, "Omeera Bahen [sister], I goin home and I go bring back Sumita right here. She go give yu the whole story."

"Yu do that. When Shiv come back from his early morning fishing trip with Roop, we go talk."

Nothing happened for a couple of days. I asked Aunty Omeera, what was Uncle Kedar complaining about. She told me that I would not understand. It was big people talk and it was not for the ears of children. I did not ask any further questions.

Uncle Shiv, Aunty Omeera and Roop had a private talk about the allegations made by Uncle Kedar. They told me to go outside and play so that I could not listen to their big people talk.

On the following Sunday, Uncle Kedar, Tanty Dulcie, and Sumita came to talk with Aunty Omeera, Uncle Shiv and Roop. I was told to go to my room. They did not send me outside to play because it was raining. They all sat down in the open eating area. They were offered drinks and savories. I peeped through the crease in the corners of the green locked door in my room. I could see Sumita's tear-stained face and the angry faces of Uncle Kedar and Tanty Dulcie. Roop kept quiet until Uncle Shiv screamed at him. "What have yu got to say Roop? Did yu give this child belly?"

Roop remained silent as a lamb, his face pale with shame. Roop started crying.

Sumita joined him with tears running down her cheeks and said, "Roop, I love you, I love you only. This belly that I carryin is yours. You are the only one who brush me. We brush so many times it has to be yours. I never brush with nobody else."

Uncle Kedar, Tanty Dulcie, Uncle Shiv, and Aunty Omeera remained quiet, as Sumita and Roop wrapped themselves in each other's arms. Sumita's parents wanted an immediate marriage.

Uncle Kedar said to Uncle Shiv, "I think that Sumita and Roop should live together here starting from today. They are lovers like the Indian movie stars. We don't have to have a big wedding. Just call pundit Ramdial, pay him some money and let him fix them up right away!"

Uncle Shiv scratched his head, looked at Aunty Omeera, "What yu think gyal. Yu think this is a good idea?"

Aunty Omeera shouted angrily, "Roop and Sumita ain't goin to live here at all. Dey go have to go to Roop fadder house in Felicity. Roop fadder and dem eh know bout dis baccanal. We can't make marriage arrangements. We go have to get Roop's family and Sumita's family together very quick before this child barn."

Kedar retorted, "Shiv, Roop is living in your house, you have to look after Sumita. I ain't goin to talk to people I do not know."

Uncle Shiv became very annoyed at Uncle Kedar's suggestion and shouted, "Look man, I go arrange a big get-together here next Sunday with Roop parents and yu family. Yu will decide what to do. Roop is goin back to Felicity right now. Yu are not leavin Sumita here."

With these closing words, the meeting ended. Two months later, Sumita and Roop got married in the temple in Charlieville. I attended the wedding with my uncle and my aunt. I never saw Roop again.

*****

In addition to the hunting, fishing, rice planting and reaping experiences, I learned a lot about Bollywood movies, Indian movie actors, playback singers, and beautiful, lilting, romantic and melodious Indian music, songs and dances. I loved the Indian music, the rhythmic dances and the melodious songs. They have remained etched in my heart, my brain and my memory. I become emotionally happy as soon as songs from Bollywood movies such as Barsaat, Dulari, Mela and Babul are in the air. The following classics would forever be ingrained in my musical soul: "ooo mujhe kissi she pyaar hogaya and Suhani Raat dhal chuki." Aunty Omeera had a melodious voice and I was given full charge of the music library by my aunt.

I organized all the records according to the movies and knew exactly where each 78 r.p.m record was located. I was fully in charge of all the records. And I played them on the gramophone at the request of my aunt or any of her visiting friends. She sang along with the artists with her sweet lilting melodious voice while she was sewing or doing her household chores. I cleaned the records regularly and made sure that there was a large supply of needles for the HMV [His Masters Voice] gramophone. I had to crank up the record player and carefully place the record so that it would not be scratched. A scratched record did not give a good sound reproduction. Living with Aunty Omeera and Uncle Shiv, allowed me to be exposed to the rich East Indian songs, music, and language.

*****

My life went through a sudden turn when Papa told me that Mama was going to have another baby very soon. I did not know anything about how babies were conceived or why they die so young. I, as well as my sisters, knew that when Mama was pregnant with the baby she had to return to the Chauhan Village home. Mama was very sick, and was not too mobile. She had to be hospitalized. In her absence, my elder cousin, Chan, volunteered to take care of us whenever Papa had to attend to Mama's medical affairs and Ajah had to supervise his employees in his various fields.

Mama gave birth to a baby girl. She had another blood transfusion. Apparently she had a history of hemorrhaging after she has given birth. She was in a critical life-threatening situation after this last baby's birth.

Late one Sunday evening, Papa told us that we had to accompany him to the hospital to see Mama. It was already dark when we left for the hospital. On arrival at the hospital, he left us in the car in the parking lot and went inside to speak to the nurses. After a short time, Papa came back and told us to come with to the waiting room. A nurse in blue uniform told us that we were to see our Mama, one at a time. The rest of us had to wait our turn in the waiting room as she took Ushi to see Mama. Papa was crying as he hugged me and Elyana. He looked very worried and sad.

"Papa, what is wrong with Mama? Is she really sick?"

"Yes, Mitra, the doctors are trying their best to do what they can to make her better," replied Papa.

Ushi came out with the nurse. She looked normal and showed no concern. Elyana went in next with the nurse. She came out eating a cookie. The center of the cookie was filled with my favourite strawberry jam. Elyana had an extra cookie in her little hand, and she gave it to Ushi and said, "Mama send you this cookie."

I was taken in next. I entered the room that had a drawn white curtain. The nurse pulled open the curtain. Mama was sitting on the bed. She was wearing a pink nightgown with pretty little flowers patterned around the top of her nightgown. She looked yellow and her cheeks were stained with chocolate. Her hair was uncombed and her gold tooth was stained with food. She held me close to her, hugged and kissed me as she sniffled and softly sobbed with tears running down her cheeks, and said, "Mitra, I am going home today. I give you all my blessings and love. Don't you stop going to school. You are a good child. God will take care of you. Go son, be good, and tell Papa I want to see him again."

"OK Mama."

She hugged and kissed me again. I looked at her, not aware that it would be the last time that I would be seeing her alive. Then I saw the last jam filled cookie which was on the saucer next to her on the bed. I looked at it with longing eyes.

As I turned to leave, she said, "Mitra, come and have my last cookie."

She gave me the cookie with strawberry jam in its center. The saucer was left empty in her hand.

"Thank you Mama," were the last words I said to her.

I slowly walked out of the room. The nurse held my hand and took me to Papa who was talking to Ushi and Elyana outside in the full bright moonlight. I slowly chewed the last jam-filled cookie that Mama gave me as I walked to rejoin my sisters and Papa.

Papa left us with a nurse and went inside the building to see Mama for the last time that night. The nurse asked us about our school and our friends. She did not say anything about Mama's condition.

Papa came back after a long time. At least, it felt like a long time. I was tired and my sisters were asking, "When we goin home?"

Papa said that it was too late for ice cream and cakes so he drove directly to our home in Chauhan Village. On our arrival Ajah had hot tea and hot milk with Ovaltine for us. We had dinner and were told to go to bed. Ajah and Papa remained talking quietly in the living room.

I fell asleep quickly. Then I felt someone shaking me to become awake and saying, "Get up Mitra, yu Mama dead."

It was Ajah. I could not understand what he meant. She was alive when we left the hospital. Still not quite awake, I fell back asleep without answering.

The next morning I got up, completely oblivious to the news that Ajah gave me. I went outside in my pajamas to do my regular morning ablutions before facing the world. I was very surprised to see the neighbours and family members cleaning up the yard. I did not see either Papa or Ajah. My sisters were still asleep.

I asked my Uncle Shiv, who was carrying chairs with my Aunty Omeera, "What is happening?"

Uncle Shiv calmly replied, "Yu mudder dead last night."

"Who say so, Uncle Shiv"?

Uncle Shiv told me that last night a policeman brought a telegram which informed Papa that Mama died at 11:30 p.m.

Later that morning, after the neighborhood learned of her death, our yard became a very busy place with neighbours, families and friends of our family.

Papa made very quick arrangements with Monsiggy, the local undertaker, to have her buried as soon as possible. In the afternoon, the hearse brought Mama's body home. She was dressed in her best outfit that Aunty Omera had chosen from Mama's collection of dresses. None of her beautiful jewels was placed on her. I watched Mama's body as it lay peacefully in the small grey casket. She looked asleep. I was neither sad nor happy. There were many people surrounding her casket.

The baby girl that Mama shed her last blood for was only three days old and was brought home on the day Mama's body arrived. Before the Hindu Pundit gave Mama the last ceremonial rites, the three day old baby was passed around, and across the casket so that the spirit of Mama would not haunt her according to some superstitious belief of the old people. Those who were Hindus sang Bhagans, recited verses from the Bhagavad Gita, the Ramayana and other sacred writings. All those who were present paid their last respects. Some followed the hearse by foot to the St. Aquinas village cemetery. The Hindu priest and the immediate family were in front of the hearse. One person was beating the brass gong with a traditional two bang rhythm as the funeral procession made its way through the main roads in Chauhan village and Benevolence. It was a Sunday so the streets were relatively quiet and all businesses were closed. Mama's body was buried next to her babies in the family plot in St. Aquinas cemetery.

We returned home with many of the family friends and extended families. The Pundit had people prepare Neem leaves drink for everyone. The Neem drink was supposed to calm your nerves and reduce stress. Some more religious singing and prayers were recited and before dusk, everyone left for their homes. Life went on as if nothing serious or significant had occurred.

*****

The next day, Papa decided to get rid of all of Mama's belongings except for her expensive jewels. He brought out five canisters of clothing, all her cosmetics, shoes, purses, belts, and any artifacts that my Mama treasured. He placed them on the lawn in front of our home. The public was invited to take whatever they wanted. I stood with my two sisters and watched the human vultures of the neighbourhood as they rifled through all of Mama's personal belongings. They took everything. All they left was their shoe prints and footprints on the grass.

I stood at the open window with Ushi and Elyana looking at the flower garden with its blooming marigolds, zinnias, bachelor-buttons and petunias. The tomatoes and eggplants which were planted in between the flower beds added a special variegated look to the garden. Some of the tomatoes and eggplants were ready for harvesting. The flowers with their various colours, surrounded the vegetables forming a natural bouquet. The front yard looked fresh, clean and vibrant after last night's torrential showers.

Elyana whispered, "Mitra, I hungry."

I clearly recalled what Papa said to me in the morning before he left to drive his taxi: "Mitra I want all of you to stay home today as a day of respect for your mother. You are in charge whenever I am gone to work and your Ajah is not at home. You know how to cook and whenever any one of your sisters is hungry, you look after them."

I nodded in agreement.

Papa continued, "Do not knock about on the main road and the back roads. If the school police see you, he will lock up all of you."

After talking to us Papa left to drive his taxi.

I was given the responsibilities to feed my sisters and to protect them from the liver harvesters. I went into the kitchen followed by Ushi and Elyana who claimed that they were very hungry. I went into the garden, picked some ripened tomatoes, boiled them and made tomato choka laced with onion, garlic and shadow beni, and chowkayed it with green mustard seeds. There were two sada rotis left from the morning breakfast. The roti remained very soft in the cloth bag. I got a ripened zaboca, which was hidden in the rice box. We ate sadha roti, tomato choka, and zaboca with hot, milky tea.

For the next few weeks, Papa, Ajah and I looked after cooking. Some of the neighbours would bring some of their leftover food for us. We were very thankful and happy to experience the cooking of our neighbours. A few of my Creole friends would either come to my home or wait for me on the road to accompany them to school. There was Alwyn who took me many times to the presbytery where his mother worked and I would have breakfast with his mom and him. The breakfast was quite different from what I was accustomed. I loved the toasted bread, marmalade, bacon, ham, cheese and hot chocolate. The breakfast was similar to those served by the late Massa's mistress, Carmalitta. I did not tell Papa or my sisters about the breakfast that I shared with Alwyn. I knew that they would not approve of me eating the bacon and ham.

*****

Mama's death had affected the lives of many people.

A few weeks after Mama's funeral, Papa told me that he was unable to look after all of us by himself. He needed people to adopt a few of us. I did not understand clearly what Papa meant.

"What do you mean, Papa?"

He went on to explain his situation by telling me that he has decided to give our little brother, Sharma, to Aunty Omeera. She has no children and is most willing and very happy to take baby Sharma as her own. He said that I could always see him and play with him, because he would be living in the shop in the junction, fourteen houses away. My father's best friend Deo, who lived next door, told Papa that his wife, Tanty Seloni, would take the little baby girl, Seema, and would adopt her as her own. Tanty Seloni had lost her first baby and the doctor had told her she would not be able to have babies again because she had some type of disease.

"What are you going to do with Ushi, Elyana and I?" I asked Papa.

"You children will live with Ajah and me. We will take care of you," he said.

I was very happy. We would see our little brother whenever we visited our Aunty Omeera and we would see our little baby sister, Seema, next door at Tanty Seloni's home.

I noticed that Tanty Seloni was either visiting us very frequently with food and drinks, or inviting us to come over next door to her home. She treated us as her own children. She fed us and looked after our well-being. This routine continued for some time. I had no idea what was going on with Uncle Deo, Tanty Seloni and Papa.

I vividly recalled that it was one afternoon, after school, when we were at Tanty Seloni's having a very early dinner and Papa arrived. He joined Tanty Seloni and us at the dinner table. Uncle Deo was at his barber shop. After dinner, Papa and Tanty Seloni spoke privately.

He happily announced, "Children, will you like to go for a car ride?"

"Yes, Papa!" we replied.

"Well, go home and quickly change into your going out clothes, and when you are ready, meet me in the car," Papa ordered. We left Papa with Tanty Seloni and baby Seema and ran home and got dressed. Papa was in the car waiting for us. I was sitting in the front seat and Ushi and Elyana were in the backseats. He drove the car along the southern main road pass Lendor village, Cunupia, and was approaching the sugarcane plantations outside Warren, when he said, "Do you know where I am taking you?"

"No Papa," we replied.

"I am taking you to a place where there are lots of children like you. Children play games all the time, listen to nice music and get lots of nice things to eat. Would you like to go there?"

"Yes! Yes!" We replied.

"Well, we will be there just now," he said.

I remembered looking at the Northern Range on the road going in the direction where Aunty Runala and our cousins lived. Papa did not go in that road but turned towards the airport after crossing the Caroni river bridge. We were passing through familiar territory.

Finally, he drove on a side street where there were many cars. He stopped the car and parked it. We all came out and walked towards a large building. The building was enclosed with a high see-through wire fence. Behind the fence, I could see many children playing ball games, tennis, football, some were on swings and others were skipping rope. It was like my school yard with children of all colours. I was very eager to join those children who appeared happy and having lots of fun.

"Papa, can we play with them?" I asked.

"Not yet, we have to check at the office. We have to give our names and other things," replied Papa.

"OK, Papa."

Papa told us to sit on the long bench in the front foyer and wait. He left and went to one of the ladies at the counter. They had a conversation with him while we sat quietly waiting like well-behaved children. We heard an orchestra playing this song:

Oh My Papa, to me he is so wonderful.
Oh, My Papa, to me he was so good
No one could be. So gentle and lovable
Oh, My Papa. He always understood.
Gone are the days when he could take me on his knee
And with a smile he'd change my tears to laughter.
Oh, My Papa, so funny, so adorable.
Always the clown so funny in his way

Oh, My Papa, to me he was so wonderful.
Deep in my heart, I miss him so today…

I could never ever forget that song. How ironical! Papa came back, looked unhappy and said, "The lady who is responsible for taking in new children will be here next Tuesday. We have to come back."

"Can we play today?" I inquired.

"No."

I was very disappointed. I asked Papa, "What is the name of the school?"

He replied, "Tacarigua Government School."

We walked back slowly to the car looking at the playing children. He kept hugging us and just before we got into the car, he asked, "Would you like ice cream and cakes from Coelhos bakery?"

"Yes! Yes! Yes! We love you Papa," we cheerfully responded.

He took us for ice cream, currents' roll and coconut filled pastries. I loved any cake with coconut. In fact, I love any food with coconut.

When we got home, it was very dark. Ajah was home and the 'Home Sweet Home' shaded lamps were all lit. We had hot Hong Wing coffee and freshly squeezed milk from one of the many cows. The milk was always boiled before it was served to us.

Ajah asked, "Whey yu went with de children, Roshan?"

Papa said, "I take them for a drive."

I piped up. "Ajah, we went to a place with lots of children playing games. They were having lots of fun. We are going back next week to play." Ajah looked puzzled but did not make any comment.

We drank coffee with milk and brown sugar. Papa did some reading with us and we went to sleep. We continued eating, drinking and, sometimes, sleeping at Tanty Seloni. Uncle Deo would be seen almost everywhere with Papa whenever they were not working. They were like shotgun partners as portrayed in stage coach scenes in Western movies.

On the appointed day, Papa took us back to the same building in Tacarigua. We sat on the bench and waited. Papa returned with discouraging news. "The lady cannot accept you. They do not have any space for any more children now."

Papa took us for icecream and cakes before we returned home. We never returned to Tacarigua Government School again.

Ajah asked, "Mitra, whey yu fadder take you this time?"

"Papa took us to the same Tacarigua play grounds, Ajah, but the boss lady did not want us to play," I sadly answered. Roshan, "Why yu taking the children to Tacarigua School? Dat is not a school. Dat is an orphanage. What de ass wrong with yu. Dey is my nathins (grandchildren). If yu kan't take care of dem, I go take care of dem meself. Yu leave dem at home and lay dem go to school. I go look after dem. Yu don give away Sharma and Seema. What kinda fadder you be?"

Papa was quiet. Ajah hugged us with tears running down his cheeks. From that unforgettable day, the relationship between Papa and Ajah became very strained.

We continued shuttling between Aunty Omeera's and Tanty Seloni's homes.

*****

It was less than four months after Mama's death when Tanty Seloni left Uncle Deo and went to her father's home in Kalcutta Settlement to live. She did not move in with Papa because we lived next door.

Uncle Deo became very enraged when Tanty Seloni told him that she was leaving him for Papa. Uncle Deo attacked Papa with a very sharp pooyah [a cutlass]. He chopped Papa on his hand when they started to fight. The neighbours heard the loud shouting and swearing and quickly intervened.

Papa and Uncle Deo stopped liming together and talking to each other. But he was still friendly to my sisters and me.

Papa told Uncle Shiv and Aunty Omeera about the problems that he had created by taking away Uncle Deo's wife and was not comfortable living next door to him. Papa told us that he needed a new place to live with his stolen wife. He rationalised that it would not be safe to live with Tanty Seloni next door to Uncle Deo. He might attack his former wife with the same pooyah and kill her.

Uncle Shiv, Ajah and Papa decided to build two bedrooms, at the back of the business place, at the junction, to temporarily accommodate Papa, his new wife and his children. We shared the kitchen with Aunty Omeera. Papa's children, although they had the same biological parents, were living under different parental guidance. Aunty Omeera and Uncle Shiv were the parents of my little brother, Sharma. Tanty Seloni considered Seema to be her own daughter. Papa had taken us to the orphanage which refused us. Ushi, Elyana and I were 'pseudo orphans' in Papa's new marriage arrangement.

*****

Later in life, when I felt comfortable to converse with Papa, he confessed to me the secrets of his affairs with Tanty Seloni.

"Mitra, my father married me to a woman I did not know, wanted or loved. I had no choice but to honour the wishes of my father. I was too young for her. She told me that she had to stay at her father's business as often as possible to prevent her stepbrother from sharing in her inheritance. Whenever she got pregnant, which was almost every year, she was always very ill. She was either in hospital or at her father's. Tanty Seloni and Uncle Deo were very good friends to all of us. They felt very sorry for me. I was in their home very frequently and Tanty Seloni became interested in me. She was younger than your mother, more loving, respectful and caring. Gradually we became secretly involved. Whenever Uncle Deo was away and your Mama was not around, and Ajah was in the plantation, and your sisters and you were at school, we used to have an affair. This went on for a year before your mother died, unknown to Uncle Deo and Mama."

I smiled with approval. I then interjected, "Papa, one night when you were not at home, I asked, Mama where is Papa?" Mama responded, "He is with the other woman."

I was too young to understand what she was saying.

I informed Papa that Mama believed in Obeah [voodoo]. Papa inquired, "How you know?"

"One night, when you were not home and Tanty Seloni was upstairs sleeping in her house, Mama woke me up and gave me a tharia [a brass plate container] on which were a blue candle, kala nemac [black salt], garlic, lavender, red sindoor, tumeric, black peppers and some other things. She told me to take it next door and to take everything out and hide them below Tanty Seloni's steps."

I was scared but I had to do it or else get a beating. I asked Mama what would the things I placed under Tanty Seloni's steps do to her.

Mama said, "It will kill the bitch."

"What you tell me is strange. I didn't know that she believed in that kind of hocus pocus superstition. Well, she is dead. Let us forget about her," retorted Papa.

"Papa, why did you take us to the Tacarigua orphanage?"

"Well boy that is another shameful story. I got myself in a lot of hot boiling water by only listening to other people. Don't tell your stepmother, Tanty Seloni, that I was talking to you about this, okay? If she hears what I telling you, I don't know what will happen to me and you."

I promised Papa to bury his secret talks and advice within my heart.

Papa said that when Mama died, it opened the door for Tanty Seloni to enter our house freely. She agreed to look after only Seema. Tanty Seloni was only twenty years old and he was thirty two when Mama died. She told me to give away Ushi, Elyana and you to any relatives or anybody who will take you. Sharma was already given away to Aunty Omeera and Uncle Shiv.

Papa went looking for new homes for us, in Palmetto Bay, Chauhan Village, Benevolence and St. Helena but no family was interested. When he told Tanty Seloni about all his futile attempts, she suggested, the Tacarigua Orphanage. She claimed that she was too young to take on the responsibility to look after four children. All his attempts to get me, Ushi and Elyana in the orphanage failed. The administration said that Ushi, Elyana and me were not diaper babies. They also claimed that he was a young, strong and an able man who could look after his own children. Ajah was not going to have any part of getting rid of my two sisters and me. I was not pleased with Papa's explanations.

*****

Living in the small rooms at the rear of the shop was very challenging for both Papa and Uncle Shiv. There was always bickering and derogatory remarks between them. Many times they were in fights and swearing matches.

One year later, Uncle Shiv and Aunty Omeera secretly built a new business place in another part of Chauhan on the land that Ajah gave to them.

Without informing Papa or Tanty Seloni, Uncle Shiv and Aunty Omeera left for their newly constructed business property. While we were away spending holidays at Tanty Seloni's parents in Kalcutta Village they took everything movable from the building and left for their new place.

Papa and his new family were left living in the two small rooms. The shop was closed and all the other rooms in the main building were empty.

Papa was highly stressed. His blood pressure rose so high that a blood vessel burst in his head. He bled for hours and was placed in intensive care in the Port Of Spain General Hospital. Fortunately, the doctors and nurses took excellent care of him and he returned home after a week.

*****

Ajah, on realizing the plight of his son, decided to take action. He called the family together and made the following suggestions. After reassuring Papa that he would be strong, healthy and energetic to return to normal life, he told him that he should stop driving taxi, and continue to collect the income from the other taxis. However, somebody had to work and bring in new money. Before he could finish, Tanty Seloni interjected,

"Baph, I could open the rum shop for now and if it start doing good, then I could fully open up the grocery section."

Ajah replied, "Dulahin, you no have any bijness sense, how yu go do it?"

She responded, "Give me a chance. I can learn. You give me the money and me and Mitra could do it. He wok with Massa and Shiv in their rum and grocery shops. He can help plenty. He smart. He and I can do it. Just give we the money."

Ajah listened carefully but remained quiet for a while looking at Papa. Maybe, he was waiting to hear what Papa would say.

After the silence, Papa said, "Baph, if Dulahin want to start the business, I would help as much as I can. Give her and Mitra the money they need and let us see what will happen."

With those encouraging words from Papa, Ajah said, "Mitra yu and I go go to the bank next week and get the money. How much yu go want?"

I said, "Ajah, thank you. I and Tanty Seloni will do our best to make the rum shop business successful. After making a list of all the things that we would need to reopen the business, and do some calculations, then I would tell you Ajah."

Ajah said, "OK."

After the meeting we had lunch and we sat down and calculated how much money we would need to start the business.

Tanty Seloni asked me to make a list of the alcoholic and non-alcoholic beverages that Uncle Shiv sold in his rum shop. She told me to make a rough calculation and add some extra money. My calculations included not only the alcoholic and non-alcoholic beverages, but also all the utensils, glassware and sundries which would be needed for the business.

Since we were all novices in the operations of a rum shop, Papa and I went to one of his friends, Barly, who managed a Chinese rumshop and grocery business to gain some experienced advice on how to manage the rumshop business. We told him about our interest to open the rumshop and that we needed some guidance and advice.

Barly looked at our shopping list carefully, smiled and gleefully said, "Good luck, Roshan. This rum shop business is not easy man. It is a lot of work. You have to be on your foot all day, from early in the morning to late in the nite, even on Sundays and holidays."

Papa replied, "Does it make money, Barly?"

"Yes, plenty money," replied Barly.

"Can you help us out? Can you tell us where to purchase our stocks at the best prices?" Papa kindly requested.

Barly gave us very good advice. He told us which merchants had the best prices, efficient services and convenient locations. Also he approximated how much money we would need to start the business on a strong footing. Our calculations were not far apart.

Ajah came back in a few days and asked us how much money we needed. I told him that we got some advice from Barly and that we needed at least eight hundred dollars.

"That's all."

"For now Ajah."

"OK. Lay we go to the bank." Ajah and I went to the bank and got the money. On the following day, Papa and I went to Port of Spain and shopped at Camacho Brothers and a few more merchants on Henry Street and Charlotte Street. While we were shopping, Nancoo asked us if we had arranged for the delivery of our goods to our place of business. We did not understand his question. The merchant then told us that we had to hire someone to take the things that we bought to our shop, unless we had our own transportation. After telling Nancoo that we needed delivery service, he gave us a list of the cost for delivering each item. The next day, all our purchases arrived. We paid Nancoo and we started stocking our empty shelves. The rum shop looked completely full. However, we had only twelve cans of Trinidad grapefruit juice on the grocery section of the business.

Ajah was elated to see his dream come true and promised to give us more money should we need it.

*****

During the time I was involved in helping my parents set up the rum shop business, a Hindu school was opened very close to my home. I transferred quickly into that school. Since there was no Standard 4A Special, I was placed in Standard 5B. I sat next to a very neat and smart girl named Yasmin who had a beautiful Barbadian accent. I learnt that she had to return to her biological parents' house, due to the death of her aunt who had adopted her as a baby. We studied and did our homework together. I liked her very much. She was very kind to me. At recess, we always shared our treats while walking around in the schoolyard.

The school was a long one-room building. The various classes were separated by mobile partitions. Whenever the noise level got too high, the headmaster, Mr. Ganesh, would ring the silence-bell several times until there was complete silence. The head master had a special educational quiz show that he employed every school day after lunch, immediately after the start of classes for standards four, five and six. After the headmaster had achieved the silence that he needed, he took over control of these three classes which were directly in his view and within his voice range. His class was on the stage from where all the classes were visible to him. He challenged the three classes general knowledge of history, geography, nature study, hygiene, literature and arithmetic. Headmaster taught the standard six class which was on the stage. There were eleven students in headmaster's class. These students were the *crème-de-la-crème* of the school. They were either the sons or daughters of the headmaster, a lawyer, an inspector of schools, an accountant, the doctor or other prominent citizens of Chauhan.

Mr. Ganesh, the headmaster, would clearly ask a question in any of the subjects mentioned above, repeat it and patiently wait for a correct answer from any student in the three classes.

Fortunately, because of the mathematical teachings from Papa and the exposure to different genres of movies and serials, Marvel and DC comic books and documentaries, I answered most of the questions correctly. The habit of answering the questions correctly more than any of the other students, even in standard six, resulted in an unexpected promotion for me.

Mr. Ganesh, from his desk on the 'stage,' looked at me during one of these mental gymnastics sessions, and said, "Mitra, take your books and come up on the stage."

I heard him but I did not budge. Mr. Ganesh stood up and repeated his command in a louder voice, "Mitra, take your books and come on the stage."

I got up and was afraid that I was going to be punished because Mr. Ganesh had a strap in one of his hands. I took my books, looked at my teacher, who said "Go, Mitra headmaster is very serious."

Quickly I ascended the three life-changing steps to the headmaster's desk. He told me to sit next to Rajan whose desk was at the very back of the class. I sat quietly next to Rajan, who looked at me as an untouchable person. He was the son of the Inspector of Schools. After sitting down, I noticed that the desktop on Rajan's side was freshly stained in red mahogany. Headmaster noticed Rajan's reaction to me sitting next to him and immediately came to the back of the class and instructed Rajan to bring back the mahogany stain from his home and ordered him to stain the entire desk as soon as possible. Rajan honoured headmaster's order and completed the staining the very next day.

This promotion exposed me into a new level of academic experiences. At first, the eleven students were not very friendly and helpful. In fact, during the Christmas season everyone in the class received many Christmas postcards. But I was the only student in the class who did not get a card from any of my new classmates. They showed their cards around the class to everyone except me. Being very hurt and ostracized, I vividly recall that I bought myself an inexpensive Christmas card at Charan Bookstore. I walked slowly to the post office, bought a stamp, wrote a very cheerful note to myself in the inside of the card and mailed it to myself. It arrived at the school two days later. When headmaster called my name to give me my mail, everyone looked at me in silent surprise. I went and took my mail from headmaster and returned to my desk.

They all said, "Who sent you the postcard?"

I slowly opened it and boldly smiled and said, "My secret girlfriend from my former class." They did not believe me.

One girl said, "He has no girlfriend. He sent the card to himself."

I said nothing. The headmaster told the class to stop harassing me.

However, my encounter with these students resulted in significant changes in my life. They dressed smartly, spoke eloquently and experienced a different standard of living to which I was exposed to in my home. I had to adapt, learn and perform in this new situation.

Two weeks after the postcard embarrassment, the end of term examinations took place. I burnt the candle at both ends studying for the examinations. I had to show these prejudiced students that my unexpected promotion was merited. I wrote the standard six examinations and I placed sixth out of the twelve students. This result affirmed the "upwards and onwards" advice that Ajah preached to me. I was now in the milieu of brilliant, energetic and scholastic boys and girls. After the results were announced by the headmaster, the boys and girls who were in my class changed their snobbish attitude towards me to a welcoming and collegial one.

The headmaster's son was the first of my new peers to invite me to his home. I told Papa that I was invited by the headmaster's son to come to their home to play some special games. Papa was very happy but was concerned about the dress code and my comportment. When he learnt about the prominence of the students' parents, Papa told me that I could accept invitations from any of the students of my class.

I went to the headmaster's home. His son and my new classmates welcomed me into their big, beautiful home. In large bookcases, behind cleaned glass, there were many beautifully displayed books of all sizes, and on different subjects. There was also a radio and radiogram with stacks of records in one corner of the large well-furnished room. Also there were several small tables with chairs around them. On each table, there was a box on which was written in bold large letters the word "MONOPOLY."

I was truly amazed at the whole setting. The headmaster and his wife cordially welcomed me. The headmaster said many flattering things about me to his wife and to his friends' children. He and his warm, friendly wife left all the young students in the large living room and went upstairs. I was in a completely strange environment. The new boys and girls, friends of the son of the headmaster, were attending other schools and were very knowledgeable about a wide range of subjects. They were very intelligent and well mannered. After getting introduced to all of them, and after learning a bit about their back grounds, they started to play the board game called Monopoly.

They explained the rules and some nuances of the strategies and the goal of the game. I learned the strategies of the game, the value of different properties, trading and many more invaluable skills as quickly as possible so that I could have a fighting chance of winning. I was at a great disadvantage. These boys and girls were playing this game for quite a long time. The dice was very favourable to me and I got all the lucky breaks. After two of the three games, I had the most properties and the most money. At the end of the games, my new friends extended invitations to me to visit them in their homes to play other games. When I returned home, after a rather enlightening and interesting evening with the headmaster's son and his friends,I was convinced that a little knowledge can be very rewarding.

After getting Papa's permission, I did visit the homes of my newly made acquaintances, some of whom became lifelong friends.

INNOCENCE

The following year, most of my peers, my new friends and I went to either colleges or secondary schools in different parts of the Island. I was able to build very interesting and enlightening relationships with some of the most brilliant students in the area. Whenever I visited their homes, I met very prominent people who encouraged me to pursue my education to the highest level.

My friends showed me pictures of their elder brothers and sisters who were studying in the United States of America, England, Scotland, Ireland, India, Canada and Jamaica. Some of them were studying to become doctors, lawyers, nurses, educators, accountants, engineers and many other professions which required high academic achievement. This only motivated me to study more intensely. These new acquaintances also taught me how to play contract bridge and chess. Some of my peers' parents appreciated me and openly invited me to spend time reading their collection of the world's greatest literary works in the privacy of their libraries. I was welcome to borrow any book from their library. Also, I was invited to overnight whenever it got too late for me to go home. I thanked them for the invitation, but, I always had to decline kindly because Papa wanted me at home just after sunset on school days.

Other parents and their children considered me to be part of their family. In fact, one prominent lawyer had two sons, who attended another school, and they became my very good friends. We studied, socialised and played games and sports together. The lawyer called me his third son. On weekends, he would take me along with his own sons to weddings, social engagements and sporting activities. I was even given my own study space in their library so that I could study with them whenever I wished.

My friends read a lot of British literature which their parents brought back from the British Isles and the United States of America; books written by the Brontë sisters, Dickens, Melville, Shakespeare and many others. They also read detective and suspense thrillers. After they had finished reading those books, they loaned them to me to read so that we could visualize, identify, analyze and evaluate the stories in more details. We spent lots of time narrating the western stories in great detail to one another. Consequently, I developed a very vivid and colourful imagination. I emulated their storytelling antics and animations by retelling the plots of the various movies that I had seen with Papa and Papa's friends. I increased my English vocabulary and even learned some of the phrases and lines from many movies. I forced myself to search for the meanings of new words so that I could understand the plot of the story. Also, I was encouraged to look for new places mentioned in the movies in the atlas that Mr. Norton gifted me.

*****

Life in our new location at Chauhan Junction was quite different with Tanty Seloni. She was officially my stepmother. My father married her at the local court house unknown to me. I learnt of Papa's marriage to Tanty Seloni from her former husband, Uncle Deo.

Papa strongly believed in providing the best education for all his children regardless of their gender. Unfortunately, Tanty Seloni, who did not have any formal education, did not share Papa's opinion. My eldest sister, Ushi, was a brilliant student at all levels in elementary school, and topped her classes in all subjects. She was awarded a scholarship to attend one of the prestigious convents. My second sister, Elyana did not receive a scholarship but was admitted to Augustin Girls High School. Tanty Seloni decided that Ushi had to stay home and cook three meals a day, do all the washing, perform any other household chores as needed and also help in the shop. She was not allowed to accept the scholarship. Elyana was allowed to attend Augustin Girls High School on the condition that Ajah paid her school fees. He agreed to pay without any hesitation. Ajah also complained about Ushi not going to college. After a few months, Ajah wanted to know why Ushi was not attending college when he knew that she had won a scholarship. He questioned Papa who claimed that our stepmother needed Ushi to do the housework and also help in the shop. He was very annoyed, and decided to pay a woman to do the cooking, washing and ironing. Since it was too late to enter convent, he paid the fees for Ushi to attend Commercial College which was still admitting students.

As I became more educated and knowledgeable, I boldly expressed my frustrations to Papa. I told him that Tanty Seloni was beating Ushi and Elyana mercilessly and that she was very cruel and unfair in what she was doing. In response Papa became very enraged and made a very hurtful statement directly to me. "I should not have sent you to college. You get too smart for me now. You are learning too much about what's right and what is wrong from those smart ass families and their children. You spend too much time with those educated people. She is your stepmother and she has the right to discipline all of you as she sees fit. So you better shut up before I give you some blows too."

I was too young to express my resentment to his statement.

Although the orphanage refused to accept my two sisters and me, we were really living in worse conditions than at the orphanage. Our stepmother treated us as hired help. I related the wretched conditions at home to my guidance counsellor at college. She did not have any viable practical solution. She told me to bite the bullet, get my certificates and try and help my sisters to escape from the tyranny of our stepmother. I never told anyone about my meeting with the guidance counsellor.

The rumshop and fast growing grocery store were operated by Tanty Seloni, Ushi, Elyana and me. The business started to grow slowly and then it started to make lots of money. Much of our precious study time was spent preparing the business for daily operation. Our studies became secondary in the eyes of our stepmother. My Papa was completely under her controlling spell.

My stepmother woke me very early in the morning to do the following chores before going to college: wash all the drinking glasses, sweep the entire shop, clean out the coolers, repack all the bottled drinks, and make sure that all the garbage and empty bottles were organized for easy disposal.

Tanty Seloni and the "Pseudo Orphans" (Ushi, Elyana and I) worked in the shop almost every day when we were not attending school. We had the most successful business in Chauhan Junction at that time. On seeing how much money the business was making without us having to leave home, Papa did not renew his water transporting contract, and joined the business full time.

With the increased cash flow, Tanty Seloni decided that she had to thank her Hindu gods and goddesses for her newly acquired fortune. She decided to spend money on feeding lazy unambitious people who were deemed untouchables by their own families, and took personal responsibility to house and feed stray dogs. She purchased a large deep freezer in which she stored hundreds of pounds of chicken's backs and necks to feed the dogs. People in the neighbourhood, and nearby villages, on realizing that Tanty Seloni had became a philanthropist for stray dogs, dropped off their unwanted dogs at our front gate.

I remembered my sister, Elyana, saying to me one evening after school, "Mitra, Tanty Seloni enrolled two more stray dogs today." Elyana called our home, "The University for Stray Dogs." The highest enrollment was 32 filthy and noisy, stray dogs.

Tanty Seloni would spend hours cooking, cleaning and feeding these boisterous mongrels. It was a very expensive hobby. She spent more time attending to the needs of the dogs than our needs. We had to prepare our own meals. These dogs created serious environmental and human problems. Tanty Seloni seemed immune to their loud barking. The neighbours complained about the continuous boisterous barking and howling, but to no avail. She was on a godly mission which, to her, was more important than our human needs. Her devotion and love for the mangy dogs resulted in her contracting diseases from them. A doctor who specialised in animal contagious diseases told her that she was infected by some bacteria from the dogs. Nonetheless, she continued to do what she enjoyed doing most so that she would be guaranteed a seat in heaven in her next life.

While my stepmother was looking after the dogs, the poor people and her personal interests, Papa and I decided to demolish the old shop and construct a much larger business. We did it and never regretted that decision.

*****

One sunny afternoon, I was unexpectedly introduced into the world of sex. I had a very good friend, named Ricky, who lived two houses away. We often went together to shoot birds and small animals with our pellet guns. We were teenagers. He was three years my senior and attended another college. His family was very wealthy and owned the automotive parts shop. Ricky's mother was an angelic human being, but unfortunately was killed in a car crash. She left behind a husband and four children. His three younger sisters were charming. His father and my father were very good business friends.

After a brief mourning period, Ricky's father married a nineteen year old East Indian girl named Yana. She was very attractive, charming and flirty. In her house, she was always scantily dressed. Her large round breasts were always hanging out from her loosely fitting blouse. This was the way she presented herself whenever I went to the house to meet Ricky to go bird hunting. Sometimes the side door leading to Ricky's room would be closed but sometimes it would be open. Whenever it was closed I would knock several times before either Yana or Ricky would open it. On many occasions Yana had to open the door for me. She told me that whenever the door was closed that I should just open it and enter. On one occasion when I opened the door, Yana was stark naked. I apologized for my invasion of her privacy. She hurriedly ran into the bathroom.

I told Ricky about the nude encounter. He told me, with a big smile, that I should not worry about her. She was always naked or half naked in the house. She complained incessantly that she was too hot and preferred to be without clothes.

"Consider it an accidental happening, I do not think Yana will mind," Ricky jokingly said. However, I was not comfortable seeing Yana in the nude .

I stayed away for almost two weeks. But I did not tell anyone about Yana's nudity. Unexpectedly, Ricky visited me in the shop, and inquired about my absence. I did not answer his question. He told me to call on him on Sunday after lunch so that we could go hunting. I was not sure what time was after lunch, so I decided to go to Ricky's around two o'clock.

When I arrived at Ricky's the door was ajar. I called Ricky by his name several times. There was no answer. I gently opened the door. There, to my shocking surprise, Ricky was having sex with his stepmother, Yana. They were both completely naked. I stood looking at them in utter astonishment. I did not know what to do, when Yana said:

"What de fuck you doing here? Get out! Get out now!"

I stood there for a moment and then got out of the doorway as fast as I could. In shock, I walked back to my home. Ricky came an hour later with his pellet gun to go hunting. I told Ricky that Papa needed me to do some extra mathematics.

I never went to visit Ricky's any more. I never went bird hunting again. During the next five years, Yana had babies alternatively for Ricky and his father.

*****

One Saturday morning at about eleven o'clock, I heard a very loud and embarrassing commotion taking place in the parking lot in front of Ricky's home. From our upstairs balcony, I saw an inquisitive crowd growing around Yana, Ricky, his father, and a young lady whom I recognised as Bina. I hurried down the stairs and joined the swelling crowd. Ricky saw me approaching. He called me and introduced me to his girlfriend, Bina, whom I knew, but we pretended that we did not know each other. I inquired about the quarrelling and Ricky told me that Yana was in love with him and not his father. She wanted Ricky for herself.

Bina, who was Ricky's secret girlfriend, had come to surprise Ricky at his home on his birthday. Bina had a birthday gift for Ricky and knocked on the front door of Ricky's home. Yana opened the door and warmly greeted Bina. Yana did not know about the loving relationship that existed between Ricky and this gorgeous, and amorous East Indian girlfriend.

Yana asked her, "Who are you? Who you looking for?"

Bina replied, "My name is Bina. I am looking for Ricky."

"What do you want with Ricky?"

"Ricky is my boyfriend. Today is his birthday. I come to surprise him with a gift and to go out with him for lunch."

"Look woman, Ricky is my man. You better get your whoring ass out of here before I strangle you."

Ricky was in his room and clearly heard Yana's loud cantankerous voice.

He immediately rushed to the door just in time to stop the physical cuffing Yana was dishing out to Bina. Ricky hugged Bina and led her into the parking lot, closely followed by Yana who was fully enraged. Ricky's father and one of Ricky's sisters stood quietly as Yana continued to verbally assault Bina. It seemed that Ricky and his father, because of his age, had a special relationship with Yana.

Finally Bina and Ricky got married. I was invited to the wedding but did not attend. After two years, Ricky died. He left Bina with a baby boy and a bakery store that they owned and operated. I visited Bina at her bakery shop to express my sincerest condolences. She hugged me and cried on my shoulder without saying a word. She was no longer the vibrant and beautiful woman that she used to be. I remained silent and looked at her with pitiful and compassionate eyes.

*****

I had just opened the three doors of our shop to do business, when suddenly there were brilliant and blinding flashes of lightning quickly followed by the thundering voices of the rain gods. I looked at the large drops of water as they completely inundated the landscape in my view. The sunshine disappeared. This unexpected torrential downpour forced the villages' Catechist to seek shelter inside our shop. He was wet. I offered him a dry towel which he graciously accepted.

"Good morning Catechist."

"Where are you going in this thunderstorm?"

"I am going to meet Fanny, the principal of Augustin Girls' High School. But let's not talk about that."

"Sorry for being inquisitive."

"What are you reading?"

"I am reading the sports section of the *Trinidad Guardian* newspaper."

"Anything interesting?"

"I am reading the profiles of the football players on the Intercol teams."

"Intercol teams!"

"Don't you follow the Intercol game?"

"Which colleges are playing in the Intercol?"

"Today the annual football match between Queen's Royal College and St. Mary's College will be played before full capacity stands at the Queen's Park Oval in Port of Spain. It is one of the greatest sporting events held in Trinidad."

"Are you going to see the game?"

"No. I have to help out in the shop. I will listen to the live commentaries on the radio".

"Mitra, have you dropped out of college and working full time in the shop ?"

"No Catechist. I attend Excelsior College in Benevolence. I am in Form 3A."

"Do you enjoy going to college?"

"Yes Catechist," I replied.

The rain started to ease. Catechist continued his questioning.

"What do you like about college life?" he continued.

I was not prepared for a question and answer session so early in the morning, especially on an empty growling stomach. I had to impress the Catechist. He was one of the villages' most respected and influential personalities. His words and recommendations could be more powerful that my certificates.

In response to his question I said, "My college experiences have been very enlightening in many ways. I have a few superb teachers, a handful of trustworthy friends who are intelligent, have very high ethical standards and are very cultured. My friends' families treat me like their own son.

A great caring and dynamic friendship exists between me, and their family. A few of us have formed the 'Eclecticans' study group." He asked me to explain the 'Eclecticans.'

I told him that a couple of the brilliant boys in my class carefully observed the performances of all the students in our class for each of the following subjects: arithmetic; algebra; geometry; geography; history; English, English literature, French, Latin and scripture. After the results of the first few tests, those of us who have excelled in any subject or subjects would meet secretly in either a vacant room in the school or in one of our homes. Then they analysed the various marks of the high achievers and performers in our different courses. They select the top performers from the various subjects to form the 'Eclecticans' study group. I was selected to teach any of my classmates who was doing poorly in any of the mathematics courses [algebra, geometry and arithmetic], only if they ask for my assistance. This was an overt tutoring session, held after classes in any available vacant classroom."

The Catechist was very interested in this study model. The rain continued to fall; but the Catechist remained silently listening to the details of the study patterns practiced amongst some of the students in my school.

I continued to relate to the Catechist: "There is a dougla [mixed breed – between East Indian and an African black] boy, named Cameron, who learned about our private tutoring sessions from one of their parents. Cameron was in a higher form and was an honour student in every subject. He met me one morning at recess and told me that he and his friends have formed a similar 'Intelligentsia' club. Cameron said that he had one piece of special advice for me, which I should share with our 'Eclecticans' study group. He said that "during his lunch time when he would walk from classroom to classroom while eating his sandwich, whenever he saw any novel information written on the blackboards in the different forms, he would copy the information in a special notebook."

I asked Cameron, "What academic advantage do you reap from such practice?"

Cameron said, "Whatever was written on the blackboard was considered important and valuable by the teacher of those students. I am a student seeking more knowledge. I am getting a free review of what I should have learnt when I was in the lower forms, and a preview of what I should know in the higher forms."

I expressed my gratitude and shook his hand.

The Cathecist just smiled and thanked me for the educational insight and remarked that he would definitely tell the principal and administration about some of the interesting student practices at Excelsior College.

*****

Twice a week, after school, Tanty Seloni (stepmother) allowed me to play 'wind-ball' cricket in the back streets of the village. The pedestrians were disgusted and expressed anger as the players inconvenienced and impeded them as they walked to their homes. This cricket activity which kept the young boys active and physically fit had been around for years. Most parents were happy to know that their sons were playing sports rather than getting into mischief. Sometimes there were spectators who wished to participate in our game. We welcomed all interested males regardless of their age. It should be noted that any female who showed any interest were welcomed to play. But none accepted the offer.

One evening, during one of the games, Tanty Lolita, one of our customers, was a spectator. I was between fifteen and sixteen years of age when Tanty Lolita tried to stop me as I was running to fetch the cricket ball from the bushes. I pushed her aside because the batsmen were scoring runs as they ran between the wickets. I had to get the ball back into play as quickly as possible so as to restrict the number of runs scored against my team. I did not know her reason for wanting to stop me. She was beautifully dressed and attractive even to a teenager.

After the game, she was still standing at the corner in the shade of the plum trees looking at the players as they headed in different directions for their homes. It started to get dark and she remained standing at the same place. I wondered whether she seriously wanted to talk to me. Since she did not make any attempt to call or approach me, I just waved to her and left for home.

I did not see her at the beginning of the next wind-ball cricket game. Towards the latter part of the game, Tanty Lolita came and was standing at the same location below the plum trees looking at the game. One of the players who was fielding close to her, called out to me, "Mitra, Tanty Lolita wants to talk with you, after the game and before you go home."

"All right," I replied.

"What question does she want to ask," I wondered. I called her 'tanty' because in the village the custom was always to respect your elders. Anyone older than you, regardless of their color, race or religion, one addressed the female, as tanty and the male as uncle.

Just before dark, I approached Tanty Lolita.

She said, "Mitra, I need you to help me to do some work in my garden. Since Lawrence's death, I have no one to climb the trees and pick the oranges, pomerac, mangoes, breadfruits and many other fruits. My husband, Lawrence, used to pick all the fruits and shared them with the village people.

After his untimely death, there are so many fruits on the trees, ripening, falling and rotting. Can you come any time after school and help me pick them?"

"I have so much school work to do Tanty Lolita. I don't know whether I can help pick your fruits. I will have to check my schedule and organize my school work before I could give you a definite answer. Tanty, you come to the next cricket game and I will tell you if I can help you."

Tanty Lolita said, "Mitra, I will pay you very well for the work. Don't worry." The mention of the word 'money' greatly appealed to me. I could have some extra pocket money to buy expensive after shave lotion, under arm deodorant and better shoes. I became interested and excited and I decided that I was not going to mention her offer to anyone.

I returned home very happy after playing. My parents, on noticing my unusual gaiety after cricket, commented,

"Mitra, why you so happy?"

"Finally my team won a game, Papa."

"That why you so happy?!"

"Yes, Papa."

Nothing else was said, and I went upstairs and had a shower. After dinner, while I was in bed, my mind was running wild with all kinds of surreptitious plans on how to outsmart my parents to get to Tanty Lolita's place unnoticed.

Another evening for wind-ball cricket finally arrived. I told my stepmother that I would be a little late coming home. She wanted to know my reason.

"Tanty Seloni, my friend Naveen is having some problems with geometry and today, after school, he asked me to help him at his home."

"I go tell yu Papa, what yu say. He go understand."

My plan was just accepted. I was thinking more of the money than the cricket game. Already I was counting how much money I could make, and what I was going to do with it. My intentions were to purchase Brut aftershave lotion, more expensive underarm deodorant, Nivea cream and Brylcreem for my hair. I was quite aware that my sisters and parents would ask me where did I get the money. First they would say I stole it from the shop.

*****

I started the cricket game and participated fully. However, after batting, I sneaked away to Tanty Lolita's cottage.

Her home was an English designed two bedroom cottage, which had been custom-built by her wealthy husband many years ago, when they left England to settle in the warm tropical climate of Trinidad and Tobago. Lawrence had included most of the amenities, conveniences, and luxuries that he had been accustomed to in Kent County, in England.

No one saw me, as far as I was aware, as I entered her large property, which was covered with countless types of fruit and ornamental trees. There were three houses on the street on which she lived. Her cottage was on the very last street of the village, next to the sugarcane plantations and one house away from the river. Directly across the street in front of her cottage, Tanty Jamiron lived on an elevated forested piece of land. Tanty Lolita's cottage was on a lower elevation than Tanty Jamiron's, and was partially hidden by small fruit trees, a hibiscus fence and bushes which gave her much privacy.

Tanty Lolita was very happy to see me, and she gave me some freshly squeezed orange juice and a piece of sponge cake. She then showed me around the property and pointed out some of the fruit trees (soursop, sapodilla, mangoes, zaboca, chenette, chatigne, papaya just to mention a few of the fruits). Many of the trees were over-laden with ripened delicious and brightly-coloured fruits. She told me that she was a member of the Orchid Society in Port of Spain and showed me her exotic collection of orchids. Also she showed me the patches of roses that she planted in every corner of her property. There were also wild poinsetta, heliconia, bourgainvilleas, red cattails, anthurium, red and yellow gingers and wild pineapples, tastefully planted all over to make the garden-scape look like an impressionist painting. I was able to recall the names of these flowers because we had them in our yard.

There was a butterfly garden filled with colourful and fragrant flowering plants. It was a paradise haven constantly inhabited, temporarily by beautiful humming birds, and a wide range of colourful birds serenading the flowers and fruits of the gardens with melodious and lilting songs. She was the proud owner of many small perfume gardens surrounding her cottage.

Then Tanty Lolita told me which fruits she wanted me to pick. As I was picking the highly scented Valencia oranges my body was attacked by swiftly moving black biting ants. I quickly, but carefully, descended the tree, fighting off the stinging black ants, and at the same time avoiding the sharp needle-shaped thorns on the tree trunk and branches. The ants were ferociously gnawing away at my genitals and my full head of black hair. I pulled out my shirt and had to drop my pants to get rid of the stinging creatures. My dark brown coloured skin was polkadotted with red burning blotches.

Tanty Lolita noticed my discomfort and rushed to help me get rid of the ants on the parts of my body that I could neither see nor reach with my hands. She had a very good view of my partially nude body covered only with my sliders. I was rubbing and scratching every part of my body accessible by my hands and was definitely hurting. Tanty Lolita went inside her cottage, and having fetched some cocoa butter cream proceeded to cream the ant bites in the areas that I could not reach. Playfully, she tried to cream my groin and my private parts which I did not allow.

After all the commotion created by the biting black ants, Tanty Lolita invited me into her kitchen for a cup of English tea, shortbread and a choice of jams. I did so with pleasure in her beautifully decorated English country-style kitchen. She had many tea sets and many exotic dishes, flatware and silverwares proudly displayed in a relatively large glass cabinet in her spacious kitchen. The teapot was an artistic masterpiece. In fact, she had a collection of teapots from around the world.

I had seen a few like them at my friend's home during one of my visits. It seemed to me that those who were educated in England loved to have tea, with either shortbread, or jelly-filled cookies. Her kitchen was decorated with many beautiful, colourful and scented orchids and other potted house plants. They were placed, not only on her large bow window but on almost every sidetable in the various sunlit rooms. What a civilized and cultured woman! She thanked me politely for picking the fruits, and was very apologetic about the unexpected black ants attack. She asked if I would spray the orange trees as soon as possible and said that she would buy the ant spray next day from the farmers' supply shop. As I was about to leave, she gave me five dollars. After thanking her for her hospitality, kindness and generosity, I left her premises extremely happy.

I went back to the cricket game on the street. Most of the players had already left as the game was coming to an end. I remained on the street corner talking with the few older players who were in no hurry to go home.

I arrived home at my usual time. But I felt uneasy about my visit to Tanty Lolita. I thought that I had compromised my integrity and my moral standards, by lying to Tanty Seloni. Did I commit any of the deadly sins? Did I sell my soul for only five dollars by telling a lie?

The following evening I came home right after the end of the school day. I told my parents that I had to talk to one of my friends about our homework. My parents granted me permission and told me to return before dark. I went to Tanty Lolita to spray the orange and any other trees which were ants infested but she had already done the spraying earlier in the day.

I told Tanty Lolita that I was very pleased she solved the ants problem by herself. She said that it was imperative to get her garden back in the shape it had been when Lawrence was alive. I promised to do my best in the restoration of the garden. For the little time I spent to come to her home to inquire about the ant problem, I was given five dollars which I reluctantly took but was thankful. Before leaving, Tanty Lolita told me that she still needed me to harvest her fruits and that I should organize my studies and sports schedules to accommodate the harvesting of the fruits.

Unfortunately, the following week the wind-ball cricket season ended. What excuse could I use to leave home?

I could not leave school and go directly to Tanty Lolita's garden wearing my school uniform. First, I had to go home, have something to eat, help out in the shop, and I had to fabricate a credible story so that I would be allowed to leave home and be back at a respectable time. I had other friends of both sexes who were attending either colleges or convents in Port of Spain and San Fernando. These students were my contemporaries. I told my stepmother that I had to meet the two boys, who attended Queen's Royal College, at their homes, who lived a few streets away, to discuss some questions in English literature. My alternate excuse was to tell her that the 'Eclecticans' study group was meeting at one of the boy's home in Benevolence.

Ajah bought me a new Raleigh bicycle, on account of my excellent term report card. I used the bicycle to quickly get to Tanty Lolita's cottage whenever I had to help her in the garden. At times, I would tell my parents that I was going to ride my bicycle with my friends around the village; and promised them that I would help out, on my return, in the shop until closing time. They were happy with my proposal.

Carefully, I rode to Tanty Lolita's cottage as quickly as possible, hoping no one would notice me and report me to my parents.

We sat and set a date and time when I should return to pick the fruits and help out in the garden. She was very excited and elated. As I was leaving, she handed me some money for keeping my appointment. I greatly appreciated it, and started to wonder whether she would become a benefactor to me as Abel Magwitch was to Pip in the novel *Great Expectations*.

Soon I realized that Tanty Lolita had a completely different standard of living from her neighbours and the village people. Her husband, died unexpectedly from a massive heart attack, leaving her with large sums of money and properties. She was very wealthy, always well dressed, groomed and attractive.

I arrived punctually on the agreed date at her cottage. She welcomed me with a big smile. Then, she hugged me and kissed me on my cheek. She expressed her joy in seeing me, but immediately gave me instructions on what I had to do.

I told her that I would prefer to pick the zabocas first because the trees were taller than the oranges trees, and it would be dangerous to climb the tall trees in the fading light of the day. She agreed. At first, I wanted to use the cocoa knife to pick the zabocas but I changed my mind because the zabocas would be bruised if they fell to the ground. After picking the zabocas, I then picked all the ripened oranges.

I was very happy and about to leave when she firmly held me and said, "How is your girlfriend?"

I told her that I did not have a girlfriend and that I had to get my Senior Cambridge School Certificate first before I could think about a girlfriend.

"That is a very wise decision. But there is no harm in having a little fun with girls once in a while Mitra," she responded with a big smile.

I said, "Tanty Lolita, I will have to think about that. Maybe you can get me a girlfriend when I graduate. I do not know anything about girls. Besides, all the girls that I know are interested in getting their Cambridge School Certificate before getting boyfriends."

Tanty Lolita told me that she would find a nice girl for me.

I was amused but was not interested. As I was about to leave she handed me ten dollars. Again I thanked her for her kindness and generosity. This picking fruits was turning out to be financially rewarding.

On my next visit, I climbed the tall chenette tree and picked sufficient fruits to full a ten pound 'harvest queen' paper bag. I also picked some papayas and sapodillas. Tanty Lolita was very happy and invited me to come inside her cottage. We sat in the kitchen and had some freshly brewed Earl grey tea, English shortbread cookies and small pieces of soft square-shaped bread with butter. As I was sitting next to her, she said to me, "Mitra, should I get you a beautiful and an educated girlfriend what would you like to do with her?"

I said, "Tanty Lolita, I haven't got the slightest idea what to do."

"Well Mitra, this is where I can help you. I can teach you a few things that you will find very useful as you get older, and you have a girlfriend."

As she was uttering that statement, she quickly slid one of her hands, up my short khaki pants and held on tightly to my totee. I did not have time to get my hands down because I was holding the teacup in one hand and the shortbread cookie in the other. In my attempt to get away, the teacup and cookie fell. In vain, I fought to get her to let go of my totee. With one hand she held on to it and with her other hand wrestled me down to the smooth mahogany floor. Being much stronger than me, she got on top of me, and first licked my face with her tongue and finally forced her tea-floured tongue into my mouth. I did not know what to do and started to wriggle and struggle to get away. Finally, being exhausted, I surrendered to her powerful manipulations. She knew fully well what she was going to do with me. I was scared that she would damage my totee but I surrendered to her.

While laying on the highly polished slippery floor afraid to scream or resist her, she forcibly took my short pants and sliders off. I feared that she might seriously hurt me with her powerful arms. She stopped rolling her tongue around my mouth, licking my face again and again and caressing my neck with her nose and face. I felt very abused, dirty and frightened. I remembered how Tanty Tina threatening to cut off my little pee pee when I was a little boy, after she had rubbed my face and mouth all over her wet, sticky and smelly Tarantula. I lay helplessly on the kitchen floor as she used her feet to kick away the chairs from around us.

She told me to relax and enjoy what she was going to do to me. She said, "I am not going to hurt you. You are mature enough to learn what adolescent boys and girls must do before they get together." I remained quiet but very frightened not knowing what she was going to do to me. Tears started to roll down the sides of my face. Was she going to do what Yana and Ricky were doing when I surprised them in Ricky's bedroom?

She skinned back the foreskin of my totee fully with her soft but firm fingers. My erect totee started to burn at first. She placed my erect totee in her mouth and started to suck it as if it was a lollipop candy. She kept sucking it while she made grunting and funny sounds as though she was eating a sweet juicy fruit. I looked at her hoping that she did not bite it off. She kept massaging my testicles, which hurt, and continued her sucking. I did not struggle anymore. The corners of my legs became very wet and sticky with saliva from her warm mouth. At times, I thought that she was going to bite my totee off. I started to get strange funny lightheaded feelings as she continued vigorously sucking my totee which was getting harder and harder. I thought that it would explode. Something startlingly and frightening happened to me. My body started to convulse and I thought that I was going to go blind or even faint. She continued. She stopped sucking and pulled me up to her face and smilingly said, " How did you enjoy that? How do you feel?"

"Am I going to die? I feel very weak and scared, Tanty!" I pleaded softly with watery eyes.

"No, you will be fine. It is just a new sweet feeling for you. This is only the beginning of a world of wonderful pleasant emotions for you," she assured me. I felt drained as though something was vacuumed out of my body.

She said, "I just sucked out your 'come'."

"What is 'come'?" I asked.

She said, "Next time I will show you what is 'come'. You go home and don't tell anyone. I mean nobody should know about what I am teaching you.

You have many sweeter things to learn from me. Just work with me and you would not have any regrets."

Before I left, she gave me twenty dollars and told me to go to the washroom and wash out all the dry saliva from my face and my neck. She dusted off my clothes after I got dressed. I went home very confused and abused. I did not anticipate this type of behaviour from Tanty Lolita. I did not dare tell anyone about my sexual epiphany with Tanty Lolita, fearing that I might be ostracized.

I completed my reading assignments and I went to bed without any delay. While I was in bed, my totee was hurting and burning slightly. I decided to inspect it to see whether it was damaged or whether any part was missing. Fortunately, it was not damaged. But it did not have a good scent. I went into the bathroom and washed myself with sweet scented cucumber soap.

On the following day, when I returned to school, I was seriously tempted to tell one of my trusted friends about what happened at Tanty Lolita's cottage. But I recalled clearly that Tanty Lolita warned me and advised that I should never tell anyone about what she did to me. I thought that my friends would laugh at me. I carried with me a very guilty and dirty feeling for days.

The day arrived for my next appointment with Tanty Lolita. Should I keep it or miss it? I did not know how to answer.

It rained cats and dogs all day. Were the rain gods telling me to stay away from her? Since the fruit trees would be very wet to climb, I decided not to visit her. Instead I helped serve our customers in the shop. For the next two appointments there were thunderstorms and thunder showers. Although, she paid me very well on every visit, I realized that I had made a very big mistake by allowing her to have her own way with me. I should have cried out for help. But who would have heard? Was it absolutely my fault? These were unanswered rhetorical questions I asked myself.

A few days after I had missed three appointments with Tanty Lolita, she appeared in the shop. Papa, Tanty Seloni and Elyana were in the shop with me. As soon as I saw her I became very frightened. Was she here to tell Papa about what happened between us? I had to wait patiently and behave as normally as possible.

Papa knew Tanty Lolita very well. He said, "Hey Lolita, I have not seen you in a long time. Since Lawrence died, you are hardly coming to buy anything. What happened?"

"Roshan, what can I tell you. I am living as a free independent woman of leisure. But it hurts me to see all those delicious fruits on my fruit trees in my garden, maturing, ripening and falling to the ground to rot. I have large amounts of fruits to pick and I can't get anybody to pick them. My two small grandchildren and my son and his wife are coming to spend the weekend. I am hoping they could help. If you know anyone who would pick the fruits, could you tell them that I will pay them well.

After hearing about grandchildren I felt like vomiting. I told Papa that I had some geometry problems to solve. While sitting on my bed, looking through the glass window, I felt very ashamed of myself for allowing an old lady to make love to me. I would have to live with that shame secretly with my conscience for the rest of my life. I lost my virginity to an old lady mouth instead of a young punani. I could not tell her age because she looked young, glamorous, slim and physically fit. She easily overpowered me and wrestled me successfully to the floor and took control of me.

*****

Our shop's prime location at the Junction of three major roads, served as a large watering hole for most travelers. Our shop was a living learning centre. Whether the customers were drunk or sober, they were always discussing politics, religion, metaphysics, education, gossips, newspaper articles, peoples' business and anything you could imagine. I only had to stand behind the counter and listen to the words of wisdom or utter nonsense flowing from the mouths of the young, the old, the educated, the illiterate, the restless, and the drunks. The customers, whether from near or far, were quite aware of the talented people who frequented our shop and the mathematical skills of Papa, and, they regularly used to drop off all sorts of questions, riddles, problems and any brain teasers to be solved.

*****

Only on Thursdays was the shop usually closed after one o'clock in the afternoon. One day there were rather loud knocks on our galvanised gate. On opening the gate, standing before me, was the village drunk and 'canal conch' (promiscuous woman). She was a middle aged woman who was married to a man who was much older. The village people called her Perfidia. She wanted a few drinks and some "cutters." She loved talking to me about the vicissitudes of life. She ordered a nip of Black Label rum and a Pepsi cola as a chaser. She also ordered a quarter pound of cheddar cheese with Crix biscuits and Matouk's pepper sauce.

This was her first drink for the day. I told her that I had a few questions to ask her. She laughed, mumbled a few phrases in Spanish and said, "What do you want to know my hero?"

I told her that one day last week as I was passing by her house, I heard familiar voices coming from her back room. I wanted to know what Sony and Roots were doing in your back room. I did not see Pedro, her husband, so I decided to investigate. She started to laugh as she took another drink of rum and bit into the cheese which was laced with very hot pepper sauce.

"What did you see?" Perfidia asked.

I told her that I noticed that she was completely naked on her bed with Sony on top of her. He was naked and was brushing her while Roots had his pants off waiting for his turn. They did not see me as I hid behind the bushes planted in front of her bedroom. After, Sony finished, Roots slowly climbed on her and started brushing her. As Roots started to brush her, she asked, "How come you get so heavy boy?" No one answered her question.

I left the scene as quietly as I had entered it. They did not know that I was looking at them. They were both married men.

"Perfidia! Did they pay you?" I inquired.

Perfidia remained silent for a few minutes. She looked at me and said, "My hero, I won't brush with you. You are young, intelligent, and have a great future ahead of you. Anyone who brushes with me will pay for it with their life."

"What do you mean?" I questioned.

"I have syphilis. They will get very sick and die without medical care."

I became very worried. What was I doing next to a woman with syphilis? She said to me, "Hero today I am going to teach you something that you will be able to use for the rest of your life to protect yourself from getting syphilis."

I thought that the last time a woman told me that she was going to teach me about what to do with my girlfriend, I was sexually abused. I stood up and was about to ask her to leave, when she got up and swiftly lifted up her dress. I was looking at her naked body from her belly button down to her shoes. Her body looked clean and young. She told me to pay close attention to her instructions. I wondered what she was going to do. She held my right hand, took my index finger and middle fingers and pushed them inside her punani which was covered with bushy yellow pubic hairs. She told me, "Push your fingers deeper Hero. Push them as far as they can go into me punani."

I did as she ordered.

"How does it feel? Does it feel warm and slimy?"

I said that it felt hot, sticky and grimy. She told me to move my fingers in a circular motion and pull them out. She looked at me and with a drunken look said, "Smell your fingers. Be very careful not to touch either your face, or nose or any part of your body. How does it smell?"

"It is an awful stink scent Perfidia."

"That stinking scent means that the punani is sick. My personal advice to you my Hero is, before you have sex with any woman anywhere you must perform the punani scent test (PST) that I just showed you. If the punani passes the test, brush it. Otherwise, get to fuck out of her sight."

That scent has remained in my sensory scent bank.

I thanked her and did not charge her for the drinks and food. After she left, I washed my hands in the sink with Lux detergent soap, carbolic soap, and Palmolive soap before the nauseating and putrid scent left my fingers and nails. In one final act to get rid of the putrid scent, I washed my hands with Old Spice aftershave lotion.

When I had finished washing my hands, figuratively speaking, with all the perfumes of Arabia there was another knock on the gate. I did not respond. Instead, I returned to my room to reflect on the unsolicited sexual information that I received from Perfidia.

Three years after their sexual relations with Perfidia, both Roots and

Sony died because they did not seek medical aid. They infected their wives but they sought medical help and lived for many years after their husbands' death.

*****

One afternoon, Mr. Chow asked me to come to one of his senior mathematics class to show the boys how to solve a geometry problem. As soon as I had completed solving the problem, the bell for the afternoon recess rang. Since it was raining very heavily I could not get back to my classroom in the other building. The teacher left me with the senior boys and went to the staff room. I sat at his desk waiting for the rain to abate.

A few of the boys gathered around the only white boy in the class to listen to a story he had promised to tell them. His name was Emile. I was within ear shot of the story teller. Emile was telling them about his father's eldest sister who was visiting them from the city of Liverpool in England. He told them that he was having sex twice a week with his father's vacationing divorced sister. An obese fair skin East Indian boy blurted out, "You lying Emile. You expect us to believe that shit you talking. You just want to make us look like cunumunus [idiots or stupid persons]"

A tall muscular boy shouted, "Shut up your cunt fat boy. Get out of here if you don't want to listen. We want to hear the fuckin story. Come on Emile. Talk fast before next class starts. The rest of you keep your asses shut."

I got up to leave when he started to relate his very colourful and erotic story about his promiscuous old aunt, who was holidaying with his family in Cunupia. He had a captive audience. He commenced his eagerly awaited story of his sexual experience. "Boys I always had a burning desire to experience sexual intercourse with a woman. Not a man. I am not a bullerman [gay] boys."

Emile continued that three weeks ago, his aunt, Ellen, came to spend two months with them to escape the brutal winter of England. His father was very elated to have his eldest sister holiday with his family for the first time. She had not met any of his father's family members. At Piarco airport, Aunty Ellen was officially introduced to his mom, his elder engaged sister, her fiancé and him.

On the first Sunday after her arrival, his parents went out to Arima to an East Indian wedding. His sister was with her fiancé spending the weekend with his family in Maraval. He was home alone with his newly met aunt. He got up late and was still in his pyjamas went in the bathroom to pee. The bathroom door was closed but not locked. He opened it and approached the toilet bowl. Much to his surprise, his aunt was having a bubble bath in the bath tub. He said, "Sorry."

She instantly responded "Oh no Emile you can pee. I have seen many pricks before."

He wanted to pee badly. He pulled down his pyjamas and held his erect pee-filled totee and started to pee. He did not look at her while he was peeing. She was looking at his erect totee.

Aunt Ellen said, "You have a fat and long prick, Emile. I have to hold it to feel how hard it is."

In a flash, she got up, and stood completely naked in front of him with soap bubbles and water slowly running down her slim looking body. She had two large breasts and looked young and wrinkle free. Before he could say anything she was squeezing his erect totee in her hand. He was flabbergasted. He did not know how to react.

"Have you lost your virginity as yet?" she smilingly said.

"What do you mean?"

"Have you had sex with anyone as yet?"

"No aunty."

"Well you and I are about to commit incest today."

Emile said that he did not know what she meant as she wrapped her wet soapy arms around him and led him to the guest bedroom in which she was staying. She stripped him completely. With her body still wet and soapy, she bear hugged him and pushed him on her bed. While on top of him she forced his very hard totee into her punani and started to brush him vigorously. It was the first time he 'came' in a real punani. She kissed his face and sucked his tongue so hard that he was afraid she would bite it out. Her body started to tremble as she was loudly yelling and moaning. She continued brushing as long as his totee was hard and erect. His totee was still very hard after two 'comes'. She brushed the hell out of him. What an initiation.

After Emile told his story a few of the elder boys ventured to tell about their sexual experiences with their cousins. But the bell rang to signal the beginning of the next class.

*****

I returned to my class. All through my scripture class, I could only visualize the scenarios in the bathroom and in the bedroom with Emile and his aunt. He mentioned that his aunt was an over fifty year old, divorced woman. Tanty Lolita was about fifty year old. Should I revisit her so that she could continue her private lessons that she started? Her lesson might be as valuable as Perfidia's lesson about the punani scent test.

I had two new pieces of information which I could use to decide my future involvement with Tanty Lolita. I was about sixteen years and Emile was seventeen years old.

Should I or should I not revisit Tanty Lolita at her home?

Emile's story affirmed to me that a woman in her mid-fifties could be full of sexual energy and could ravenously want sex. Also, with the test that Perfidia taught me, I could check out Tanty Lolita's punani before I got involved. I was tempted to talk privately with Emile about all the sexual experiences that he had with his aunt and tell him what Tanty Lolita did to me.

I was afraid that he might tell me that I was too young to be talking about sex. He might also tell Mr. Chow that I was a pervert.

*****

On the very next Sunday, I got dressed, and told my parents that I was going to ride my bicycle to Freeport with one of my friends. Papa wanted to know what was so important in Freeport. I told Papa that we were just exploring the nearby town to see what it looked like. He reluctantly approved. I left home, fully knowing that I was going to pay a surprise visit on Tanty Lolita.

On arriving at her home, I hid my bicycle behind the bushy hibiscus fence and, when I was in front of her kitchen door, called her name. I called twice. She answered upstairs from her bathroom. She was completing her bath. She opened the bathroom window and told me to sit in the drawing room downstairs. She finished her bath and joined me. She invited me to have a cup of tea with her in the kitchen. I sat down at the kitchen table eating the sandwiches she had made earlier, and drinking tea sweetened with condensed milk. I told her that her flower gardens were very beautiful and colourful and that her house plants were very healthy, colourful, and highly fragrant. She thanked me for my honest appreciation. She told me that most of the flowers were grown from seeds and seedlings that they bought from the Horticultural Club in the city.

I asked, "How did you become so strong and look so physically fit?"

She said, "Mitra, one of these days I will spend lots of time with you narrating my life story. I am positive when you hear my story you would have a lot of probing questions to ask."

She looked at me, held my hands, looked into my eyes and softly said, "Are you mad at me, Mitra?"

"Why should I be mad?" I replied shyly.

"Well you have not contacted me in over one month. Did I hurt you? Did I frighten you? I came in the shop and I told your father about my problem while you were present. I was pleading for help. You did not respond to my call."

"I was going to come, Tanty, but it rained for three weeks consecutively. I told Papa that I was riding with a friend to Freeport. Instead, I came here to see how you are doing."

After tea, she told me to accompany her upstairs. The air was very tranquil and serene with only the soft sounds of the breeze whispering through the branches of the fruits and ornamental trees that surrounded her home. We went into her large bed room which was located in the upper front part of her home. There was a sitting area adjacent to her bedroom in which were magazines, books and relaxing reclining chairs and side tables. Her bedroom was wall papered with a red landscape pattern designed similar to those seen in western cowboy movies. The room looked very welcoming. She had a large dresser on which there was a cluster of perfumes, many of which were the same that Papa collected. There were phials and bottles of French perfumes such as Shalimar, Tabu, Joy, Blue Grass and several others.

Her dressing table was covered with all sorts of cosmetics. The room was well lit indirectly with lamp shaded lights, and had an amorous scent and attractiveness. There were a few eye catching paintings on the walls. Her large ornate wardrobe and two small chairs were located around her king size bed. It was the largest bedroom that I had ever seen. While sitting on her bed, she looked at me, and said slowly, "Do you want to continue from where we stopped last time?"

I told her that she was the teacher and she knew what I should learn. And I reminded her that it was our secret.

Tanty Lolita told me to take off my shoes and lie on the bed on my back. I did as she asked. She told me to close my eyes, relax and enjoy everything that she was going to do to me. I was not afraid to obey her orders. After listening to Emile's experience, I was ready. She lied down on the bed next to me with one of her legs over my body, and started slowly to caress my head, neck and face. Her body exuded a beautiful exotic scent. While kissing me gently, periodically, she licked my face and ears. I did not like anyone licking my face but I soon learnt to enjoy it. I became very sexually aroused. I could feel my totee getting harder and erect trying to escape through the opening in my sliders. She knew fully well what she was doing. She took off my shirt and vest, and rubbed her face along my hairy chest and belly. She unbuckled my belt, unzipped my pants and pulled out my hard erect totee. She eased herself down and pulled my sliders and trousers completely off, leaving me naked. She was still fully dressed as I opened my eyes.

She said, "I will show you how to jerk off today."

As I was lying on the bed on my back completely naked, she took my erect totee and held it firmly in her hand. It felt very nice in her warm hand. She started to peel it back and forth with a slip sliding motion, slowly then rapidly. In less than a minute, I felt the same way as when she was sucking it a few weeks ago. My body started to writhe. I felt as though I was losing my sight.

She asked me how I was feeling.

I moaned, "Very sweet and nice but strange." She continued her slip sliding motion until I felt that I was going to explode. I felt as though something was coming through my totee.

She said, "look at the squirt. There is your 'come'." She placed my hand in the small pool of 'come' which was on my belly.

"Feel it, smell it, taste it, look at it."

I followed her instructions. It was warm and it smelt like bleach. She did the same thing she asked me to do with my 'come'. She hugged and kissed me and told me to have a warm shower. I got up from the bed and went into her bathroom and had a shower. I dried my body with the clean perfumed towel she gave me. Wearing a broad wicked smile, she kept looking at my nude body constantly as I was getting dressed.

She said, "You can 'come' anytime you wish. Do what I did with your totee when you are in bed tonight and enjoy the experience of your first personal jerk off."

As I was about to go downstairs, she asked me whether or not I wanted to learn more things.

"Are there more things that I have to learn?" I inquired.

She laughed and said, "There are lots of things you have to know about girls."

"I still have more things to learn?" I asked inquisitively.

She said, "Come back next Sunday. I will teach you how to make girls want you."

I thanked her for the lessons. She gave me twenty dollars as I was leaving. How fortunate was I. She was teaching and paying me at the same time. Happily I took the money and thanked her for her generosity, hospitality and her private lessons.

At that tender age I could not understand the psychology she was using on me. I was just an innocent teenager and was eager to learn anything that was interesting and exciting. My teenage hormones were racing through my blood vessels at very tremendous speeds, and I did not know how to utilize this energy source appropriately.

I went home and Papa asked me whether I learned anything new on my journey to Freeport. I hesitated to answer his question. He repeated his question in a serious tone, "Did you and your friend learn anything new in Freeport this evening?"

I told him that we learned that the Freeport area was not as built up as Chauhan Junction and was economically poorer than Benevolence. He asked me, "What was the name of the school situated at the corner of Freeport junction?"

I told him Carapichaima C.M. School.

"So you really went."

"Yes Papa," I replied.

There was no more interrogation. I did not think he believed me.

After dinner, I went to my room and worked on a few algebra and geometry questions, read some scriptures from the New Testament, and prayed for forgiveness. On reflecting on what happened in Tanty Lolita's bedroom earlier that evening, I controlled the temptations to jerk off and fell asleep.

*****

I went to college on Monday and was very interested in knowing whether my 'Eclecticans' study group members ever jerked off. In a soft voice, I asked the question, "Guys have you ever jerked off?"

They all started laughing scandalously. They looked at me and unanimously said, "Don't you Mitra?"

I responded, "Absolutely not!"

They all laughed again. Don commented that they have been doing it since they turned twelve. "You have missed out on a lot of fun Mitra."

I stood dumbfounded in their midst. "Who taught you how to do it?" I inquired.

"Emile," they all replied. I was amazed.

"Maybe they are all having sex with their aunts like Emile," I wondered. "What else did Emile teach you?" I jocosely asked.

"Where have you been Mitra? Emile runs a jerking off competition at the back of the college every Wednesday mornings during recess."

"Have you witnessed any of the competition?" I asked.

"Are you crazy or what Mitra? That show is only for senior boys."

"How do you know? Have you gone to see the show?"

"Yes. We went twice. Two big chuck-outers [bouncers] kicked our asses out before we could reach the competition zone."

I kept silent.

I decided to go secretly to the competition zone at morning recess on Wednesday by myself. There was a betting pool with the contestants' name operated by an East Indian boy, who walked with a limp. The senior boys were allowed to bet on who would 'come' first, second and third. They kept records of the 'coming' times for the academic year.

I guessed there was an annual trophy for the fastest 'comer'. Apparently the winners got money after each contest.

I got as far as the two bouncers. The big Creole boy, named Johnathan, shouted, "Where the fuck you think you going. You little shit? Get your little prick out of here fast before I put two kicks in your little ass."

Johnathan slapped my head very hard which caused me to accelerate at a high speed past the washrooms to the refreshment parlor on the other side of the school.

I could not believe that jerking off was a college competitive sport. I wondered whether it was held in every college. How did they select the team players? Was there an inter-collegiate championship?

What an exciting and interesting week. I learnt so much more about my 'Eclecticians' study groups private life and Emile's sexual business. I imagined the boys in my study group were discreetly involved in sexual activities. I decided that I should learn as much as I could while I was a healthy teenager and have fun doing it. When I thought that all my friends and peers were sacrosanct, I was totally wrong. I had to learn all there was to learn from my personal sex mentor, tutor and coach, Tanty Lolita.

*****

At last Sunday arrived for my visit to Tanty Lolita. I made another bullet proof excuse and went to her cottage. She was expecting me and I was anxious to learn more sexual skills. On seeing me, she came outside to meet me with hugs and kisses. What an amorous greeting. She was beautifully jewelled, looked very glamorous, younger, very clean and perfumed with expensive colognes. Looking gorgeous, lovable and inviting in her evening relaxing outfit, we started in the customary manner by having tea with cookies and biscuits on the kitchen table. After some recollection of her life and the conclusion of tea time, she said, " It is time to go upstairs." She walked in front of me as we ascended the stairs. My totee went instantly into erection mode as she walked up slowly, but deliberately moving her buttocks in a sexually inviting way so that I could see her panties through her partially opened flimsy evening dress.

At the top of the stairs, she stopped, turned around and slowly and delicately whispered in my ear, "My sweet lover, I have a special treat for you today." I had no idea what she was talking about. I just assumed that it should be interestingly exciting.

She sat me down on one of the small cushioned tub shaped chair which was at the side of her bed. She said that she wanted me to pay close attention to what she would be doing because I would have to repeat it later. I became very curious. "What was she going to do? What would I have to repeat?" I remained puzzled. She went into the back bedroom. She turned on her radiogram. It played a French love song.

"This is my favourite love song to which I always danced and stripped for Lawrence when he was alive," she whispered in my ear.

She was humming the tune as she danced around in the bedroom. I sat quietly as she slowly started to strip as though she was a ballet dancer. She swung and swayed in the free space between her bed and the big picture window as she delicately took off her petite red shoes. She artistically removed her see-through dress which she threw on my head.

I quickly uncovered my face to see her dancing with her black panties and white brassier. She was very excited as she jumped on the bed while removing her bra magically exposing her pear shaped, tanned, luscious-looking breasts. She rotated on the bed so as to expose her opened legs in frontal view towards my piercing eyes. Her tanned legs looked very youthful, firm and sexually arousing. My totee which was beginning to relax, automatically transformed itself into a weapon of massive punani destruction. She slowly slid her black panties down her smooth hairless thighs so that I could see her brownish pubic hairs. She was restless and kept slipping it up and down between her thighs and just above her smooth knees. Finally, she was completely nude with her partially opened punani facing me. She sat in front of me on the bed with her legs wide open, sucked my tongue, and surprisingly said, as she held my erect totee in my pants "I want you to brush me hard, hard, right now Mitra."

The music stopped. She helped me to undress as quickly as possible. I was thinking about Emile and his aunt as Tanty Lolita helped me get out of my clothes. My mind, body, spirit and imagination were completely laced with adrenalin. Momentarily, I reflected and recalled the scenarios in which Ricky was brushing Yana, and Emile was raped by his aunt. My dream was about to become true. I was about to get my first real brush.

We were both nude. Her light brown eyes were closed. She had beautiful short curly brown hair. She was perfectly groomed. She was wearing pink lipstick and a little smudge of rouge on her cheeks. Her body was exuding the scent of Shalimar. The deliciously delicate aroma was all over her body. I played gently with the back of her slim neck and chin. I started to kiss her on her face and mouth. She responded by reciprocating with her tongue and hugging me tightly with her long slim arms. I realised how fantastic, and soothing it was to be in a woman's arms romancing her without any reservations or any limitations. We did this tongue gymnastics and caressing continuously for a short time.

I gently caressed her breasts and kissed them. I slowly moved my face down her soft clean perfumed neckline through her breasts, down her smooth warm belly unto the beginning of her pubic hair line. She did not look like any old woman. Her body was flawless. It was the most beautiful nude body I had seen or touched close-up in my life. I moved my face gently down her belly and stopped at her Shalimar scented punani. She used her delicate fingers to show me the various parts of her punani. She spread apart her labia and showed me her clitoris. It was the first punani that I was able to see very close up. I ran my fingers up and down inside both of her legs up to the very top corners next to her hairy punani. I started opening her legs as wide as possible to expose her pinkish punani lips and clitoris as she did. As her legs opened wider her punani started to open. I played with her brownish pubic hairs and gently pushed two fingers up her punani as far as they could penetrate. It was warm and slimy. I slowly pulled my fingers out and lay down on top of her. I managed to get my fingers close to my nostrils without being seen by her. My first PST was negative. She was clean. There was neither a putrid nor a stink scent from the juices from her punani. She was, according to Perfidia, worth brushing. It was time to brush her. My hard erect totee pierced through her punani like a fast moving arrow. My totee was inside the punani of a real woman for the first time in my life. What a heavenly, exotic, ambrosial and erotic experience!

It was wet, tight and slippery. She adjusted herself and we started to brush. While we were brushing, Tanty Lolita was telling me how to move my waist, my buttocks and my legs to get better leverage and to create more eroticism. She moved her body in all different ways and advised me to teach my girlfriends those simple moves to enjoy sex to the fullest. She told me that during sexual intercourse that I should suck her breasts and keep on kissing her. I should use my hands to caress her all over her body. If possible, I should get my fingers into her punani to manipulate her clitoris during intercourse. We brushed for quite a long time. We were sweating and were breathless.

I had two 'comes'. Either she enjoyed or pretended to enjoy brushing as she uttered moaning and wild sounds. We remained on the bed just hugging each other in a half-asleep mode. What a wonderful, glorious and angelic experience for me to remember and relate.

I got up to get dress. She stopped me from dressing and said, "You have to have a shower before you put on your clothes. Use my tooth paste. Use this towel to dry yourself off. You have too much brushing evidence on you. If you don't wash yourself, before you go home, your Papa will know that you were brushing somebody. Always wash yourself and tell your girlfriends to do the same. You will get caught by those who could identify after-sex scents. You hear me."

I nodded in agreement. She showered again; this time with me. What a novel experience, at this age, to have a woman wash my entire body. After showering, we got dressed. I thanked her for the ecstatic and erotic learning experience. She said that next week she would teach me some more tantalising and exciting things. Furthermore, she added that she would also enlighten me on her ballet interests and some of her other cultural experiences. I was about half way down the staircase when she told me to stop. I did. She came down and met me half way and gave me about fifty dollars and thanked me. I hugged and kissed her and expressed my appreciation profusely for everything. I did not know the exact reasons for my extreme happiness. Was it the sexual experience or was it the money?

I went downstairs and left using the backyard. There were some people who did their shopping in our shop who recognised me. They hailed out to me from the river banks where they were fishing. I did not feel comfortable after they saw me coming through the hibiscus bushes.

*****

Papa was not home so I did not have to face an interrogation session. In order to maintain my first place position in geography, and history, I had to do some serious studying immediately. I did maintain my academic standing in my class when the test results were posted.

*****

The boys mentioned that they heard from Emile that I had tried to be a spectator at the 'jerking off' competition and that I was chased away. I asked them whether they were having sexual experience like Emile. They again made me look like a sexually incompetent, ignorant and uninitiated teenager of the western world. I was informed that they were all having sex.

"With whom are you having sex?" I foolishly inquired.

They were all very silent. No one ventured an answer.

After our private tutoring session at the lawyer's son home, a very close friend in the group called me aside, and told me that few of the boys were having sex with their cousins, their friends' sisters and their elder neighbours' wives. I was surprised. I thought Emile was the only one having an incestuous relationship.

*****

Sunday evening saw me walking the back-roads towards Tanty Lolita's cottage. Surprisingly, as I was about to open the gate to Tanty Lolita's cottage, the voice of the young, sexy, and charming Tanty Jamiron addressed me from the flower garden in front of her home.

"Mitra, what yu doin in the back here? What yu have with Lolita?"

Tanty Jamiron came out her garden to the find out my intentions.

I was lost for words.

"What yu doing here boy? Does your fadder know what yu doing here?" she questioned.

I quickly gathered my alibi thoughts and said, "Tanty Lolita informed Papa in my presence that she needed somebody to harvest her fruit trees, which were laden with fruits. She promised to pay good money. I am here to harvest her fruits," I proudly replied.

Tanty Jamiron looked at me with suspicion, smiled and stated, "When yu finish pickin Lolita's fruits, I want yu to pick me fruits too. My fruits sweeter than she fruits." I did not answer.

Tanty Jamiron went back into her house after her speech. I opened Tanty Lolita's gate and she met me at the back door. She greeted me without hugging or kissing me.

*****

Tanty Lolita, apparently disturbed by Tanty Jamiron's talking to me on the road side said, "That young bitch across the road is too inquisitive, she only want to know my business. You don't worry about her. I will handle her in good time. Mitra, you handled yourself very shrewdly. Let us have our usual tea time."

During tea time, Tanty Lolita revealed the story of her vibrant, colourful, interesting and exciting ventures of her life. She said that after completing her high school education at St. Raphael Convent in Port of Spain, her white Trinidadian parents from Barataria sent her to the University of Leeds in England to further her studies in literature, music, history and art. While she was attending university, she met Lawrence in her second year of studies.

Lawrence met her at the university library and invited her for tea and scones. He was reading botany, geography, history and astronomy. Being very interested in her, he invited her during reading week to accompany him to his family home. He was from a wealthy family from County Kent in England.

His family fell in love with her and wanted her to join the family. She contacted her parents and told them about the situation. Her parents went to England. Both families met in London and discussed the marriage proposal and marriage arrangements. They decided to get married at the successful completion of their degree programs. However, they got engaged and lived together as though they were already married. They travelled throughout The British Isles and Europe whenever they were not having regular classes at university.

After graduation, they both worked in Kent County for many years. Lawrence decided that they should see the world while they were still young, energetic and capable. They spent lots of time on the continent attending operas, ballets, and various cultural shows; visiting famous art collections in various parts of the world. They had visited the Louvres, Prado, Rijks and many other famous cultural centers in most large cities. Also, they had travelled all over the world in steamships across the various oceans and seas and lived with the indigenous people in the different countries.

I asked her what her favorite travelling experiences were and where would she recommend me to visit when I could afford to travel. She said that topic would be addressed at another time. Now we have to attend to the business of picking the fruits. I did not make any comments.

I was slightly disappointed as I was expecting to increase my sexual knowledge. For some reason, she was quite serious and very direct on that day. Something was obviously bothering her.

She led me to the fruit trees, and told me which fruits she wanted me to pick. She said that I had to bag them so that the fruits could be distributed the following morning to the children at the elementary school which was located on the main road.

I agreed. The evening seemed to drag on forever. There was no hint of a sexual lesson so far. We returned to her kitchen. She told me to wash and dry my hands and face in the main floor bathroom. She went to her sitting room and said that the last time I expressed a keen interest in her ballet like dancing, and that I inquired whether or not she was a ballet dancer. She said that she had attended shows at the Paris Opera Ballet, The Royal Ballet, and New York City Ballet. She wanted to be a ballet dancer but Lawrence objected. He could not tolerate seeing her in the arms and on the shoulders of another man. He wanted her for himself. He told her to dance for him at home. She said that she maintained the integrity of her marriage throughout her life with Lawrence. After he died, her first sexual exploration was with me.

I inquired about her reasons for selecting me over all the other young boys in the village. She smiled, chuckled and gave me a sweet eye (winked).

After a momentary silence, she declared that she had been purchasing her groceries at our shop for a long time and that she had observed my attitude and humorous approach to life. The value that I placed on education was revealed by my discussions with people of all ages, gender and different political and religious affinities, whether I was in the shop or outside the shop. I was especially kind, helpful and comforting when Lawrence passed away. Mentally, she had decided to adopt me when she had learned about the story of my life after my mother's death. Also, I made her feel very loved, alive, and valuable. The village people were quite aware that my stepmother did not want either me or my two sisters.

I thanked her for her candid concerns and compliments. She shed a tear, got up, came over to me and hugged me. Then, she said that she had a special gift for me.

We went upstairs into the room with the radiogram. This was a very beautiful room. I had seen similar ones at my wealthy, educated, and affluent friends' homes. She had many books, including encyclopedias, also classical records. Interesting paintings adorned the walls of each room.

She told me, that her husband enjoyed the finer cultural things in life. They had the finances to do whatever they wished to do leisurely. Her inheritance was fabulous. Lawrence left her with superb and fantastic memories and lots of wealth. Her husband's ashes were buried at the roots of the golden apple tree in the corner of one of the lots so that she could frequently pay homage to him. She did miss him immensely and had no intentions of replacing him in her life time. Tanty Lolita was quite aware that whether or not she climbed the highest mountain in the planet, or sailed the wide world endlessly, or paid visits to all the holy and sacred places on earth that nothing would bring Lawrence back to her.

After she had played her recordings from the *Sleeping Beauty* and *Nutcracker* she briefly explained the plot of each. Also, she gave me a book on ballets, ballet choreographers, ballet companies and famous ballets, and told me to read about them in my time. I did not know what to expect after these wonderful stories, cultural information and details of her personal life. She promised to get me a few records on operas. She loaned me a few classical music records which she suggested that I listen to in my bedroom at bedtime.

She said, that she had a lot of cultural enrichment for me and qualified her promise by adding that all my formal schooling in all the subjects that I was studying would get me only a high school certificate. But I would have to apply and explore the subject matter on the real world stage because formal education without cultural enrichment is like a house without a lamp. She promised to complement my geography, literature, and general knowledge with her personal world-wide travelling experiences. On the side tables there were maps of the countries where they had travelled, stayed and worked.

My education took a turn for the better. I was getting first-hand information that I could use in my classes. I was told to come back whenever I could and that she would always be ready to teach me. We did not participate in any form of sexual activities that day. I was treated as a regular college student by a woman of wisdom and panache. She gave me fifty dollars and kissed me on my cheeks. I thanked her for all her personal interest that she was extending to me and left discreetly. I continued to keep our secret.

I went home carrying the book and record of the Nutcracker ballet. No one at home saw me with them. The music was very soothing, relaxing and sleep inducing. As I was falling asleep, I envisioned Tanty Lolita's face lecturing to me about the cultural aspect of life. I felt fully elated and blessed that she included me in her life.

During the next two visits, she told me about the experiences she shared with her husband in Hawaii, Egypt, Spain, France, India, Australia and many more exotic destinations. She whetted my appetite for travelling and exploring the world. Her postcards, souvenirs, maps, diary, and her vivid descriptions of each place she visited with her Lawrence motivated me to become a global traveler when I get older and could afford to do so. Finally, there were no more fruits to pick and she had spent a lot of her time and energy enriching me.

On my next visit, she took me to her bedroom and continued her sexual lessons with me. I took every opportunity to visit her in my spare time. Every time I visited, we had sex on her big bed in her front room. She was a tantalising, fantastic and a very sensual mentor. Paramount to her personal charms and delight was the personal pride she took in the integrity of her cleanliness.

One evening while we were naked and about to have sex, Tanty Lolita said, "Do you know what fellatio is? Do you know what cunnilingus is?

I looked at her very perplexed.

Innocently and softly, I replied, "No."

She said, "Would you like to know what they are?"

Being curious and unaware of these words, I shyly questioned, "Are they good things or bad things? Would they be useful for me?"

"You tell me whether or not they are good or bad after I have given you the lessons. So far you are learning and performing excellently."

She sat up on the bed and looked at my hard young, virile and fully erect totee. She held it, squeezed it and said softly, "This looks and feels very edible!" She placed her warm, wet and delicate mouth over the head of my very painfully stiff totee and started to suck it as she did many times before. She did it for a few minutes and suddenly stopped and commented that what she had just done to me is called in sexual lingo, 'fellatio.' She went on to say that she was going to teach me how to perform cunnilingus. What was about to happen to me was totally unexpected. I was unaware that people did these things since the beginning of time. I was very curious to learn the meaning of this word. She sat at the edge of the bed, completely nude with her feet on the floor. I kept looking at her and fondling her soft breasts. Her body, beauty, and scent were all driving me crazy for sex. She knew how to set my loins on fire. Her husband must have regretted that he had to die and leave his goddess to be worshipped and serviced by other gods or goddesses. She motioned and told me to kneel down in front of her. She opened her legs as wide as possible and positioned me very close to her tanned physically fit body, and told me to get my face as close as possible to her punani. She spread apart the labia with her fingers and showed me her clitoris engorged with oxygen laden blood. She held her bulging clitoris between two of her fingers, and explained to me that her clitoris had billions of nerve endings and by stimulating and sucking it I could drive her or any woman raving mad. She wanted me to drive her raving mad before I left her bed room.

It was another close up view of her clitoris. I did as advised. She slowly showed me how to locate her clitoris with my fingers. It felt slimy and rigid to my sense of touch. Her eyes were sparkling, her face was flushed and she appeared to be in a state of utter exhilaration. I started to wonder why she wanted my face so close to her opened punani. Was she going to rub my face into it like what Tanty Tina did to me when I was younger? The view in front of me did not look black and hairy like Tanty Tina's tarantula. I became very apprehensive. I recalled the unpleasant scent of the former experience and the burning sensation that my eyes and face felt after Tanty Tina rubbed my face into her dirty Tarantula. Tanty Lolita lay on her back on the bed with her feet hanging over the bed's edge with her legs wide open. She parted the lips of her punani. All I had to do was to find the clitoris with my fingers and then hold it between my lips and suck it as a lollipop candy. I heard her instructions clearly and did not do anything. I became frightened. My inside was telling me to get out of the room.

I did not want or wish to put my clean mouth in the place where her pee pee came out. I felt nasty. What about the nasty scent? What about the taste? I was caught between a rock and a hard place. Was this normal in life, or was she just trying to take advantage of me? Do people really do these nasty things? I felt like a fly caught in her punani hairy spidery web.

I looked at her gaping punani which she spread open with her fingers with the fleshy, juicy looking red clitoris looking, and apparently enticing me. She looked at me from her prostrated position and exhorted, "Suck it." I hesitated. I giggled, scratched my head and my erection disappeared. I could not believe that I was about to perform sexual hari-kari. Would I be the same in body, mind, spirit and soul? Would God curse me for fulfilling her request? My prolonged hesitation made her impatient.

"If you refuse to do what I want you to do now then I will not have sex with you again! So, suck it now."

I wondered whether or not my classmates were already doing this. To date, everything that I mentioned to my peers resulted in me being the laughing stock of the class. I moved my mouth closer and closer to the clitoris. Tanty Lolita had her labia spread opened. I looked at the red clitoris and pretended that I was about to put a small sweet and delicious cherry candy into my mouth.

Finally, I felt in my soul that what she was asking me to do was wrong. So, I said, "Tanty, I do not want to do this I think it is very dirty, I might get sick."

She got up, and looked at me angrily, and said, "I really wished that you had done it now, maybe next time you will have the courage."

She told me that when I do have a girlfriend and I do have the opportunity to perform it on her, do it without reservation, but only, if she is totally clean. I would drive her insane with delightful pleasure whenever I do perform it. She might object first but when she has experienced the sweetness and delightful orgasms that would result, she would want more. She said, in all fairness to both of us, we should brush. We had fantastic sex. She was a wonderful sex machine. After we had shared a pot of English Earl Grey tea and a few shortbread cookies she gave me lots of money. I thanked her endlessly for the private lessons, her generosity and her flattering comments. Quietly, I opened the gate and slowly walked the back roads to my home. No one saw me when I left her place or on my way home, at least, so I thought.

*****

I went to college and asked my classmates whether they knew anything about fellatio and cunnilingus. They looked at me and said, "You now hear about that? Those are old things. Where did you hear about this?"

I told them that there were men who were drinking in our rum shop and they were talking about it. The boys in my class said, that I had to get with the program very fast, otherwise I would miss out on all the fun in life.

I said nothing and pretended that I did not know anything about sex. They believed that I was a book worm and only wanted to study while they were not only enjoying their sexual activities but were also doing their studies. I continued my studies with them and we all did very well at college. I got promoted to the next form with most of the members of the 'Eclecticans.'

*****

However, I did not stop paying my social visits to Tanty Lolita. She always treated me respectfully and generously. Sex was always on my evening agenda. She was looking younger, happier, and more cheerful than when I first met her.

Unfortunately, one evening, after having sex with her and was leaving to go home, Tanty Jamiron's loud voice addressed me from her upstairs balcony. "Mitra, I want to talk to yu and to show yu something. Come upstairs."

I stood on the road dumbfounded. She came down her steps and approached me with a very big smile. She placed one of her arms around me and said softly, "Come, I want to show yu somethin very interestin." I continued to remain on the road. I wondered what interesting thing she had to show me. I was very confused.

"What do you want to show me?" I questioned.

"Just come, na boy. Yu go see what I go show yu," she insisted.

I was perplexed. My brain was rapidly searching my memory bank for a possible reason for her surprising request. She forcibly led me through her garden and up the concrete steps to her upper floor.

"What would Tanty Jamiron want to show me?" I wondered. I never had any serious discussion with her, except when I saw her in our shop purchasing her groceries and the day she asked me to look after her fruit trees.

As she was leading me towards the steps that led to the upper floor of her home, a passerby shouted,

"Mitra, whey yu doin in this part of the village?"

As I looked back there was one of our well known regular customers. I wondered what he would think on seeing Tanty Jamiron hugging me and literally dragging me upstairs in her house.

"Tanty Jamiron wanted to show me something a long time now, but I could only come today," I answered.

There was no further dialogue with the passerby.

I accompanied her upstairs. She led me through her front gallery into her bedroom. Having led me to the glass windows in her bedroom, she looked at me and said sweetly, "Yu must be wonderin why I bring yu here?"

Quietly I remained in extreme suspense. She opened the window and told me to look through the branches of one of the three mango trees which were directly in front of her house. The trees completely obscured the front of Tanty Lolita's home which was directly across the street. I looked at the trees but I had no idea what I was looking for. She asked me what I saw. I told her that all I could see was the mango trees and the road in front her house. She told me to look again through another specific branch that she pointed out to me.

"Look through dat branch over dey, that big one with the dead leaves," she insisted.

I looked and looked. Again, I looked through a very narrow slit between the branches. Eureka! I could clearly see Tanty Lolitas's bedroom and all the furnishings in the room. Her bed could be clearly seen from the window through the spaces between the leafy branches of the mango tree.

"Do yu see Lolita bedroom?" she exclaimed smilingly.

"Yes."

"So yu see she bed?"

"Yes."

At that moment, I became very fearful and scared. An extremely tingling chill seized my entire body. I did not respond to her questions. I sensed serious trouble. She pushed me unto her bed and told me in a hush voice that she saw everything that happened in Lolita's bedroom from the very first day. She mackooed me every time I was at Tanty Lolita's home to see whether I was picking only her fruits. So she always stood at her upstairs window and peeped into Tanty Lolita's bedroom to see what would happen after the fruit picking. She confessed that she would stand at her window and patiently watch to see what would happen in Lolita's bedroom. Finally, her patience paid off handsomely. She witnessed all the sexual activities that were taking place. Now, it was her turn. I kept quiet in a state of mental uncertainty. Being guilty of all the observations and claims Jamiron lustily described, I realised that I was in deep shit. How was I going to escape from Tanty Jamiron's imbroglio?

Tanty Jamiron continued by making the following demands: "I want some of everything yu giv to that old bitch Lolita. My punani sweeter, and better than she any day. Look at mey body boy."

Tanty Jamiron got naked in a flash.

"I much younger than she. I can do moor tings than she could ever do."

I looked at her naked body standing in front of me. She had a slim, gorgeous and alluring body. She walked away from me, revealing her sexy ass as I stood completely bewildered, looking at her nude body. She closed the door leading to the gallery and looked at me with a passionate smile and lay down on her medium size bed with her legs spread widely apart and said with a gesticulating motion, "Come brush me now Mitra. I want some of de sexy stuff that yu was givin to Lolita. If yu don't brush me now, I go tell yur fadder and the people in the shop that yu comin by Lolita all de time and yu only brushin she and doing all kinda nasty ting with she," she threatened.

I stood looking at her young, beautiful and smooth body. Her body was very slim, looked very fair, clean and inviting. I was tempted to rush to the door, open it and run out the room. Instead, I just stood looking at her but not really focused on brushing her.

"Com on. Hurry up. I feelin very hot. I want to brush bad, bad. Lay we stat right now. Nobody home. Meh husband have a part-time job, cookin in the Indian restaurant in Sando, he go be home late," she pleaded.

I wanted to cry. I felt that if I did not have sex with Tanty Jamiron at that time, she would not hesitate to create a scandal in the shop in front of my parents and among the village people.

She kept on telling me to, "stop stallin and start brushin."

I told her, "What about tomorrow? I am too tired now Tanty."

She got up, put on her clothes. "You sure yu go come back tomorrow," she inquired.

I told her I will definitely arrive tomorrow at four o'clock. She said that was too early because her husband would still be at home. She exhorted me to choose another day. Reluctantly, I gave her another date. She agreed and I left quietly feeling guilty and shamefully trapped. I left Tanty Jamiron's home very confused and looked across at Tanty Lolita's home. Tanty Lolita was standing at her gate. She signalled me to come to the gate. I went.

Tanty Lolita said, "Don't admit to anything Jamiron accused you of. Don't give any information to anyone. Deny everything. I will support you. I will proudly claim that I was educating and teaching you about classical music and the fine arts. You have the records and the books as evidence."

I told Tanty Lolita that I would not admit any charges that were laid against me. I went home a very worried and frightened adolescent. No longer was I an innocent teenager when it came to sex.

I had a sleepless night, only thinking and envisioning Tanty Lolita. For the next week I was very uneasy, quiet and carried around a troubling lump in my stomach. I went to school as usual, did my homework, helped those who needed help in mathematics and participated in the 'Eclecticans' study group.

*****

I used the money that Tanty Lolita gave me to purchase a cuckoo clock, a jacket, a camera and many other items which were illustrated in the *WARDS* catalogue from England. The clock arrived at the post office after a long time. I collected the clock and installed it in our main living room. It played the *Blue Danube Waltz* every half hour. This cuckoo clock brought some much needed soothing relief to my dilemma.

The day arrived when I had to visit Tanty Jamiron. I was very surprised to see her in our shop. I started to wonder whether I was hallucinating. What was she doing in the shop? She gave me her grocery list and softly whispered, "Mitra, me husband lost he cookin wok and he home right now. I doh no how long he go be home. So don't ever come near me. If he see me talkin with yu or any man, he go kill me for sure. Don't come near me or talk to me in the road or when you come by Lolita."

I breathed a great sigh of relief. My guardian angels were flying and working overtime for me. I thanked my lucky stars. I followed Tanty Lolita's advice and said nothing to anyone about my affairs with her. After I filled Tanty Jamiron's grocery request, she left, and I never had to worry about her threats again.

*****

A week later, Papa called me into his bedroom. He, calmly but sternly informed me, "Son, one of the villagers reported that you are having sexual intercourse with Lolita and Jamiron. You should spend your precious time and energy studying for the examinations you have to write soon. You need your energy for your studies. Don't waste it on those old women. There will be plenty of younger girls who will want you when you get your high school certificates. Stop going by them. You are giving the family a bad reputation in the village. Smarten up. I hope that we will not have to discuss this issue again. Remember we did not have this talk."

I thanked Papa for his fatherly advice and left the room.

*****

One day, I paid Tanty Lolita an unexpected visit during the school week, after recalling that she had promised to tell me about the prints of some of the famous paintings that she had on the wall in her home. She was more than ecstatic when she saw me. After hugging and kissing me, she brewed a pot of one of her special tea collections. No mention of Tanty Jamiron or anyone else was made. She wanted some feedback on the regional geography discourse she had given me about Lawrence and her travels around the world. After tea, I reminded her about the paintings of her prints on canvas on her walls. She was elated that I was so keen to learn about the wonderful world of art in all forms. She accompanied me from room to room and showed me all the prints and canvas that she had bought in different parts of Europe. She emphasised four of Lawrence's and her favourites. She expounded on the lives, the periods and the styles of the artists and the masterpieces they left to the peoples of the world.

After our cultural mini tour and commentaries, and giving me a few books on art appreciation she said we should sit down on the love seat where she and Lawrence used to sit after tea. We sat down and she talked more about her travels, her classical music collections and about her dreams for the future. I listened carefully. She talked about the uncertainties, the great hopes and unexpected disappointments that could befall anyone at any instant in life. She suggested that we should see each other socially but with no sexual relations. I was deeply disappointed, but acknowledged that she did prepare me to go into the world a more enlightened and astute adolescent.

As I was opening the gate to leave, she called out, "Mitra! Come back."

I stopped, turned around and went back to the kitchen door. "May God bless you, Mitra," she said, and gave me some money.

"Thank you very much Tanty Lolita. I will use this money to buy a set of encyclopedias and classical music records."

Also, I thanked her for her kindness, generosity, life lessons, and for being part of my life. With tears in my eyes, I left feeling emotionally drained. I wondered why she gave me so much money. What did I do that made her think that I was worthy of such a large monetary reward? However, I left her home in a very sullen mood. I never entered her home again until her death a year later.

*****

I successfully completed my Cambridge School Certificate at college. I distinguished myself in mathematics, geography, history. My principal took me to the affiliated college in Marabella where I was accepted and given a scholarship to continue my studies in pure mathematics and applied mathematics. All the players in the 'Eclecticans' study group also did excellently in the Cambridge Examinations and got scholarships to further their education in schools in other towns. Their parents allowed them to accept and to attend the schools and their chosen programmes with blessings and good luck.

I was very happy to tell my parents about the great opportunity which was given to me by the principal. Papa and my stepmother had a meeting with me in our living room. They bluntly said that I could not accept the offer. They asserted that they needed my help in the shop and that, after learning about my sexual exploits, they could not trust me. They agreed that I should study whatever courses were offered by Excelsior College. It was offering French, Latin and Spanish.

I was not in favour of my parents' decision. I loved mathematics. They forced me into studying languages.

Their decision dealt me a great blow. All my close classmates left to continue their studies in their chosen fields. I was still in my teens and completely under the control of my East Indian parents. In spite of all my pleadings and crying they were very adamant. I was forced into courses that I did not want and only studied these subjects for my parents. I realised that my stepmother was forcing Papa to make decisions against his true beliefs. Papa strongly believed that all his children, regardless of gender, should get the best available education. My stepmother had already forced him to deny my sister, Ushi, a high school education.

*****

My life changed. I started to drink all brands of alcohol, became promiscuous with the unfaithful village wives and unmarried girls. I got involved with girls of my age or younger and decided to have a great romantic life with the help of my new acquaintances and so called friends. I decided to hone my social skills with those people who were not academically inclined. I learned to dance a wide range of Latin-American dances; I read French romantic novels; I dressed in style with the guidance of the best tailors in Benevolence; I associated and socialised with the fun loving people who loved to party and to have a very good time. They believed that life was too short to waste and that we should live happily moment to moment.

*****

Towards the end of my days at Excelsior College, several of my classmates and former members of the 'Eclecticians' would meet on weekends to do exciting and adventurous activities that I did not do before.

After school, during the week we would get together and brainstorm for possible fun-loving activities. Being a daring bunch of teenagers we did things which were illegal as well as legal.

One such adventure we went on a 'river lime.' It involved purchasing and consuming alcohol and non-alcoholic beverages, and fresh meat which we barbecued on the bank of the river.

Since it was an all boys lime, we bathed nude in the cool mountain water which flowed in the bend of the river in one of the naturally formed pools. Pats and I decided not to go swimming because we were feeling feverish. We sat on the bank of the river looking at our youthful friends exhibiting swimming and diving skills. Some of them had fun playing water polo, while others just stood in the pool of water eating, drinking and exchanging jokes. I sat on the bank of the river just looking at what the various groups were doing. Some of the boys were jokingly simulating homosexuality, others were comparing erection while the more modest ones decided to harass Pats and me. They splashed water, threw mud and small stones towards us. Many times they succeeded in hitting me with the mud and the stone. I became rather annoyed when a stone struck me painfully on my shoulder. In my anger, I took up all their clothes and threw them into the water. I thought that would have stopped them from harassing us. Immediately, they stopped whatever they were doing and swam to salvage their clothes. I stood up and enjoyed the chaotic situation that I had created. After getting their clothes from the water, they wrung them as dry as they could and hung them on the bushes and short plants in the sunshine. They were very quiet. There was no sign of anger or displeasure on their part. They returned to the water, but did not say anything neither to Pats or me.

I went to the cooler, got a beer while Pats remained where he was. Suddenly, while I was at the cooler, they all came out of the water, ran towards me shouting, "You bastard, your ass is dead."

I dropped the beer and ran for my life along the bank of the river, closely pursued by my nude and angry friends. I ran until I came to the sugarcane plantation, jumped across a drain, and ran into the sugarcane field. They pursued me relentlessly into the field. I kept running until I came to an open patch of land that separated a small village from the sugarcane fields. They followed me to the edge of a small village. Fortunately, a wedding ceremony was taking place at the first home in the village. I ran into the wedding. They stopped as they got into the full view of the guests and ran back.

Many of the guests asked questions about my plight. I did not say anything. I enquired about getting a taxi to Curepe Junction and one of the guests volunteered to take me to the taxi stand. I returned home.

When I returned to school on Monday, I got the cold treatment from all those boys who were with me at the 'river lime'. For the entire week, they deliberately refused to associate with me. I went to our regular liming spot, the bicycle stand, but none of the boys were there. I wondered what had happened.

Finally, I went to the 'Garage Club,' where we had weekly meetings to discuss the social issues of the boys. The 'Garage Club' was a private club only for boys from our class, the 'Eclecticans' and members of our sports team. Apparently I was sent to Coventry for commiting a grave misdeed.

One of the boys' sister saw me at the 'Garage Club.' She came and informed me that the 'Garage Club' would be having a meeting on Sunday morning to discuss my indiscretion and ostracism. She handed me an envelope and left. The contents of the envelope echoed her words.

On Sunday, I attended the meeting. Everyone was present. They were very cordial and unusually friendly. I became very apprehensive as they locked the doors and called the meeting to order. They discussed my over-reactions at the 'river lime,' their reasons for ostracizing me and the penalty I had to serve.

Then, they held me down, stripped me to my underwear, and proceeded to bathe me with stale stink water from a washing tub, stagnant water from the drain and urine flavoured water. Everone relished doing it. I closed my eyes, hoping that they would not kill me. Then, they dressed me in a blue maternity frock, took away my shoes, and led me onto the main street of the village. I felt very humiliated and dirty. I walked the main street to my home. As soon as I arrived at home, my father started laughing and my stepmother became very concerned.

My father, "What happened to you?"

I did not answer and ran upstairs into the shower. I had a warm shower, followed by a cold one.

When I came out, my family's interrogating team was anxiously waiting to learn about my new dress style. I told them what happened and they all remarked humorously, "Mitra, you are too wicked. It good for you!"

*****

One of the customary function of the boys of the 'Garage Club' was to celebrate the birthday of each member of the fraternity. During the monthly meeting many different issues were discussed and debated. Sometimes we would discuss our aspirations, dreams and future careers. Also, we would narrate the memorable things we had experienced and commented on the experiences we would like to have.

One of the member, named Ralph, had no sexual experience with a woman. So far he has only masturbated.

After the meeting, and in the absence of Ralph, we made arrangements to get him sexually initiated. We decided to pool our money to pay for his initial sexual experience with a woman. We planned a boys night out and went to the capital city, Port of Spain. We travelled by two cars which our parents loaned us.

Ralph had no idea what were our plans. We got to the city, parked the cars in one of the parking lots in Marine Square. A few of us asked Ralph to accompany us to meet some young beautiful girls. He was extremely excited. We went to George Street, where the whores operated their business. None of us had ever done this before. We were operating on the advice of the elders. It was dark when we arrived. Beneath the street lights, and in front of the brothels, the beautifully dressed and strongly perfumed ladies of the night were mingling with passerbys and potential clients.

On seeing us, two young and beautiful girls came towards us and softly told us the costs for various sexual activities. When one gave us a price the other one underbidded her.

We were very surprised and confused with their bidding behaviour. Before we could make a deal, Ralph said that he wanted no part of the activity and started to walk briskly back to the parking lot. No sooner he started to back track, we saw the police van coming down the street. As the prostitutes saw the police, they scampered through the open doorways of the buildings. The two women left and also ran behind the nearest buildings. On seeing everyone scurrying, we ran down the street as fast as we could, jumped over garbage piles along the side of the Cathedral and hid between the cars, face down in the parking lot. We waited for a while. Then we saw the police car coming down the street towards us. It did not stop but continued and went out of sight. We returned to our cars very scared. The other boys asked what happened. We told them.

At that point Ralph wanted to know what we were doing as he trembled. We told him about the plan we had. Surprisingly, Ralph did not object to our plans. But he wanted no street walker. He would prefer a woman of a higher pedigree who operated in a respectable establishment.

We consulted with one another to find out how much disposable income we had. In order to get more information about a possible woman for Ralph, we went to a well known night club. At the night club, after purchasing drinks and fried chicken, we spoke to one of the waitress who was serving us. We told her what we had planned and if she could recommend us to a place where there was a stable of thoroughbred girls. She spoke to another waitress, they giggled as they talked. Our waitress told us that her friend recommend the 'Perfume Gardens.' We found out the address, and as we were about to leave, another young, beautiful girl came to our table and asked who was the young man who needed to be initiated. A few of us, on seeing how gorgeous and charming she was volunteered to take Ralph's place. When Ralph told us he wanted her, we all acquiesced to his wish. She asked a very high price. One of the boys, whose parents were very wealthy business people in Benevolence, volunteered to pay whatever she wanted. He spoke to her privately, and we had no idea what he told her. We assumed that he told her to give Ralph the full works. Ralph left with her and went upstairs.

We remained downstairs drinking and eating until Ralph returned, looking very happy, he commented that he would be seeing her again privately at another time. We returned home after midnight, feeling very satisfied that Ralph was no longer a virgin. Those days when we were young and restless would never come back.

*****

During one of the wind-ball cricket games in the Market Square I hurt my foot while running for a ball. Although I limped around I still played. After the game, a few of the 'Bicycle Stand Boys' (BSB) sat down on the benches in the square just old talking and looking at the girls who were going to the movies.

We did not have a lot of money so we decided to perform a prank. It was dark, and the street lights were on. Located at the end of the market street was the 'Grill' restaurant. There was no one else in the restaurant, except the young lady who was in charge. We ordered for a large box of french fries.

She left to make the fries in the cooking facilities located behind the dining area. The young lady could not see us from where she was preparing the fries.

On the front counter, and directly in our view was the rotating rotisserie, fully loaded with BBQ chickens. One of the boys suggested that we should steal a couple of the chickens while the girl was in the back cooking. Most of us consented. Two chickens were taken out of the spit and brought to the park. When the girl returned with the french fries, she had not noticed the vacant spots on the rotisserie. We each bought a drink. At first, we walked away slowly, then ran into the Market Square, which was partially dark.

In the Market Square, we ripped the chicken apart and shared the meat. After our meal we were about to leave when I decided to throw the empty soft drink bottles into the waste paper barrel which was about ten feet away. I successfully threw most of them into the barrel. Two of them broke as they fell on the concrete. In the quiet of the dark night, the loud sounds of the breaking bottles could be heard across the Market Square. I did not think about cleaning up the broken bottles in the dark, so I left to join the other boys.

Within a minute, I heard the voices of two policemen, who were standing in the dark under one of the trees, shouting for us to stop. At first, we ignored the call. Again they shouted for us to stop. We all ran out of the park in all different directions. Because of my injured foot, I was the last to exit the square. The policemen started running and shouting for us to stop. As I got under the street light, I stopped and walked back to the policemen.

At first, I thought they were coming after us because of the chicken we had stolen. Instead, they asked who threw the bottles. I told them my story and they decided that I should accompany them to the police station.

Meanwhile, the residents of most of the homes on the main street of Benevelonce came out on their balconies to see me accompanying the policemen, as we headed for the police station. As we got closer to the police station, my friends, who were following closely behind, kept on shouting for the policemen to set me free. Their pleas were ignored and as we entered the police compound, the policemen warned my friends that they could be arrested for interfering with their duties. They remained on the sidewalk outside the police station and watched as they escorted me inside.

It was the first time I had ever been in a police station. As I stood with them, the sergeant told me to sit down on the bench which was opposite the two prison cells. There were prisoners peering at me through the bars. I did not know what was going to happen. The sergeant asked the policemen for their reasons for bringing me in. On hearing their reasons, he became very annoyed and told them to go to his office. Then, he called me, apologized and told me to go home. I rejoined my friends on the sidewalk. I told them what happened. They did not say much as we all left for our homes.

The rumours of my encounter with the law spread like wild fire throughout the village of Chauhan and Benevolence. My father, after hearing it from several customers, was very annoyed at me and remarked that I brought shame to the family. I was very apologetic to Papa and my entire family, especially my Ajah.

*****

After learning how to dance the merengue, bolero and Samba dances, I bought the records that my teacher was using to teach me to practice at home. My ballroom dance teacher, Vasso, told me that he would ask his sister, Anita, to be my dance partner. At the next dance lesson, he told me that his sister had agreed and would accompany me to dances on either

Saturday evenings or Sunday afternoons. We entered many dance competitions under the tutelage of Vasso. At that time, we danced to the music of Choy Aming, the Dutchy Brothers, Fitz Von Bryan, Joey Lewis and many more bands. Whenever Anita was not available, I was able to attend dances without a dance partner because there were always many unescorted girls at the dances who loved to dance and could. I finally found a dance partner, Cathy, who was younger than me.

After dance dating her on several occasions, and because we had so much fun together I wanted her to be my steady girlfriend. Unfortunately, Cathy went out to dances with me only when she was at her parents' home in Benevolence. She was attending Belvedere high school in San Fernando and stayed with her cousins at their home during the week and occasionally would not come home for weeks. Whenever Cathy and I were alone, I would try to kiss her. She resisted all of my attempts to kiss, to fondle, or to romance her. On many occasions when I forcefully kissed or fondled her breasts she slapped me and walked away. I realized that she was just patronizing me at the dances.

There was really no romantic relation between us. She was a Christian and I was a Buddhist. Her family did not appreciate her dating a boy from a different religious background. One of her brothers strongly objected our association because of religious differences and made it a great issue with his mother in their home when I was not around. But being one of my better friend, he never objected personally to me about dating his sister nor prevented me from visiting their home. His mother was very open-minded and did not have any objections to the budding relationship between her daughter and me.

One day Cathy's mother cornered me in the kitchen when no body else was present at home, and told me, that she knew that her daughter, Cathy, was in love with me, and should a strong love bond be realised between us, and should I ever consider marriage, I would have to convert to Christianity.

I looked at her with great amazement and did not respond. I had no intention of marrying her or any one. I definitely had no intention of making any religious conversion of any kind. That relationship could not and did not go any further. I also learned later from one of my sister's friends, who attended the same high school as Cathy, that she had a steady boyfriend where her cousins lived. Then, it dawned on me why she resisted all my advances to kiss and fondle her. I was disappointed at my first attempt at teenage romance. Despite all the misunderstandings and assumptions, a Platonic relationship existed between us. I had learned many romantic skills from Tanty Lolita, but I had no opportunity to practice them as yet.

*****

On many occasions, I was asked to help out my friends whenever they were experiencing dating crises. In one such situation, when one of my cricket team mates who was also a very good friend, Raja, who was dating one of the most gorgeous and charming girls in the village, named Nancy, came to me at my home and sought my help. Raja told me that Nancy's mother would not allow Nancy to go out with him to the dance unless he found a date for the other sister, Gina. I was chosen.

"Gina!" I protested, "She is a very loose girl [Jagabat]. I am not going with her. If my other friends should see me taking her out to dance, I would be the laughing stock of the village. Also, if my father should only hear that I went out dancing with Gina, I don't know how he would react."

Raja pleaded with me, giving me all kinds of reasons why I should help him out. Finally, I agreed.

Raja accompanied me to his girlfriend's home which was not too far away. I met Gina and her mother, who looked like another Tanty Lolita. Raja, Gina, Nancy and I went to the dance in Benevolence. I became very embarrassed by the scandalous behaviour of my attractive and alluring companion. A few of the single men, who were at the entrance to the dance hall, were very interested in Gina's sexy and gorgeous body. They flirted with her openly and wanted her as a dance partner. She told them that I was her boyfriend and to get away from her. I did not get involved in the argument. I was never a fighter and was not going to fight for any woman. I paid the entrance fee for both of us. Raja bought tickets for Nancy and himself. We entered the reception area and got a nice table for four at the edge of the dance floor. As I started to dance with Gina, many of my sister Elyana's college friends questioned me about Gina. I told them that I was just helping out my very good friend Raja. I tried to explain the predicament of my friend but they did not buy my story.

I was fully aware that should these girls tell my sister about Gina, it would not augur well for me at home. I did not anticipate their macocious (spying) eyes would be on me for the entire dance. On my part, I had to be very careful, to avoid being too loving, caring and romantic with Gina. I had no way of knowing what Gina had on her mind as she continuously kept smiling and hugging me on the dance floor.

Raja bought the first round of drinks and East Indian snacks. Calypso and Latin music were just what I wanted. I was sweating and tiring as the hours passed away but I kept on doing what I loved – dancing.

Before the evening sunlight could change fully into twilight, Gina approached me at the table and told me that she needed some assistance with her strapless bra. I was totally flabbergasted and surprised at her request. She told me that her strapless brassiere fell down and needed me to help her fix it. I did not know how to respond. She held my hand and led me outside the building through the backdoor. There was no one at the back of the building. She pulled the top of her dress down exposing her two lemon size breasts and told me what I had to do with her bra. It was the first time I had to help a girl put on her bra. We went back to the dance floor. Raja inquired about my absence. I explained briefly Gina's dilemma. He could not stop laughing. We were having a great time dancing, eating, talking and joking when it suddenly became dark outside. Night had fallen suddenly as it usually did in the tropics.

Raja told me quietly that we had to leave because he needed some extra time to make love to Nancy before taking her back home.

We left the dance. Gina and I led the way through the front door closely followed by Raja and Nancy. As we got on the main road, Raja told me that we would be taking the back road to go home. I looked at Gina and asked her what she wanted to do. She said that we had to chaperon Nancy. We all headed for the back roads. There were no street light or houses on the road that Raja took. Frequently, Raja stopped to kiss, fondle and romance Nancy. I dared not follow suit because Gina was not my girlfriend. Remember, I was just helping out Raja. However, Gina decided that she would kiss and romance me. Being a jagabat, she was accustomed to making love with other teenage boys.

As we walked towards our homes in the dark back streets, I got more than I expected. Gina was a wild love-making machine. She was all over me. She gave me her signature love bite. While we were kissing, Gina deliberately bit deeply into my lower lip. I felt her teeth piercing my delicate thin lip which bled instantly. I became very worried and immediately stopped all bodily contact with her as we slowly made our way home. I wondered, how I would explain my bleeding lip to Gina's inquisitive mother, my curious Papa and my sisters, who were very protective of me. My sisters loved me unconditionally.

When we arrived at Gina's home, immediately her mom noticed my bruised lip and commented with a smile, "Gina bite you Mitra. She too dam bad." I smiled and did not respond.

I thanked my friends Raja and Gina for a very memorable evening. I left them and went home.

I hoped that my detective-minded father was not at home. The news had already got to Papa that I had taken Gina to the dance. He was patiently awaiting my return. I realised that our shop was a hub for information on anything and everything that took place in either Chauhan village or Benevolence. Papa noticed me sucking my lips as I tried to conceal my bruise. Papa remarked, "What happened to your lip boy? Some girl buss your mouth?"

I defended myself and said, "Papa, while I was dancing, a guy made a fast spin and his elbow hit me in my mouth."

"Let me see that bruise," challenged Papa.

Papa looked at the bruise and smilingly professed, "You think I was born yesterday. Gina bit you while you were kissing her. I warned you about wasting your time on girls. You have to stop going by Gina and her family. The mother is a whore, therefore, the children will have a tendency to be whorish too. If the tree is rotten then the fruits will be rotten."

Taking my father's advice, I stayed away from Gina.

*****

Frequently I helped in our shop with my sisters and parents. As a result, I was privileged to see and to hear, on a daily basis, from our customers about the infidelity and debauchery that were rampant among the village people. From the shop windows and from the upper level of our home, I witnessed my neighbours' wives and husbands having affairs with other neighbours' wives and husbands as soon as either their husbands or their wives left for work. It dawned on me that I could get free sex from a few of my neighbours wives by threatening to black-mail them. Smiling to myself, I started to seriously consider the idea. Secretly, I went to the home of one of the married women, who was very attractive, young and sexy. She was horning (cheating on) her husband when he went to work. Being quite aware that her husband would not be returning from work for another eight hours, I visited her and told her that I wanted to have some of the sexual activities that she was sharing with the other man. She became very annoyed and shouted, "What kinda sexual activities? What de hell are you talkin bout Mitra?"

I did not expect such a brave reaction from her. I was speechless.

"Get out of my fuckin room before I start screaming rape," Zora shouted.

"Shut up Zora! I know everything you doing as soon as your husband, Kamal, leaves for work. On many occasions, as soon as Kamal leaves, I notice that Faiz would meet you at the corner and both of you would come here. You would close the window by the zaboca tree. After about forty five minutes, Faiz would leave and come in the shop and talk about how he horning Kamal."

"What do you want me to do? Please don't tell Kamal about Faiz. He will leave me," she anxiously begged me with tears in her eyes.

I felt very sorry for her as I quietly stood in her bedroom. In fact, I felt very embarrassed at the emotional turmoil that I had caused Zora. There was no dialogue between us for a few minutes as she sobbed and begged me not to say anything to Kamal. She got up from her bed where she was sitting and said, while holding me, "I beg you to keep this a secret. I will talk to my younger sister to brush with you. My sister, Laila, is engaged to be married in a few months to Imtiaz. She will brush with you anytime. She is only getting married to him because he got lots of money."

I was confused and very startled at what I was hearing. I thought marriage vows were sacred. I became very curious to learn about the truth about Zora's claim. She told me that she would talk with her sister, make all arrangements and would come in the shop, and would relay the time and place to secretly meet Laila. I knew Laila and her future husband who both lived in the village. Patiently I waited for her relay. Zora came into the shop when I was alone on duty, bought a few items and passed me a piece of folded paper with the pertinent information concerning Laila.

I memorized the information and destroyed the evidence. I was supposed to meet Laila after eight o'clock at night in two days. I was expected to be at Zora's place to meet Laila when it was dark. I was very puzzled at the arrangement.

After eight o'clock in the evening, Zora's husband, Kamal, would be at home from work. How was I going to have sex with Laila at Zora's while her husband Kamal was at home? Was this a sting or an entrapment?

I realised that we had the biggest business in the village. Every sensible female would like to get romantically involved with me so that I would marry them. Were Laila, Kamal and Zora planning to hook me? I decided to honour the appointment and I was prepared to face the consequences.

Later that evening while I was reading the evening news Kamal appeared in the shop. He greeted me in his usual friendly and cheerful manner. Kamal told me that he would like me to go with him to see the movie, *The Grass Is Greener*, at the night show the day after tomorrow.

I was lost for words as my brain started to overheat with a conspiracy theory. What was unfolding before me? Why would Kamal invite me to go to the movies on the night that I was expected to have sex with his sister-in-law at his home. I agreed to his request. Kamal told me to meet him at the gas station at six o'clock when it would be dark. I had a very restless night.

I told Papa that my college friends, on the recommendation of one of our teachers, were going to see the movie, *The Grass Is Greener*, and had invited me to join them. Papa, after speaking with my stepmother, hesitantly agreed. I met Kamal and as we were walking to the movie house, Kamal informed me about his surreptitious plan. He told me that he was made aware by his wife, Zora, that Laila wanted to have an affair with me before she got married. Kamal was making sure that I would be at his home to have an affair with his sister-in-law. I was amazed and shocked! His plan was to pretend to be going to the movies with me. But he had a secret agenda.

Kamal and I went to the Sunset Cinema house to find out for certain who was starring in the movie and what the movie was about. We found out that Cary Grant and Deborrah Kerr were the stars. We also inquired about the plot of the story from a few of our acquaintances who were seeing the movie for a second time. I needed that information in the event Papa wanted me to validate that I really had gone to the movie and was not visiting a woman. I did not think that my father trusted me. Why should he, after learning that I had been associated with Tanty Lolita.

After I was satisfied that I had sufficient information about the movie, we doubled back under the cover of darkness to Kamal's home. While we were walking back from the Cinema, I asked Kamal why was he doing this.

He said, "Mitra, my sister-in-law, Laila, has a superiority complex because she thinks she is too good for any man. Once, I asked her for sex, and she told me that she will never have sex with me in this lifetime. She continued by saying that she will only have sex with her husband. So, when Zora told me about the arrangement she had made, I had to be present to see it happen. If this goes as planned she will never be able to talk down to me again."

I was amazed and shocked by what I was hearing.

When I arrived at Kamal's home, he told me that he would hide behind the bushes at the side of the house, so that Laila would not know that he was involved. He added that if she knew he was involved, she might change her mind to maintain her integrity and prudence. Kamal was going to peep through the cracks between the boards on the room's wall to witness the sexual activities that was going to take place. As Kamal went behind the bushes I went and knocked on Zora's door. She greeted me and said, "Come inside quick Mitra. I do not want anybody to see you coming by me in the night. If they see you they go start talkin. You know how people mouth is."

I hurried inside and she closed the door. Laila, who was sitting quietly on the bed, got up and said to me with a smile, "So you really serious boy? Yu eh fraid yu fadda get to know?"

I did not answer. Zora, then advised us to go to the adjacent room and have sex. We went to the next room and closed the door. The room was indirectly lit by the light rays that streamed through the glass louvres.

Laila hurriedly took off her clothes and I did the same. Since there was no bed in the room, we lay down on the hard wood floor and we started making love. We kissed several times while I fondled her breast. I gradually got my fingers into her punani and performed the PST on her which she passed. While we were having sex I realised she was not as experienced as Tanty Lolita. In the meantime, after we finished, she told me that I should not tell anyone that we had sex, but also she would like to have sex again with me.

I left through the backyard, where Kamal congratulated and thanked me. Then I circumvented the neighbouring homes and patiently waited in the dark to join the crowd of people returning from the movies. After joining them, I spoke about the movie by asking them their opinions. I got more salient details which became very invaluable under the cross examination of Papa when I arrived at home.

*****

I went to school and boasted to my peers about my sexual experience with Laila. They wanted juicy and detailed stroke by stroke action of the actual sexual events. I exaggerated the details as much as I could. My peers kept on repeating, "You damned lie. You too damned lie, Mitra. You couldn't fuck two times. You fuckin lying bitch."

I kept my appointment with Laila on the following week. She was in the room but there was a mattress on the floor. Before I could ask, she said, "Last time my back and my ass pained for days after brushin on the hardwood flooring. You brush me much sweeter than my future husband. I had a great time, but I cannot stand all the after pain. My fiancé was asking all kind of serious questions. He even asked me whether I was cheating on him. I told him that I love him only and that no other man can come between us."

"What a wretched hypocrite," I thought.

I listened very carefully to the remorseless and hypocritical voice of infidelity. We had sex. However, my conscience bothered me. I was having sex with her, fully knowing that she was getting married in a few weeks. She has been unfaithful to him even before her marriage. I believed that I was equally responsible for her infidelity. Women usually cheated after they got married according to my teachers. She was having either a prenuptial last sexual fling or fulfilling a fantasy.

I started to wonder about the integrity and confidentiality of the sacred marriage vows couples took in the presence of their parents, justice of peace, the legal marriage ministers, pundits, holy men, holy women and their trusted friends. How ironical to witness Kamal's participation in the infidelity of his sister-in-law in his own home when he was unaware that his own wife, Zora, was having regular sexual intercourse with Faiz in his own bed when he left for work! I started to lose faith in the sanctity of the marriage vows.

My peers and I had some serious discussions with our teachers at college about the infidelity of married couples. I expressed my concerns about the pros and cons of marriage. Two of my teachers apparently were having doubts about the fidelity of their female companions. As we were the senior students of the college, we were privileged to have frank and honest discussions with our teachers. I was totally against marriage for myself, after all the cheating that I witnessed and participated in.

I recalled Papa's advice to me. He told me that I should never leave my wife in the company of other men unsupervised. Men had a natural propensity to seduce any attractive women of any marital status. They asked the relevant questions that would lead any woman to either have the man take off her underwear or she would pull it down faster by herself than any man could.

*****

My convictions against marriage were reaffirmed by my experiences. One evening, I was drinking Italian vermouth with a few of my married friends in a Chinese restaurant located on the main road in Benevolence. A very good friend, who was a teetotaller, came in to the Chinese restaurant, called out and got the attention of Justin, one of my drinking partners. Justin went outside with the trusted friend who spoke with him for about ten minutes. On returning from his brief meeting with our teetotaller friend, Justin called me from the drinking table and spoke to me privately.

Justin asked me to accompany him to his home to be his witness. Being very apprehensive and a bit reluctant to participate, I asked, "Witness to what?" I could not believe what he angrily and anxiously later told me.

We excused ourselves from the drinking party and left on foot for Justin's home which was about half mile away. We did not say a word to each other on the brisk walk.

When we arrived at his home, he told me to be very quiet. He climbed up on a wooden box which was outside his bedroom window and without saying a word stood looking. He came down as quiet as a mouse and after whispering told me to climb on the box and to look through the slightly opened glass louvres. After, mentally recording what I saw, I carefully and quietly climbed came down from the box. What I saw was repulsive and degenerate. Justin's wife and one of his best friends were romancing each other in complete nudity on his bed.

Justin held me around my shoulders and we walked away from the house. He looked very disappointed and defeated and asked me for my advice. I asked him whether he had a camera. He responded in the affirmative. I advised that he should open the back door quietly, take his camera, enter the bedroom and take photos of them in the bedroom in whatever posture they were in. Furthermore, I assured him that should he want me to be a witness to the affair, I would accompany him to the bedroom.

He said, "You are coming with me now. We are going in together and keep very quiet."

Justin opened the kitchen door which was at the back of the house and furthest away from the bedroom. As he opened the kitchen door, we could hear the sweet and romancing sounds of the Tijuana Brass coming from the living room radiogram. Justin entered the kitchen and signalled me to follow him very closely.

He took his camera and we stealthily headed for the bedroom. The door was partially opened which made it very easy for Justin to swiftly push it wide open. They were fully engaged in fornication. Justin entered with his camera shooting rapidly and continuously at them in *flagrante delicto*. He caught his wife in the act of adultery. He had the evidence and an eye witness.

The marriage ended in divorce. Justin and I remained friends until Justin's new wife did the same thing to him. He later left the village and went to live in another town far away from all his friends.

*****

I finally completed my studies and left college. I applied for positions with the Trinidad and Tobago Government Civil Service and The Ministry of Education. Many months elapsed without a response to any of my applications. I became very depressed. I no longer wanted to work in the rum shop and grocery store. In spite of my disenchantment, I spent most of this period helping my parents operate the business.

Many of our customers would inquire about my future career. They wanted to know whether or not I would continue to work in the shop and take over my parents' business or would I open my own shop, or would I be seeking a job with the government or a private business company. I did not like the shop business, even though it was making money. Working in the shop was too time consuming and too laborious. I wanted to be free from the confines of shop business.

I had reached a very crucial crossroad in my life. I was no longer a teenager. In the eyes of the public and my parents, I was a young and educated person, who should get a good paying job, get married and start a family as soon as possible. I was not interested in marriage at that stage of my life. However, I was worried that if I did not find a job within a very few months, I might end up as a shopkeeper for the rest of my life. That thought terrified me extremely. I prayed and waited patiently, but hopefully, for a favourable response from one of my job applications. It was immensely stressful and discouraging. My Ajah was very caring, comforting and compassionate. He advised me to stop worrying and to have patience, courage, understanding and determination to meet and overcome the inevitable difficulties, problems, and failures in life. I listened and heard him loudly and clearly.

IMPUDENCE

IMPRUDENCE

A fter the majority of the boys with whom I associated completed college and were in search of employment, we frequently limed (gathered) at the 'bicycle stand'. It was located opposite the only cinema and adjacent to most of the business places on the main street in the town of Benevolence. For many years, we had observed and listened to the words of wisdom from many self-proclaimed budding evangelical prayer groups. The prayer group was a collection of elderly women and men who preached from the four Gospels. Every Thursday, at twlight, five middle-aged men and five middle-aged women, all dressed in white, sometimes wearing coloured head bands, would assemble under the Tops Tailoring store. They would teach and preach about the parables, miracles, morals and any topic they thought would make a difference in the lives of their followers. They needed only a small table, covered with a green cloth, on which they placed a large bell, a tall lighted candle and a few Bibles. On the floor in front of the table, a clean white sheet was spread on which all offerings were collected. One of the men acted as commentator. First, he would ring the bell several times to get the attention of the curious and the regular listeners. Then, he would announce the chapter, verse and Gospel from which a member of the group would be reading. The readings were directly related to the topics announced. The crowd grew slowly and the cash offerings continued to pile higher and higher as they preached.

At the end of the prayer session, a few of the boys, who were executives of the 'Garage Club', and who were also members of the 'bicycle stand' decided to have an emergency meeting.

It should be noted that all the 'bicycle stand' boys were also members of the 'Garage Club'. Many of us inquired as to the reasons for the emergency meeting. The president told us that the agenda would be revealed in a few minutes. Hurriedly, we assembled and the meeting was immediately called to order. The secretary told us that we were all losing out on a great opportunity to collect some easy cash. There was a deathly silence on hearing his statement. Most of the boys asked him to explain his declaration. He said that it dawned on him as he was sitting on the bicycle stands listening to the older folks preaching the word of the Gospels, and collecting money effortlessly for doing it, that we should be preaching instead of them. These people were not college graduates and were making easy money by only ringing a bell, lighting a candle and reading from the Gospels. The treasurer joined in the speech and claimed that we all had attended a Catholic school, studied scriptures and were more knowledgeable about the words in both the Old and New Testaments than they were. One of the floor members asked what was he suggesting. Three of the executives, and many of the members, suggested that we take over the preaching group route. Two of the boys got annoyed and shouted, "Are you bastards insane? Do you want to go to hell?" Few of the heavy drinkers questioned the motives of the club for taking such a blasphemous act. One of the executive said that he carefully observed the amount of cash collected within ninety minutes of effortless readings. He claimed that we could preach better and could draw a larger audience, and maybe influence more people because we were young, educated and unemployed. "What are we going to do with the collection?" A member inquired. The answer shocked almost everyone. The President said that we would use the collection money to purchase all the alcohol and non-alcoholic drinks, Chinese food and curried rotis that we regularly consumed. The meeting went out of order. Heated arguments ensued and a skirmish between a couple of the Catholics and the non-Catholics had to be pacified before the meeting could be brought back to order.

The originators of the idea suggested that we find out when and where they preached. Having found out their schedule, we should go one or two days earlier to their scheduled meeting place and do our preaching.

We were advised by one of the boys to seriously think about what we wanted to do, and what could be the possible repercussions from our teachers, our parents and the general public, when they learn about our motive. We all vowed not to disclose our real motive. If we were ever questioned about our reasons for preaching, we would tell those concerned that we have intentions of furthering our education at university and we would need to start collecting seed money.

A feedback meeting was scheduled for a week later. Many of the Catholic boys were absolutely against the idea. They asked me for my opinion. I told them that I would have to think about it seriously.

One week later the plan was passed with an overwhelming majority. We had to rehearse our various roles several times. When we were confident that we could face the public fearlessly and intelligently, we implemented the preaching plan. It took us two weeks to go public. We were well received at the two sites we selected. The collections were more than we anticipated. With all that cash at our disposal we had to be very careful how, when and where we spent it. We had to go to other neighbouring villages and towns where we would not be easily recognized as the young preachers from the neighbouring village.

On the third week of our preaching mission, in front of our village people, the unexpected happened. Towards the end of our preaching session, the Benevolence police squad car slowly approached, drove by and stopped across the street. No one came out from the police car. At that moment panic ran through my heart and soul. We continued preaching, as the crowd looked around at the parked police squad car. Finally, the doors of the police car opened and two uniformed police men slowly alighted. We looked at one another and unanimously decided that it was time to immediately pick up our belongings and run. One picked up the collection, another took the bell and others ran in various directions. We thought that someone from the 'authentic' prayer group had complained about our encroachment of their preaching territories. As I ran towards the open park, I could hear the bell ringing as the bearer ran with it. I ran as fast as I could through the corn fields at the back of the school and ended up in the swampy fields. The stars were bright and I could clearly see the street lights in the town and the lights in all the business places and homes. I stood in the mud for a long time. Then, I realised that the creepy and crawling reptiles would be searching for prey. Being very afraid of snakes and frogs, I ran out as fast as possible on to the gravel road. There was no sign of a police squad car so I headed for my home. When I arrived at home, everyone was in bed. I used the downstairs shower to clean up and I hid my wet and muddy clothes among the other soiled clothes in the laundry basket.

On the following day, I made no mention of the disgraceful event either to anyone at home or anyone who came to shop. By noon, the news had not reach our shop as yet. I decided to stay home that evening and help my parents in the shop. At approximately five o'clock the two policemen who were at our preaching congregation came to our shop in the same squad car. I became extremely terrified. I thought that I would be arrested and taken to jail. Surprisingly, they were very calm and pleasant as they spoke to my Papa. They called me as I tried to avoid their glances. They started laughing loudly and said, "Why did you run last night from the preaching?" Papa became curious and started his investigation. Before I could say anything, they said that they had heard about our preaching and the large crowd that were attending so they decided to pay us a courtesy visit. They were very apologetic for frightening us. I was the first member of the 'Garage Club' to learn about the reason for the police visit. After informing the 'Garage Club' about my talk with the policemen, we never stepped on a preaching podium again.

*****

Early one Thursday morning as Papa was en route to Port of Spain to buy stocks for the shop, he stopped in McBean village where I was spending the weekend with relatives. He met me in their front yard and after greeting me, he proudly told me that the headmaster of Chauhan Hindu School, Mr. Ganesh, wanted to see me as soon as possible. I hugged, kissed and thanked him for delivering the message. Papa was very excited and happy for me. I was more than happy and excited to meet Mr. Ganesh. Immediately, I got dressed and took a taxi to my home at Chauhan Junction. After a quick shower, I got dressed as though I was going for an important job interview. Although it was a hot sunny day, I wore my suit and tie and made sure that my shoes were clean and shining.

I went to my former elementary school and met with Mr. Ganesh, my former headmaster. With a broad smile, he greeted me by my first name and shook my hand. He inquired whether I was employed. I told him that I was not and that I was in search of a teaching position. Mr. Ganesh offered me a teaching position which I gracefully and gratefully accepted. Without any delay, he gave me the curriculum guidelines from the Ministry of Education for the subjects taught in the standard three classes. He told me that I must design lesson plans for the standard three classes in all the subjects mentioned in the guidelines, and must have them prepared and available for him on the following Monday morning. I was to assume the duties of a primary school teacher with the Hindu phalanx of the Ministry of Education. He shook my hands and congratulated me. He proudly said, "Welcome back to your educational home base, Mitra."

Mr. Ganesh escorted me to the various classes to meet the new teachers and also a few of my former teachers who were still employed at the school.

My prayers were answered. At that time in my life, I was not aware that I would be embarking on a lifelong teaching career. Vividly, I recalled a sermon that Mr. Ganesh gave many years ago to all the students in my Standard Six class.

He calmly asked these very simple but profound questions: "Students of Standard Six, how old are you now?"

"Eleven years old," we responded in unison.

"How old would you be in five years?"

"Sixteen years old."

"How old would you be in five years if you do not further your education at the high school level?"

"Sixteen years."

"How old would you be if you further your education at the high school level, study diligently and successfully pass the Cambridge School Certificate Examination?"

"Sixteen."

"Do you want to get a high paying job which could lead to a better life?"

"Yes, sir."

"Well, the choice is yours to make. Either you decide to advance your education by studying diligently or waste your time doing foolish and wasteful things."

I applied these same lines of questionings whenever I had an opportunity to advise or motivate students of any age.

The following Monday morning, I reported to school very early. I presented my lesson plans to the headmaster.

Mr. Ganesh sat down and went through my lesson plans with some very constructive and critical comments and recommendations. I had to present my lesson plans for the next week every Friday evening before I went home.

Mr. Ganesh always returned them to me early every Monday morning with his constructive comments and invaluable suggestions for improving my teaching practices.

I found myself in a new learning and working culture. I had spent my college life studying under the Roman Catholic education system. I was now returning to the Hindu education system in which I received my early education. I did not know that I would be spending the next few years learning and teaching. However, I made sure that my lesson plans and pedagogy were acceptable to the headmaster and the senior trained teachers. My tutoring background and my enrichment experiences from my 'Eclecticans' study group became very valuable in my pedagogy. Very quickly I gained the respect and acceptance of all those I considered important and influential in the school system. Meaningful and friendly relationships formed with a few of my trusted colleagues.

*****

I was ready to have a steady girlfriend, not a wife. I was young, somewhat handsome, educated, employed, unmarried and a sportsman. My family and I were prominent and respectable people in our village.

At the end of my first term of teaching, several of my former college mates who were employed as educators in different parts of the island but still lived in the village, decided to rent a beach house in Mayaro. They invited me to join them for the two week vacation. The roaring sound of the ocean's rushing tides could be heard loudly throughout the house. The rear windows afforded full views of the endless Atlantic Ocean. The coastline was lined with several coconut plantations, and tropical seashore vegetation. In the beach house, we played card games, chess, checkers, backgammon and mathematical brain teasers. Every morning just after sunrise, we played either wind-ball cricket on the smooth sand or skimmed wind-ball cricket in the waist high salty water of the ocean.

We cooked lots of seafoods and also ate bake (bread) and shark. Our main alcoholic drinks were Antiquary Scotch whisky mixed with fresh coconut water and Mount Gay Sugarcane brandy rum often diluted with Pepsi cola. The neighbours were very patronizing because we looked like respectable young men who were all budding educators. On many occasions, we were invited to join them for either lunch or dinner, or just cocktails which we greatly appreciated.

After playing wind-ball cricket in the morning, we usually went swimming and running along the sandy beaches which extended for several miles in either direction from our beach house. We climbed coconut palm trees which were everywhere along the seacoast and helped ourselves to the fresh green coconuts. Sometimes after lunch, some of the boys had siestas. Others went into the seaside village to do grocery and personal shopping, while the rest of us either read or went out girl hunting. When no one was asleep or trying to sleep the radios and record players were played loudly.

In the evenings, just before the sunset most of us went for walks along the beachfront properties to people watch. We admired the late evening swimmers and young, middle-aged, and mature lovers, as they hugged and held hands displaying their true love for one another without reservation.

One of those evenings, as I was looking through the rear window of the beach house at the impressionist like seascape, I beheld a wonderful sight. Walking into my full view was a young, attractive and charming woman. Unknown to her, I admired her delicate beauty as she slowly walked barefooted on the golden sand at the water's edge. I was instantly magnetized by her graceful walk and slim figure, clothed in a light blue swim suit.

I wondered, who was this young and beautiful woman? Where was she staying? Was she engaged or married? I needed answers to these questions as quickly as possible. She melted quickly away into the mass of beachcombers and evening strollers. I hurried outside and ran along the beach, winding my way through the evening strollers and lovers in the hope of finding her. I searched and wandered, but I did not find her. I walked up and down the beach until it was too dark to see clearly.

On the following evening, at about the same time I decided to sit outside our beach house. I hid behind a clump of short coconut palm trees hoping to see the beautiful woman as she walked along the beach again. As I patiently waited in an ambush mode, she appeared. My heart started to accelerate as I dared to approach her. Slowly I walked behind her for a few hundred yards. In my great desire not to lose her in the growing beach crowd, I greatly increased my pace to catch up with her. As I walked, I could not resist admiring her slim tantalizing body, her exotic yellow patterned outfit. Mentally I stripped her as I got closer.

When I finally caught up with her and was next to her, I said, "Good evening, Miss Beautiful. How are you doing?"

She stopped. She swizzled her head around about forty five degrees and replied with a soft sweet voice, "Very wonderful!"

I said proudly, "My name is Mitra. What is your name?"

"Pryanka"

"Where are you going Pryanka?"

"I am going to walk to the end of the beach where the rocks and hilly landforms begin. I have always wanted to know what was behind the hilly area. My parents did not allow me to explore the landscape by myself when I was younger. Now that I have voting rights and adult status, I think I can venture out on my own."

"Can I join you?"

"Yes. You can walk with me."

We walked and exchanged pleasantries. She told me that she was holidaying with her family and her relatives at the big blue beach house on the other side of the road and had to be very careful in crossing the street to get access to the beach. She continued talking and told me that they would be staying for two more days at the rented beach house.

I told her that I was holidaying with my friends. She asked me where I lived and whether I had completed high school. I told her that I successfully completed high school and was employed as a teacher at the Chauhan Hindu School. She smiled, then, laughed and said, that she attended St. Gabriel Girls High School and had passed all the examinations with distinctions. She was presently teaching at the San Pedro Hindu School.

We continued our walk very close to the water's edge. We reached the end of the flat open beach and decided to be adventurous. Pryanka was about to fulfill her wish to see what was on the other side of the hills. We walked along the very narrow rocky beach surrounding the hilly area. Being so deeply engrossed in exchanging personal information about our lives we did not notice the incoming tides. The high rushing waves forced us to climb up the rocky hills.

We were now surrounded by seaweed and sea water as we looked down. We were stranded and it was becoming dark as we tried to hike over rocks to get back to the open beach area. The only light came from the colourful sunset reflections from the waves. The light gradually diminished. An eerie feeling came over me as we looked at each other for comfort and support. We were strangers when we met less than an hour ago. Now we were seeking safety and survival as two people stranded on an isolated island. At that stage of our brief encounter we were no longer strangers because we depended on each other's support to get back home safely. We spoke and cautioned each other to watch our footsteps, to be careful and to stay close to each other. Suddenly, one of the rocks that I was climbing broke and I fell down on the rocks below me. I was much too close to the raging waves which I was trying to avoid at all cost.

Pryanka yelled, "Are you OK?" I shouted that I was OK. She told me that she was climbing down to help me up. Before I could respond, she fell down on me, crushing my private parts. She was on top of me with one of her feet firmly anchored in my crotch. She quickly moved her foot from my crotch, apologized and asked how I was feeling. Groaning in pain, I remained on my back with my knees pulled towards my belly. She wore a very frightened and worried countenance. We remained there for a bit. Darkness was rapidly swallowing both the land and the sea.

With the help of some unseen force and sheer determination to live, we managed to crawl over the rocky terrain. Pryanka was unscathed while I nursed my sore ankle and knee from my unexpected fall.

Fortunately the seaside night time reptiles were not on their prowl as yet. We stretched out on the beach in the moonlight and did some face kissing and caressing. Nothing too serious. Slowly, we hugged and retraced our steps to her beach house. Before leaving her at the gate, I told her that I would like to meet her on the following evening behind our beach house. She agreed and slowly walked to her holiday house.

The following evening, we met as arranged. We walked the beach in the opposite direction for a very long time until the Monet like sunset painted the evening sky. We slowly walked back, hugging and kissing each other. She told me that she informed her family and relatives about what happened to us the previous evening and how I fell and was hurt. Her parents wanted to meet me.

In the morning, Pryanka came to our beach house, knocked on our door and invited me to join her, her family, and relative for breakfast. I told her that I would join them in half an hour.

Much to my amazement, the person who greeted me at the door was the teacher, Mr. Yadav, who had taken me to the nurse when I fell and cut my chin on the edge of the concrete drain on the very first day that I went to elementary school many years ago. He remembered me immediately, not only from the elementary school but also from playing cricket against his son.

Mr. Yadav warmly introduced me to the family. Pryanka was more than excited to learn about my sporting background from her father's most trusted relative. We all had breakfast together. Pryanka's mother asked me for my address, my work number and my home telephone number. I told her that I did not know my work number. I did not ask for any of their contact information. I was not interested in forging an intimate relationship with Pryanka. She lived far away from my little village. I would need a car to get to her home or workplace. Since I did not have a car, it meant that I would have to take a couple of taxis to meet her. I was not ready to make that sacrifice for her. All my relationships to date were in the village and with the village people. Pryanka told me that they were leaving later that morning because her dad had to do business in Arima. I extended warm goodbyes to all of them.

As I was leaving, she looked at me with sadness in her eyes, and bade me farewell with a hug and a kiss on my cheek. Her mother also hugged and kissed me. Mr. Yadav also hugged and kissed me. Her father and brother shook my hand and slapped me on my back to express their friendliness.

*****

Holidays ended and every one returned to their workplace. On my return to my school, I related to my very close colleague and trusted friend, Lagan, about my encounter with Pryanka. I had to be very discreet because I was already wooing one of the newly hired female teachers in the school. Lagan asked me whether or not Pryanka was a better looking girl than Dulcina. I shook my head in affirmation.

I had known Dulcina since we were in elementary school. I was one year older than she. She was from a very wealthy and prominent family in the village. Her parents had held me in high esteem from a very tender age. I was always welcomed to their home either to take Dulcina out on dates or to remain at her home to spend private quality time with her. I was not aware of their ulterior motives. My motive was to make puppy love to her and hope that she would go away and study like the other career-oriented girls in the village.

However, I was secretly nurturing a love relationship with her since the beginning of the academic school year. We went to the movies, weddings and socials together. Every morning, I waited for her at the junction so that we could walk together to the school. After school, we would walk together up to the junction, where we would say goodbye until the next day. On Friday evenings, just before we parted to go to our homes she would tell me what she would like to do on the weekend. Sometimes she would invite me to spend some private time with her at her home if we did not have any other engagements. Occasionally she would spend the weekend with her older married brother who lived in one of the neighbouring towns.

The village people gossiped and everyone was talking in our shop about the close relationship that they imagined existed between Dulcina and I. They were all hearing wedding bells, except me. I realized very early in our relationship that she was a flirt and an opportunist. Dulcina was not a knock-out like Pryanka but she was young and vibrant. But neither too kind nor romantic. She was playing a very conniving love game with me during the school days and with another boy on weekends when she visited her brother out of town.

*****

I became very disenchanted with her after a very frightening event in which she coerced me to participate. Dulcina and I, together with two very good friends, were returning from a Valentine's Day dance which took place at the Aparima Club in San Fernando. On our way home we stopped to have a late night snack of roti and Carib beer at one of the many restaurants in Marabella. After snacking, as we were driving back to Chauhan Junction, at about one o'clock in the morning, Dulcina asked me and our friends to accompany her to her father's grave which was in the St. Aquinas village cemetery. I became very scared at the mere mention of the word grave, and replied, "Are you crazy girl? Do you know what time it is?"

She boldly said, "Mitra, if you love me and you wish to kiss and feel me up, you have to come with me to see my father tonight."

I was very silent as the car driven by one of my faithful friends approached Chauhan. I tried to caress her but she resisted my romantic advances and angrily said, "Don't touch me. You can do anything with me, only after I have spoken to my father tonight." She was adamant.

David, the driver, and his date were very quiet as Dulcina argued with me. I asked David whether or not he would be willing to take Dulcina to talk with her father. David had no fear of the dead but insisted that he and his date would not venture out of the car when we were in the cemetery.

When we arrived at the burial site, it was after one o'clock. She opened the door, stepped out and said, "Mitra, if you want to make love to me, you would have to walk with me to daddy's grave."

I was frightened to death. Interestingly, we had to pass the grave sites of my family. I accompanied her to her father's grave. Fortunately a full moon was hanging very low so that we were able to see the graves clearly. When Dulcina arrived at the site, she started to sob. I neither hugged her nor remained close to her. I thought that she was a witch or some sort of supernatural character parading as a normal human being on planet earth.

Dulcina stood at her father's grave and cried and cried aloud. I was intensely terrified. I did not know whether or not she was attempting to invoke her deceased father or appealing to the gods of the underworld to be kind to him. Ironically, she slowly but loudly started to recite the eulogy that she recited at her father's funeral. I listened to her as she emphasized each word of the anonymous poem on death. She spoke as though her father was listening to her from inside the grave. She assumed the voice of her father. I listened in the hope that the reward she promised would be worth more than the harrowing ordeal that I was forced to endure.

> Dulcina spoke thus:
> Do not stand at my grave and weep;
> I am not there. I do not sleep.
> I am a thousand winds that blow.
> I am a diamond glint on snow.
> I am the sunlight on ripened grain.
> I am the gentle autumn's rain.

> When you awaken in the morning's hush,
> I am the swift uplifting rush of
> Quiet birds in circled flight.
> I am the soft stars that shine at night,
> Do not stand at my grave and cry;
> I am not there. I did not die.
>
> -Anonymous.

After her lamentations, she hugged me and we slowly walked back to the car. Not a word was uttered by anyone as the car sped away from the cemetery to re-enter the brightly lit streets of Benevolence. In the backseat of the car, I cupped one of her breasts and fondled it as she hugged me. I French kissed her frequently. Finally, I got one of my hands into her underwear and slowly masturbated her as she gradually opened her legs to accommodate my fingers. Her punani was very wet. It also passed the PST. I kissed her good night, and accompanied her to her front door. After seeing her go inside, I left with David and his girlfriend. My friend remarked that I should stay away from Dulcina. She was not normal. I made no comment.

*****

I must confess that I never professed any true love to Dulcina at any time. After that acutely distressing and dreadful experience at the cemetery, I was completely convinced that I did not want to be romantically involved with her. Truly, I was never seriously in love with any of the girls I ever dated. I was out just for a good time with no intentions of impregnating anyone. I loved clean, perfumed, fun loving beautiful girls, and women.

I was a fanatic for romantic movies. I always appreciated and adopted many of the love styles of the young movie actors. I watched carefully how they held their women before kissing them, how they touched and looked into their lovers' eyes. I also observed how they held them when they were dancing. I adopted many of their romantic movements.

As long as Dulcina and I continued to teach at the Chauhan Hindu School, we continued to socialize as though we were involved. Never did I express any intention of marrying her, either implicitly by my actions or explicitly in my dialogues with her. I ceased visiting her at her home and stopped asking her to go to the movies. In short, I started gradually to show less interest in her and always found an excuse to avoid associating closely with her again. She did not comment on my lack of romantic advances. Her indifferent reaction to my nonchalant attitude convinced me that she was sincerely interested in another person.

A few weeks after Valentine's Day, just before eight o'clock in the morning, as I was opening the grocery and rum shop doors, Dulcina's mother came and asked for my father. Papa was reading the morning papers. I told him that Dulcina's mother wanted to talk with him in her new automobile which was parked in front of the shop. Papa went outside and spoke with her privately. After talking with her for about half an hour, Papa returned and did not say anything to me or anyone else.

Later in the day, I asked Papa for the reason for Dulcina mother's visit. I felt that it had something to do with me. Papa told me that he would discuss it with me at the end of the business day.

At dinner time, I was told that Dulcina's mother would like me to marry Dulcina and settle down. She would help out financially to get us a home and would provide any assistance we would need later in our married life.

Papa asked, "Mitra, do you want to marry Dulcina?"

"No, Papa"

"Is Dulcina pregnant for you? Have you dishonored her in any manner?"

"No, Papa"

Papa, after having asked those direct clarification questions, informed me that he told Dulcina's mother that the children were too young to get married. He recommended that we should be allowed to further our education so that we could obtain certifications that could get us honourable and respectable professions. Papa was convinced that when we had secured respectable employments with good salaries, then marriage could be a possibility.

The following week Dulcina discussed with me what her mother had proposed to my Papa. I reiterated what Papa told me. We decided to remain good friends. At the end of one year of teaching, she went to study in Canada where she married an Italian businessman.

*****

As this marriage proposal fizzled, another marriage proposal reared its ugly head. I was in my class teaching, when Mr. Ganesh, the headmaster, came and told me that there was an urgent telephone call for me at his home next door. The headmaster told me that he would take care of my class while I answered the phone call. I left my classroom completely baffled. I was not expecting any phone call from anyone, especially at my work. I took the phone from the headmaster's wife and said, "Hello."

The person answered, "This is Rajev. We were in Standard Six together. Do you remember?"

"Yes Rajev. How are you doing? What's going on?"

"Mitra, one of my relatives, Pryanka, asked me to call you and relay this message to you."

"What kind of message?"

"Her parents were very impressed with you when they met you at the beach house in Mayaro. Mr. Yadav highly recommended you to them and painted you as the perfect husband for their only daughter. Her parents strongly advised her to marry you because she is in love with you. She told me that she would like to marry you as soon as possible. I do not know what happened between Pryanka and you. She is crazy to see you and marry you."

"Rajev, this sounds like serious business. I do not have time to address this issue. My students are waiting for me in the classroom. Please tell Pryanka to phone me at home. She has my phone number. Rajev, thanks for the information, but I have to return to my class. It was a pleasure talking with you. Bye."

I hung up and returned to my class. I thanked the headmaster for taking care of my students. He left and I continued my lesson. About ten minutes before the end of the last class of the day, the headmaster returned to my classroom. He told me that he wanted to speak to me privately before I left for home. I did as instructed. The headmaster became very enraged at me.

When I entered his office he shouted, "Why did you give out my private home telephone number to the public? You should manage your personal business with your home phone number."

I protested, "Sir. I did not give your telephone number or the school's telephone number to anyone. I do not even know what the numbers are."

"How did the person who called you get my home telephone number?"

Out of great respect and gratitude to my headmaster, I decided to relate my encounter with Pryanka. I was very mindful of the fact that this was the headmaster that promoted me years ago from Standard Five to Standard Six. It was that promotion which gave me the opportunity to meet many brilliant students from the wealthy middle class, and more recently, it was he who employed me as a teacher at his school.

Headmaster was not only my mentor but a surrogate father to me. Headmaster knew Pryanka's family very well. In fact, he was related to them. He was also related to Rajev who made the phone call. Thus the reason why the headmaster's wife did not object to calling her husband to fetch me. She was fully briefed by Rajev as to the contents of the call which she did not have time to relay to her husband, the headmaster.

I found myself in a new marriage conundrum. Headmaster was very excited and was very eager to do anything to get me married and settled down as a member of his 'pumpkin vine' family. Everyone wanted to get married to me but I was not ready for a marriage commitment to anyone.

After arriving at home, Papa told me that a girl named Pryanka called. She left her phone number and she wanted me to call her as soon as possible. Papa did not ask any questions or made any inquiries or insinuations. However, he looked rather concerned. At the dinner table, where all important family issues and business were frequently discussed, Papa asked me to explain the reason for the phone call from Pryanka. Papa unleashed a battery of questions on me. "Who is Pryanka? Where did you meet her? Why is she phoning you at our home?" Papa wanted full coloured details and a panoramic view of the relationship.

Once again, I retold the same story that I had told my headmaster.

"Are you interested in this girl, Pryanka?" inquired Papa.

"Papa, I do not know much more than what I told you. I will have to visit her and her family and try to ascertain the intentions of Pryanka and her parents. I have not made any commitment or promise to anyone, Papa. Please allow me to meet the girl and learn some essential information about her and her family before I could tell you what I would like to do. Will that be fair, Papa?"

Papa remained quiet for a minute, looked at me and said, "I hope that you know what you are doing".

Papa warned, "Mitra should you commit such an unpalatable deed as impregnating any one out of wedlock, and should you refuse to marry her, then you would be ostracized from the family and would have to find another place to live."

I left very confused. I was getting mixed signals from all directions. Headmaster was all in favour of marriage to Pryanka while Papa was very opposed to marriage. I was caught between a rock and a hard place. Papa did not ask for details about my dating and my courting of Pryanka.

He was patiently awaiting my final decision, whether to marry or not to marry.

The following school day, I called on my *Fidus Achates*, Lagan, and discussed at length the series of dialogues that I had over the past few days with Headmaster, Pryanka and Papa.

Lagan and I trusted each other implicitly and explicitly with our love affairs. I was venturing into a new love relationship and I did not wish to break anyone's heart including my own.

Pryanka and I made all our dating arrangements by telephone. On my first official date, I accompanied her to a Hindu Temple in St. James.. She wanted to pray and to ask her deities to bless our relationship to be happy, successful and fruitful. What a blessed and surprising way to initiate a loving relationship!

Pryanka was a very spiritual, respectful and charming young woman. She was very gentle and loving. I vowed not to hurt her in any way. I loved her in a very special way. Her petite hands and her sweetly perfumed body felt wonderfully in my arms. She was alluring, gorgeous and respectful and I could not resist kissing her whenever I had the opportunity. We went to the movies a couple of times and we spent some time together with her at her home. I was very respectable and discreet with her. I was warned, on several occasions, by her to keep my hand and probing fingers out of her crotch. I was not allowed to touch her flesh below her navel. I could fondle her breast, caress her upper body abdomen and kiss her as much as I wished. But I dared not venture in her private area. Constantly, I was left with painful erections. She was very protective of her punani area.

She bluntly told me, "You are not going to get into my punani until we are married. I will be a virgin on my honeymoon night for my husband."

I honoured her request. I told her that I was not ready for marriage. I had to further my education and become a well paid professional. Consequently, I encouraged her to go overseas and further her studies in a discipline of her own choice.

After a few months, Pryanka took my advice and resigned from her teaching job. I wished her the best of luck and all success in her studies as she left me at the departure lounge at the Piarco Airport.

*****

At the end of the second year of my teaching career, I received a phone call from one of my former class mates, Seth, from Excelsior College. He invited me to attend a surprise birthday party. I loved to party and graciously accepted his invitation.

I asked Seth for whom was the surprise birthday party. He told me that the party was for one of his cousins. Seth told me that this cousin knew me and that she wanted to meet me. I tried to inveigle Seth to reveal the identity of the secret guest but he did not disclose any information.

"What is the girl's name?" I inquired.

"I am not privileged to disclose her name," responded Seth. "It is supposed to be a great surprise for you."

Being a very kind and a thoughtful guest, I brought two very beautifully designed scarves, handmade locally with Indian silk, for the mystery birthday guest. I loved to see women wearing beautiful scarves. In my opinion, they added much sex appeal and glamour to a woman's innate beauty and charm. In time, I would realise that my introduction to the mystery guest would not only be a surprise birthday party for Seth's cousin but also a very shocking and most beautiful surprise for me.

The evening of the party arrived and I was welcomed by Seth. There were many other former classmates and former cricket team-mates present. It was a great unexpected reunion of so many old college boys.

We were trading jokes, sharing pleasantries and reminiscing about the old school days when the host got my attention, and told me that the surprise guest would like to meet me. I was more than eager to meet and to discover who was this mystery person. Seth took me to the last room in their very spacious home. He stopped in front of the doorway of a room, smiled looked at me and whispered, "Do have a wonderful time Mitra." Seth walked away to the main party room.

I stood in front of the closed door. My imagination was running wild. My heart rate increased as I was about to see who was behind the white door. I knock gently three times on the door, but there was no answer. I became concerned. Was Seth playing a nasty trick on me? I was quite aware of the idle and absurd pranks and capers our classmates played on one another when we attended college.

I slowly opened the door not knowing what to expect. When the door opened, it was Pryanka standing in front of me with her charming familiar face. She jumped and threw her arms around my neck. She immediately started to kiss me in my mouth. I reciprocated. She just ravished me. She stopped her kissing and said, "Mitra my love, I have been longing to see you and for you to romance me again."

"Pryanka," I exclaimed, "What the hell you doing here?"

Before she could answer, we were rolling on the bed. I caressed her soft body lovingly and sensuously She got on top of me and lay on my chest with her face between my chin and my chest. Not a word was uttered by either of us for a few minutes as we caressed and kissed each other. I could feel the warmth of her soft body seeping through her very fine garments. I relished her aromatic scent, and enjoyed passing my finger through her beautifully groomed hair. She was more beautiful than ever. We kept gazing into one another's eyes as though we were searching for some lost treasures. Finally, I asked her to reveal the purpose of her visit and the reason for meeting me in this surprising way.

Pryanka confessed that she did not have my unlisted phone number and was afraid that I might not accept the invitation sent out by her cousin, Seth, to attend the party. She wanted to see me in person to discuss her life story since I bade her farewell.

Pryanka started to sob and warm salty tears escaped delicately from her beautiful brown eyes. I hugged her, kissed and tasted her tears as they dampened her blemish free face. I became emotionally saddened to see her shed tears. I held her closely as we both sat on the bed.

I asked her, "Why are you crying? What is bothering you, Pryanka? You can speak to me," as I kept looking at her in sheer ecstasy.

She broke the silence with, "Mitra, Are you married?"

To which I responded, "No, I am not married. What about you? Are you married?"

"No. I am divorced."

"Divorced! What happened?"

"Mitra, I made many very grave mistakes in my life. I married an American man who was very charming, wealthy and handsome. I thought that I had struck the jackpot of marriage. Little did I know that he was a sadistic philanderer and guilty of bigamy. Our marriage lasted less than fourteen months. I divorced him and got a great part of his wealth. Fortunately, we did not have any children. I returned home a few months ago without completing my studies. I am planning to complete the degree at Glasgow University in Scotland. Now that I am here on holidays, my heart and soul are focused on getting involved with you again. I knew when we departed at the Piarco airport that you had a great love, admiration and respect for me.

"On my return, I asked my friends who knew us when we were courting and my extended families in Chauhan, whether or not they knew how to get in contact with you. I want you to be my husband. I cannot forget how you made passionate love to me on the sandy beach in the moonlight in the presence of the raging tides of Mayaro Beach. You can do whatever you want with me. There are no restrictions. No one will bother us in this room. Seth promised me. Brush me Mitra!" She was lying flat on her back with her legs partly spread apart to expose her beautiful legs.

The temptation was too overpowering for me. I did not know how to manage the risky situation that was staring at me. I did not know whether she was telling the truth or just setting me up for a fall. Quickly and conveniently, I recalled that when we were courting I was not allowed to touch or play with her punani. She was very protective of her virginity.

Since she was a divorced woman, she might no longer be a virgin. I looked at her, with my face directly in front of hers, and asked her simply and explicitly, "Pryanka are you serious? Do you really mean what you are saying? Do you really want me to brush you?"

She nodded. I looked at my watch. It told me that it was five minutes after seven o'clock. I was experiencing a very rigid and adventurous erection beneath my blue cotton pants. I looked at her and realised that Pryanka was used and abused by her husband and was in a very vulnerable emotional state. I became a bit saddened to see her in such a desperate and vulnerable state. Albeit, I was made an offer I could not and would not refuse. I was not assuming that she was free from any sexually transmitted disease. Consequently, she had to undergo and pass the PST. As she lay on the bed, I lay beside her and she pulled her black bikini underwear off and placed it under the pillow beneath her head. She was very aroused. I told her to get completely naked as I got up and locked the door. As she started to undress and while I was still standing, I embraced her and gradually slid two fingers into her warm slimy and wet punani, after delicately playing with her soft and curly pubic hairs. She was very cooperative and very happy to allow me free access to any part of her youthful, slim and blemish-free body. I nibbled on her smooth and well-rounded breasts and bit her on the inside of her sensuous legs. We had sex. I confessed and told her that I had no intention of getting married to anyone until I had secured a professional career and a good paying job. She quickly responded and assured me that she would pay for me to further my education. In fact, she wanted me to accompany her to Glasgow. She also said that she had more than sufficient finances for both of us to lead a wonderful and happy life. I told her that the more than generous proposal would need some serious consideration before I could either accept or reject it. I left her and wished her bountiful success in all her life's endeavours.

I went to the washroom and followed the advice of Tanty Lolita as much as possible. I rejoined the party which was in full swing. The host asked me whether Pryanka and I had made any resolutions. I replied, "Not as yet. We need more time."

A few minutes later, Pryanka emerged from the back bedroom looking as ravishing and beautiful as though she did not have a worry in the world. She joined the other guests and behaved as though she was there to have a tremendous and fabulous time.

I danced with her for most of the rhythmic musical selections – boleros, calypsoes, and meringues. We behaved as though we were young lovers which she greatly appreciated. The night was young and long and we had a great rollicking time together. I kissed her for the last time in public and left her with the promise that I would keep in touch and inform her about my decision.

I never contacted her. We never communicated with each other again. I would sometimes reflect when reviewing my life story, whatever happened to Pryanka.

*****

I told my trusted friend, Lagan, about what happened at the surprise party to which I was invited on the weekend.

Lagan could not understand the kind of tight squeeze I was able to innocently get myself into and to escape unscathed.

Lagan and I were 'riding shotgun' partners. We looked out for each other whenever we were liming in the towns and villages looking to woo good looking young unmarried girls who wished to have some fun.

Lagan was the main harmonium player of the Naya Sangeet Orchestra which was based in the Chauhan Hindu School. The orchestra was often invited to perform at several Indian celebrations throughout the Island, in major concert halls, and at wealthy business peoples' homes. As a result, Lagan, as well as all the members of the orchestra, were exposed to a wide variety of people from the poorest socio-economic level to the wealthiest aristocrats on the island.

On one such musical engagement, a very affluent and beautiful fair skinned East Indian teenage girl from Marabella, who was attending Vistana Girls High School, fell head over heels in love with Lagan. She was enchanted with the melodious songs and music that he made with the harmonium, his charming personality and his positive attitude. She was always present wherever the orchestra was performing. Lagan and Primala fell deeply and seriously in love. She was a crazy teenager from a very wealthy Brahmin family who was madly in love with a simple, young and poor country boy. Lagan was not only talented and handsome but intelligent as well.

Lagan, however, faced much opposition from Primala's parents. He was running head on into the Maharajahs' old caste system which originated in India. He did not believe in any caste system and never claimed to be either a Brahmin or from a Maharajah family. This was definitely not an issue for him. He was educated, respectable and an eligible bachelor. Primala knew that she loved him and he knew that he loved her. Whether it was infatuation or just simple puppy love, no one could discern at that time.

Lagan was very interested in marrying her. He was quite aware that, should he get married to Primala, he would be financially secure for life with her inheritance. He was made aware by Primala's very trusted and beautiful friends that her family was filthy rich.

The irony of the situation was that Primala's parents liked me and thought that Primala and I were in love. Primala knew me because I was Lagan's faithful friend and I had no intentions of stealing my best friend's girl. Little did both of them know the important role that I would play later in their love life.

Primala parents learned about her love affair with the harmonium player from their personal friends, who were the parents of Primala's classmates. They were very unhappy with her choice of a boyfriend and curtailed and controlled most of her movement from her home to any place they suspected Lagan may be present.

I was always welcomed to Primala's home but Lagan was not. I had to work very closely with Lagan and Primala to coordinate all the dates and events that they had planned. I had to be very discreet in handling the clandestine plans that had to be executed in order to get Primala on time for her dates with Lagan. But I was free to visit the Maharajah's family at any reasonable time any day of the week. All I had to do was make a simple phone call to either her mother or her father.

Whenever I visited the Primala's parents, they were very happy, excited and most inviting. After serving chai and Indian sweets and savouries, they would talk about the politics of the nation, the state of the sugarcane industry, the economy and any topic *au currant*. Apparently, they were educated business people, who were very interested in the welfare and wellbeing of their only daughter.

Primala would tell her parents that she was going out with me for the evening. Her father would ask all sorts of thought provoking questions which Primala answered to her father's satisfaction, or at least so it seemed. They believed that Primala had given up Lagan and that I was her new boyfriend. If Lagan and Primala were going to go to the movies, I had to be given all the details of the movie which they planned to attend before I visited her home, in the event her parents inquired. Also, I had to be able to describe the plot and summary of the movie to the parents – especially her father – when I returned from the movies. This was a great challenge for me.

Lagan and Primala were obliged to arrange for dates for me so we could double date in the movie house, so that I could get first-hand knowledge about the movie. I did not mind double dating with a new girl every time that I had to help out Lagan and Primala, either at a dance, or a house party, or the movies. I was used to doing favours for my trusted friends. Most of the time, the blind dates turned out to be very gorgeous, lovely and charming young teenagers.

Primala finally had to reveal the truth to her parents. They were very annoyed and disappointed in both me and their daughter. At first, Primala was grounded for over a month. Lagan contacted her only by phone. Primala ran away from home and did not return to school for a week, while she stayed at friends.

Her parents finally located her. Primala called Lagan and told him that her parents wanted to talk to all three of us. We honoured Primala's father request. After the meeting, her parents yielded to their daughter's wishes and allowed the marriage to take place. Her parents attended the marriage ceremonies under great duress and showered the bride and the groom with their personal approval and their blessings for a fruitful, successful and happy married life.

Lagan and Primala seemed very pleased and delightfully happy with each other. Lagan resigned from his teaching position at Chauhan Hindu School and got another teaching job in Princess Town where they bought a home.

However, as the months marched on, a very strained, and discordant relationship developed between Primala and her parents. Her mother became very depressed and died less than a year after the marriage. One year later the marriage ended in a divorce. Her father was happy to have his daughter back home.

*****

One Sunday afternoon, just before the start of the new school year, I was in front of our business place, doing some touch up painting to the façade of our building. As I got down from the ladder to retrieve my fallen paint brush, I saw the beautiful young lady, Rangeela, exiting my neighbour's front door and walking towards our business place. I had heard gossip about her from other young men in the village who were interested in wooing her. She had recently graduated from St.Raphael's Convent and was eligible for courting.

I had learnt from my very close neighbours, who were colleagues at the Chauhan Hindu School, that Rangeela Kapoor would be joining our staff as a teacher. Her mother was a well respected and admired politician and a member of the most prominent family in the village. Although her own family circle and family were neither prominent nor wealthy, she lived vicariously through her extended families' fame.

As she passed in front of our business place and was in front of me, I said to her in a polite manner, "Namaste, Rangeela. I understand that you will be joining the staff at the Hindu School tomorrow."

She replied, without stopping or looking at me, "I do not know anything about that, and by the way, it is none of your blasted business, painter boy."

She did not stop, and continued on her way home. I looked at her and realised that she had insulted and scorned me. With the paint brush in my hand, I followed her as she walked towards her home across the open spaces. Her pair of fair skin legs united at her hips to form a beautifully shaped buttock. She displayed a gorgeous body which entitled her to be pompous and to be filled with hubris. Maybe that was the reason for the rude and crude response to me. Regardless of the outcome, I was determined to pick up the gauntlet that she had just dropped. I was not going to surrender to her rude and crass behaviour. I thought about her that night with vengeance on my mind.

On the first morning of the new academic school year, Mr. Ganesh, my aging and wise headmaster, introduced the new teachers to the other teachers and staff members. He introduced Rangeela Kapoor as the new kindergarten teacher. The meeting ended quickly because another more detailed meeting was scheduled for later in the day after regular school hours.

All the teachers went to their assigned classes. I was assigned standard three which was located on the second floor. Rangeela looked beautiful with her well groomed hair, brightly coloured pink 'hubble' skirt, white embroidered New Yorker blouse, clean white shoes with flat heels and a colourful scarf. She looked ravishing and beautiful with all her cosmetics. Her alluring and delicately scented perfume turned me on. I was completely attracted and hypnotised by her charm and elegance.

Since I had no active girlfriends, I decided that I would try to woo Rangella as soon as possible. After Lagan had left, I had forged a trustworthy friendship with my neighbours and colleagues, Kareena and Vishal. Initially, I decided to win her love and affection by applying my own charisma, experience, and personality.

After a couple of weeks, I was invited by Vishal to join Kareena, his wife, and Rangeela during the morning and afternoon recess breaks in Vishal's classroom which was on the ground floor of the school. When I joined them during the recess sessions, they would usually get involved in a variety of discussions – students' behaviour, excellent restaurants, new movies, and the latest novels. I tried on many occasions to encourage dialogue with Rangella but she was very distant and critical of whatever I said. She looked at me as though I was an untouchable and was expendable. On many occasions she bluntly refused to acknowledge my "Namaste" greetings. Her vitriolic comment definitely insulted and emotionally affected me. She was more beautiful when she was not speaking. I realised that, in order to win her affection and finally romance her that I had to be more direct and assertive with her.

I was in for a very rude awakening. Rangeela lived a short distance away from my home. I could see her entire house from the upper floor of our home. We were within walking distance of the school where we both taught. I would leave my house as soon as I saw her leave hers, and, I would walk at a calculated pace so as to meet her, as if by accident, as she entered the main road leading to the school. I would extend a very cordial 'Namaste" to her. Sometimes, she would reply in a very professional manner and at other times, she did not respond. She told me that she would prefer if I did not walk with her in public. She asked that I walk either ahead of her or behind her, but not with her. Sometimes I would walk a few steps behind her or a few steps ahead of her. She behaved as though she was a very special woman who was too good for any man and needed her private space even in a public road.

Rangeela always carried an umbrella so that she would be prepared for rainy weather or too much sunshine. She did not wish to be tanned by the brilliant rays of the hot tropical sun, hoping to maintain a blemish free fair skinned complexion. She showed neither admiration nor genuine interest in me for many weeks. I tried to engage her in conversation about current events, her family, her personal activities, sports, the job and several other interesting topics but to no avail. She just did not want to be in the same air space that I was breathing. She detested me with a burning passion.

*****

One morning when I was on my way to teach, it started to rain very heavily. I dashed into the closest clothing store to avoid getting drenched by the warm torrential early morning showers. Much to my surprise, I saw Rangeela, with her umbrella, hurrying to shelter from the heavy showers. As she tried to accelerate, she slipped and fell on the wet muddy grass. She could not get up. She became drenched. I was the only person sheltering in the store. Realising, that she looked hurt and appeared helpless, I rushed out into the showers and picked her up and brought her into the store. The woman who owned the store came immediately to her. She knew that Rangeela was the teacher of one of her sons and she attended to her very compassionately. I wanted to be more helpful but the owner told me that she would take care of her son's teacher.

She took her into her back room where she cleaned, dried and refitted her with new dry clothing. As she came out from the back room, the rain had stopped. I asked her whether or not she was hurt, and she nodded in the affirmative. I left the store and walked away leaving her behind.

On my arrival at school, I signed in my time and went to my classroom. I watched her from afar as she limped around.

For two days, I did not visit Vishal's class for any of the recess, and did not mention her fall to anyone.

A week later I decided to ask her to go to the movies. She bluntly refused by saying, "I have never gone to any place or any function with any male person except for members of my immediate family circle. I have no intention of starting dating boys without the approval of my Mom. My Mom must know about everything that I plan to do with anyone. She has to approve the boys and girls with whom I should socialize and furthermore, I have no desire to introduce you to my family circle."

A long silence followed that speech. I was facing a very young, serious and tough adult who was also very hostile.

One week later, I asked her again to accompany me to the movies. She refused by saying, "You will never be in my social class. Stop asking me to go out with you anywhere. I do not have any interest or use for you. Stay away from me."

Those bitter and hurtful words forced me to mutter to myself "Vengeance would be mine." From that moment, I decided to apply new strategies to ensnare her into my love trap. She was the first woman for whose affection I had to fight a hard battle. However, I had to find out whether or not she was secretly interested in me or was just out to give me a difficult time.

During one of the afternoon recesses in Vishal's classroom, I decided to ask her once more, in the presence of Vishal and Kareena, to go to the movies. As soon as there was a lull in the conversation, I seized the opportunity to ask her for a movie date. "Rangeela I would like you to join me to see the movie, *Rome Adventure* [starring Troy Donohue and Suzanne Pleshette], on Friday for the four thirty show at the Sunset Cinema. I will come to your home to fetch you."

Rangeela got up from her chair and walked towards me, and said sarcastically and emphatically, in the presence of my friends, "I told you before and I am saying it again that you are not my type. I would not go out with any shopkeeper's son. Why don't you find some cheap girl, at your low social level from the staff, to accompany you to the movie?"

I looked at her in utter silence as the bell rang for the resumption of classes. She walked out, leaving me with Vishal and Kareena. My pride and valor were bruised in the presence of my colleagues. Feeling very insulted and extremely embarrassed, I returned to my classroom. I taught my class some geography and history for the remainder of the afternoon class time. After class, I remained seated at my desk, pretending that I was making lesson plans for the following week while I silently licked my emotional wounds. When I was satisfied that most of the staff and students had left the school, I left my classroom and slowly walked home, contemplating how to tame the wild beast which resided in Rangeela's savage-like heart.

"Where there is a will, there is a way", I muttered the old English proverb to myself as I walked in front of her home on my way to my home. I never mentioned her insulting remarks to anyone. However, Vishal and Kareena were present when Rangeela ripped me apart verbally and emotionally. I wondered what their reactions to her biting and insulting remarks were. I decided that only love can conquer her insensitivity and insensibility.

I stayed away from her direct pathways for a couple of days. I was definitely placed on the defensive mode. I decided to apply one of soccer's oldest strategies, *"reculer pour mieux sauter,"* to help me put my 'love ball' between her carnal goal post.

*****

Another good and trustworthy friend, Vijai, got wind of my dilemma from Vishal. The three of us were drinking partners. On any Friday, usually after school when we were free from any other social engagements, we met at Lady Gay restaurant. There we discussed any issue we considered worth discussing while we were drinking and eating Chinese food.

Vijai, being slightly inebriated, slurred, "Mitra, how are you going to tame and saddle that big eye bitch who dared to insult you in the presence of Vishal and Kareena?"

I said that I would flood her with flattering compliments and sweet charming remarks. I added that I was intent on making her fall madly in love with me.

"Beware what you wished for Mitra. You might be sorry when it is manifested," Vijai chuckled. Vishal remarked that Rangeela regretted what she said to me. It was inappropriate and unbecoming of her. However, she would not apologize because she believed that no man was good enough for her and definitely not worthy of any apology from her. We left the restaurant, and Vishal drove me home in his antique Oldsmobile.

During the weekend, Rangeela's hurtful and demeaning words haunted me. I was restless and could not sleep. I stood in front my wardrobe with the long mirror stark naked with a firm erection in one of my hands and with the other gesticulating at my image, as I said, "Rangeela, I will capture you, you bitch, and I will perform on you every sexual act that Tanty Lolita taught me. You will beg me to make love to you. You just wait and see, Rangeela, the power of my muscular love machine. When I do capture you, I will strip you naked and explore and exploit every orifice in your slim sexy body." Definitely there would be no turning back on my words.

*****

After school was dismissed and all the children had left her classroom, I observed that Rangeela had a tendency to slip off her shoes and to lie flat on her back on the kindergarten students' writing tables with her legs hanging over the sides. Her skirt was usually short so that when she was on her back on the table, it was possible to see part of her underwear. Apparently, no one ever mentioned it to her, maybe they enjoyed the view!

I decided that I would teach her a lesson. One evening after school, as she rested flat on her back on the table, I quietly took her shoes and left the classroom unseen by anyone. I hid her shoes behind the water cooler in the refreshment room and left for home.

The following morning, as I was signing in my arrival time in the log book, Rangeela, rather infuriated, approached me and shouted, "What did you do with my fuckin shoes, you coolie? You better bring them back. They are very expensive. You will have to use your month's pay to buy them back for me. I had to walk home barefooted yesterday evening. How embarrassing for me."

I pleaded innocence and walked away. She followed me upstairs, kept on accusing me of hiding her shoes, and even cuffed me several times on my shoulders and back.

I reported her to the headmaster and accused her of harassment and assault. Headmaster summoned both of us to his office after school to sort out the shoe dilemma and her unprofessional conduct. The shoe issue was not resolved because I denied ever taking them. She had no evidence or witnesses. Mr. Ganesh, the headmaster, severely reprimanded her for her childish behavior. A few days later, one of the teachers found her shoes and returned them to her. I realised that I could tease her and she would react either intelligently, aggressively or absurdly.

As she was lying down peacefully on one of the students' writing tables in Vishal's classroom, after school, with her eyes closed, and in the absence of any students or teachers, I could not resist the sensual sight of her tightly fitted pink panties, and her bare naked legs spread out on the sides of the students' writing table. My sexual hormones exploded through my circulatory system and I had an instant erection. I was tempted to spread her legs apart very quickly and bite her punani. My discretion and common sense prevailed over my valor – I had not checked out the health of her punani with my patented PST as yet. However, I performed a daring and lewd act. I quickly placed my hand on her punani and squeezed it. She screamed, "Fuuuck!" and jumped up faster than a track and field star and in a flash, picked up one of her shoes and dealt me a severe blow on the side of my head. I thought that I had gone blind as a starry firmament invaded my optic nerves. I ran out of the school rubbing the side of my head and looking at my hand for the sign of blood. There was a lot of bleeding. The short heel of her shoe left a large red bruise and cut on the right side of my head. It quickly grew into a bump. I confessed that I deserved the blow she dealt me. I realized that she was not an easy prey to capture. I walked home slowly, covering the wound with my handkerchief, in the hope that no one would inquire about the blood clotted bump on the side of my head. As soon as I arrived home, my very observant Papa immediately questioned me about my wound.

"Mitra, who buss your head boy?" Papa inquired.

I did not answer and hurried upstairs to my room.

Papa followed me and laughingly repeated his question, "Which woman beat you up this time?"

I told him what I did and how she reacted. I told Papa that he should not tell anyone about the incident. Papa advised me to stay away from her. I listened but did not honour his advice.

When I returned to school on the following day, students and colleagues were asking probing questions about the bandage on the side of my head. Apparently, she did not reveal the incident to anyone, as yet. When she saw me during the morning recess, she pretentiously asked me in the presence of Vishal and Kareena, "What happened to your head Mitra? Did you get into a fight last night?" She inspected my wounds and wished me a rapid healing process as she spoke to me with a scornful smirk.

I smiled and fabricated a very convincing story. I told them that I was drinking with a few of my friends in a rumshop yesterday evening when I got into a very heated political debate with a Creole man. A fight ensued between us and he cuffed me. Rangeela looked at me, smiled and before leaving for her classroom, remarked, "I like your story. I feel very sorry for your head." I was perplexed about her calm and consoling behavior. Everyone commiserated with me.

*****

Three months had slowly passed and I was not able to successfully take her out on a date. All I had gained for my loving advances were insults, abuse, ingratitude and blows. Regardless, I continued to woo her. Daily, I would leave either, candies, chocolates or Indian sweets on her desk without any clue that they were from me. During her free time, she was always in her usual prostrated position on one of the students' writing tables in Vishal's empty classroom. I saw another opportunity to be alone with her.

After school had ended and most of the students had left, I found Rangeela in Vishal's classroom sleeping in her usual position. Vishal and Kareena were in a meeting with the teachers who were preparing the selected students for the Common Entrance Examinations for Secondary Schools. I looked at her with the devil's angels urging me to ravish her. I recalled vividly the bloody blow she dealt me the last time I molested her. I looked at her youthful legs, her breasts bulging beneath her yellow blouse and her luscious pink lips. I stealthily approached her as my powerful passion to romance her propelled me closer to her body. I moved like a cheetah stalking a gazelle in the Serengetti bushes. I held her head down on the table. I proceeded to kiss her initially on her neck and finally, forcefully in her mouth. She resisted violently slapping, kicking and wriggling to break my hold. She could not overcome my powerful arms and body weight as I held her down. She did not yell for help. She relented and I enjoyed kissing and hugging her to my delightful satisfaction. Fortunately, no one interrupted. She looked at me in amazement but was serene. She sat up and looked at me as though she wanted more. I did not know how to decipher her look. We said nothing to each other. I wiped my face clean of her lipstick, looked at her and bravely pronounced, "I have a lot of hot, sexy and juicy things that I want to do with you. Stop fighting and start loving me honey bunch."

I left the classroom and walked away. As I walked away from the school, I looked back to see her standing at the main entrance to the school looking at me as I disappeared behind the homes. I was slowly but surely making her realize the sweet loving feelings that were generated when one was romanced with burning desire and passion.

*****

One week later, Vishal and Kareena invited me to their home for dinner. After the dinner, while we were having coffee and brandy, they openly inquired about my intentions for Rangeela. I was very surprised at the questions that they were asking. They wanted to know the degree of my sincerity and the extent of my love for her. I told them that I liked her very much and would like to know her more intimately before making any serious decision. Vishal looked at Kareena and they smiled and giggled at each other. Kareena remarked that she believed that Rangeela liked me very much but she was not sure how committed she wanted to become. They continued laughing and smiling.

"Why are you smiling and laughing?" I asked.

"We do not know what has happened between both of you but she was speaking very favourably about you."

"Did she tell you anything about me?"

"There is nothing in particular. Rangeela thinks that you are just a friendly person," responded Vishal.

I told them that I would like to date her but I would need to hire a car because Papa would not allow me to use his car in the night.

Vishal said, "Mitra we will do something to help you with her."

*****

Every year, all the Hindu and Vedic schools in the local school district celebrated India's Independence Day. The students and their teachers of the Hindu Schools would assemble at the Sunset Cinema to celebrate India's Independence Day. While we were at the celebrations, we were served refreshments – aloo pies, bara, pooloorie, fried chick peas, and Solo soft drinks. After the refreshments, we were shown a movie on how the people of India won their independence from the British in 1947.

On that memorable day at the cinema, I was seated with my students in the front rows in the balcony of the cinema. The majority of the other teachers were seated in the back rows of the balcony with their students seated directly in front of them. Just before the lights were turned down low, and before the show started, the powerful and authoritative voice of Miss Baijnath pierced through the babbling noises of the students with the following announcement, "Mr. Roshan, Miss Kapoor wants you to come and sit with her in the back row." Roshan was my surname.

I did not respond to Miss Baijnath's appeal. My students became excited and told me, "Sir, Miss Kapoor is calling you to sit with her."

I did not even respond to my students' exhortations. There was a definite hush when Miss Baijnath's voice repeated, "Mr. Roshan, Miss Kapoor would like you to sit with her for the show."

My students became extremely excited and urged me to go and sit next to Miss Kapoor. I looked at my students, smiled, turned around in my seat, and loudly exclaimed, "If Miss Kapoor wants me to sit with her, why doesn't Miss Kapoor call me herself?"

There was a deafening silence as the pleading voice of Miss Kapoor responded, "Mr. Roshan would you please come and sit with me for the show."

At her personal invitation, I slowly got up and went to the back where she was seated next to Kareena, Vishal and Vijai. As I walked to the vacant seat next to her, Vishal and Vijai smiled and shook my hand without uttering a word. Kareena looked at me and was beaming with a broad smile. I sat down and did not say anything to Rangeela. The show started as soon as the lights were turned off. I behaved myself very decently during the show. At the intermission period, I asked her, "Would you like a soft drink or something to eat?" She said that she would love to have a cold banana soft drink and a currants' roll pastry. Kareena said that she was joining Vishal and Vijai to get refreshments downstairs. We left Rangeela and went downstairs for refreshments.

When we were in the refreshment area, the gossip from the other teachers was all about Miss Kapoor's openly inviting me to sit with her in the presence of the students and other staff members. I made no comments. I got the requested food and drinks for her and two alloo pies and a cream Solo for myself.

When I returned to my seat, she expressed her thanks and proceeded to consume the currents' roll and drink the banana Solo soft drink. She looked lovely and happy after she had her refreshments. For the rest of of the show, we did not speak much to each other. We made a few positive comments about the celebrations and the show. At the conclusion of the show, the students and teachers were permitted to go directly to their homes. Rangeela went home with Vishal and Kareena in their car. I preferred to visit a few of my former college friends who lived across the road from the cinema.

*****

The following morning, instead of walking alone to school, Rangeela crossed the main street, stood at the bridge and waited for me as I walked slowly towards her on my way to school. I greeted her with the usual 'Namaste' to which she warmly responded. She handed me the umbrella and asked me to shelter both of us from the bright tropical morning sunshine. Her sudden change of attitude towards me was perplexing. I wondered what might have triggered such a drastic change in her behaviour. Was it my roguish behavior or was it the assistance I gave her when she fell down in the street? I was not going to question her motives. Instead, I was going to enjoy whatever delights she freely offered or whatever personal romance I could steal without life-threatening consequences.

We arrived at school together and we signed the attendance book with the same time of arrival. Mr. Ganesh, my headmaster, with a big smile commented, "It is very refreshing to see both of you with such amicable dispositions."

From the efficient rumour mill at school, the headmaster had learned what had happened during the India Independence show at the cinema.

Neither Rangeela, nor I entertained any discussions about the cinema incident from any member of the staff or students.

*****

Vishal and Kareena invited me to their home two Saturdays after Rangeela showed her open admiration for me, and her overt association with me on the streets, and at our workplace. I went to my neighbours' home at the appointed time. We sat in the front room and talked about the changes in Rangeela's attitude towards me. They wanted to know what were my intentions. I told them that I do not know her intimately as yet, and I really did not know her true feelings about me.

There was a knock on the door. Vishal opened the door and Rangeela entered. Vishal offered her a Scotch which she accepted without any delay. Kareena invited her to have a seat next to me. Rangeela and I were very surprised to see each other. Vishal and Kareena had planned this surprise meeting for us. She kept looking at me as she gulped down her drink and asked for a refill. With drinks in hand, we retreated to the dining room where dinner was served. It was a delicious and salubrious meal. Rangeela and I thanked Kareena and Vishal for dinner and congratulated Kareena for her exquisite culinary talents.

After dinner, Vishal and Kareena invited Rangeela and I to accompany them to the drive-in cinema to see the movie, *Gone With The Wind*. I waited to hear Rangeela's response. She said that she had no objections to the suggestion. I was most surprised but agreed to all and any decisions they made that evening. We left for the drive-in cinema. Rangeela and I sat in the back seat of the car. The darkness in the car was punctured only by the light from the silver screen. I thought and rethought which of the passionate and romantic tactics I should implement from Tanty Lolita's love manual. As the movie progressed, I gradually inched my way to touch her.

I held one of her hands in one of mine, placed my other hand around her shoulders and pulled her down across my lap. There was no resistance to my physical manipulations. I touched and massaged the back and sides of her neck, passed my hand through her soft and fragrant hair and started to kiss her in the mouth. She responded in an extremely cooperative manner.

We were no longer interested in looking at the movie. I opened her blouse, unsnapped her bra and gently pulled it down. I caressed her firm but soft breasts. I slipped my hand down her abdomen to her navel and rubbed her belly gently as I sucked her breasts. She softly released a peaceful and happy confirming sigh in affirmation that she was enjoying what I was doing. Gingerly, I slid my hand towards her pubic area but it was met with firm and powerful resistance by her hands. For the rest of the show, we continued making love.

Kareena, in her role as a big sister, said, "Make yourselves presentable, guys! The movie will end soon."

"What a wonderful and memorable evening," I commented after they dropped Rangeela home. "Thank you infinitely for your support and continued friendship and may God continue to bless both of you forever," as I bade my neighbor's a very blessed good night sleep.

*****

During the following weeks, we walked to school as two very good friends. Everyone was talking about us in our shop. We were the young lovers in the village. I asked Rangeela about her feelings and reactions to the loving that I made to her in the backseat of the car. She said that she really enjoyed having her breasts sucked. Also, she enjoyed immensely the way in which I simulated milking them. She laughed and said, "One day you will be able to actually suck milk out of them when I have a baby for you."

I smiled and responded, "It may happen or it may not. Who knows what the future has in store for both of us?"

We went to the drive-in cinema one more time. Rangeela decided that we should meet at her home instead of in the backseat of a car. I asked her whether her mother knew about her relationship with me. She responded that not only her mother but her entire home circle knew. Her brothers did not approve of her dating anyone. The boys were the men of the house. Although they were younger than she, they exerted control over the family affairs. Her brothers and sisters were all very friendly and inviting in the public domain but I dared not visit her when the brothers were at home.

She decided to meet me outside the village where her brothers or her extended family could not see her with me.

On Saturdays we would first arrange to meet at Woolworths in downtown Port of Spain and go for lunch at any of the popular Chinese restaurants on Frederick Street. After lunch we would take a taxi to the Queen's Park Savannah where we would alight in front of Queen's Royal College, the first of the *Magnificent Seven* breathtaking colonial mansions along the road leading to the Botanic Gardens. We would walk very slowly in front of these inspiring heritage buildings. In order to get a better appreciation of their architectural charm, we would sit on the park benches and admire the unique beauty of each mansion. Next to the Queen's Royal College was Hayes Court, the residence of the Anglican Bishop. This building was followed by a graceful and elegant French provincial-style home commonly known as 'Mille Fleurs' or 'Salvatori House.' The fourth building looked like a mini chateau and was named 'Roomor.' The last three buildings in order were the Archbishop Palace, the Whitehall and Stollmeyer Castle. These buildings were a must see for all tourists and the locals. After viewing these mansions we would vist the coconut vendors for a drink. We then would stroll through the rose gardens and enter the botanic garden where the young lovers were enjoying themselves amongst the bushes and trees. We did this love exercise a couple times but she found it not private enough and we decided to discontinue meeting in the Queen's Park Savannah.

One week later she asked me whether my parents and family would object to her visiting me at our my home. I then invited her. She came and was welcomed by Papa, my stepmother, my grandfather and my sisters. Papa, however, did not like the idea that I was inviting a woman to whom I was not married into my bed room. He did not think that his eldest son was setting a good example for his younger siblings and cousins who lived in the same home. I invited her home twice but I did not feel comfortable to make love to her in my own home.

I was very amazed to see Rangeela, who considered me an untouchable fall madly in love with me. She decided that she had to see and make love with me at least once a week. But while we engaged in passionate foreplay, we never had sexual intercourse.

*****

Our friendly relationship gradually got stronger as time passed. However, I was never invited to her home. My parents met her on several occasions during her visit to our home. I was wondering and thinking whether her family would ever invite me to their home. I did not have to bother anymore after the following conversation.

"Mitra, my mother wants to have a talk with you."

"Your mother wants to talk to me? Why? When? And where?"

"You are invited to lunch on Saturday."

"Am I going to have lunch with your entire family?"

"No. My brothers and sisters will be visiting my aunt for the weekend."

"What does your mother want to talk to me about?"

"When you come for lunch you will find out."

I remained quiet for the rest of the walk home.

Saturday arrived, and I told my stepmother that Rangeela's mother has invited me for lunch. She became very concerned and said, "Be very careful how yu answerin her questions, don't lay dat woman fool yu."

With that advice, I left for lunch.

Rangeela's mother was most welcoming. When I got inside her home, she invited me to sit with her in the living room. Rangeela offered me Indian appetizers and soft drinks, then she joined us. I anxiously sat, waiting to hear what her mother had to say.

Her mother said that she noticed the drastic and positive changes in Rangeela's attitude to everyone at home. She was more friendly, happy, and pleasant. She boldly stated that Rangeela had disclosed all the details of her love relationship with me. I became very uneasy on hearing her mother's detailed review of the things that I had done to her daughter.

At that stage, Rangeela said that she was very hungry and told her mother she can continue her talk after lunch.

After lunch, as soon as her mother started to openly discuss the topic of marriage, a car pulled into her driveway. They did not expect any visitors. Her mother got up quickly to see who came. As she was peering through the louvres, she said, "Both of you, get in the back bedroom and keep quiet. My brother is here. I will call you when he leaves."

We hurried to the room and closed the door.

I asked her, "Why is your mother so worried about her brother?"

She did not answer. We sat quietly on the bed and listened to the activities in the front room. Her uncle came in and said that he just dropped in to say hello to the family before returning to his home in Chase Village.

He was offered lunch, which he accepted. After having lunch, he continued talking loudly to his sister about his business affairs and family problems. He asked for the children and her mother told him that they were away for the weekend.

In the meantime, in this lockdown situation, I decided to take this opportunity to do exactly what I promised to do to her, after she insulted me. This was the first time we were ever alone behind closed doors and under strict instructions to be very quiet. I was fully aware, that she could neither cry for help, scream nor run outside. I removed her blouse, bra and skirt. When I held her panties to pull it down, she tightly held my hand and whispered, "Are you crazy? My mother and uncle are in the front room. Suppose mom comes in unexpectedly!"

I listened and did not remove it.

I was fully aware that we had to be very silent so as not to arouse the curiosity of her uncle. We were enthralled in deep passionate love making. While making love to her, I decided to pet her punani area with my hand on the outside surface of her underwear. I deliberately and frequently rubbed my fingers directly over her punani and massaged it.

At first, she tried to restrain my exploring fingers. Finally, she succumbed to my persistent attempts to get into her punani area. I slowly pulled her underwear off and had to decide what to do. Should I have sex with her, or protect her honour? I recalled how she had treated me as an untouchable, and insulted me, in the presence of my colleagues. This was the opportunity that I patiently waited for. I wanted to perform cunnilingus on her as was highly recommended by Tanty Lolita. Instead, I masturbated her and performed the PST on her, she was OK. She was very quiet and fell asleep. I looked at her naked body again and again, and smiled, and softly said to myself, "You little bitch. You believed that you are too good for me! Seeing is believing and touching is the naked truth. You are just like any other woman."

I positioned her nude body as Goya's painting – "The Naked Maja." Then, I covered her nudity.

I waited patiently for her uncle to leave. When he left, I made sure that she was completely covered. As soon as her uncle's car drove away, her mother knocked on the door and said that it was safe for us to return to the living room. I came out and told her mother that Rangeela had fallen asleep and was beginning to snore. She took my words as the gospel truth. I thanked her mother for the lunch. I hugged and kissed her and I left to meet my friends.

*****

The following Monday morning, we met on the road to school. Under the shade of her open umbrella, we walked leisurely to our workplace. At morning recess, she came to my classroom and said that we have to talk. While we were on our way home for lunch, she asked the following questions.

"Why did you leave me completely naked on the bed?"

"Was it a problem?"

"Mom was very annoyed. She believed that we were having sex when her uncle was in the living room talking with her. Did you have sex with me when I fell asleep?"

"Yes, I brushed you. However, you will not get pregnant."

"Are you impotent?"

"I do not think so. If you get pregnant then I will have to marry you."

I told her all these lies with a smirk on my face.

"You will marry me?"

I responded, "Only if the baby belongs to me."

"What the fuck you mean if the baby belongs to you. You are the only person who ever dabbled in my pumpum. Stop fucking with me, Mitra." I laughed and I advised her to stop talking about what happened last weekend and not to worry about any baby. Life went on in a very harmonious and peaceful manner for the next two weeks. Holidays arrived and we did not have any private trysts where we could make love. She finally got her period and she was very happy.

*****

She devised a plan whereby we could meet at her home when no one was at home. They had green curtains covering the two big glass louvered windows in the front of their home. She told me that, when the curtains on the right side of the front window were closed during the day that would be the signal that she was alone at home.

Every morning, noon and evening I would run upstairs from the shop to see whether she had given a signal. I got signals at least twice a week. I would shower, get dressed, and meet her at her front door where she impatiently started her romancing. We made love passionately but there was no sex.

My stepmother had warned me on many occasions that I should resist the erotic temptations of stealing a woman's honour; her comment was, that a woman's honour was like a grain of match. Once you light it, it cannot be relighted again. In a nutshell, a girl can lose her virginity only once. I had no intentions of stealing anyone's virginity.

I was not interested in marrying Rangeela because of the initial prejudices and discrimination she expressed to me. Also, I did not forget her mother's reaction to her uncle's surprise visit.

I was only interested in the delightful pleasures and enjoyment that I derived from making romantic and sensual love to her as long as possible with no marital commitments. I evaluated and concluded that I did not wish to join a family which treated me with such callousness and insensitivity as expressed both by Rangeela and her mother.

*****

I was very much interested in furthering my studies in mathematics and the natural sciences. Initially, I was not allowed to pursue this line of studies because of my stepmother's objection. As karma would have it, my second sister, Elyana, was attending Augustin Girls High School and was studying physics, chemistry and biology. Her best friend, Beverly, who lived in the village, was studying the mathematics courses that I wanted to study earlier in my academic years. I followed their courses of studies in my spare time at home. I did the home work they were given and all their tests. At the same time I took advanced level correspondence courses in mathematics and sciences from Wolsey College in England and successfully wrote the required examinations in Port of Spain.

*****

Holidays ended and we returned to teaching. One Thursday afternoon about two o'clock, I was with the students of my class in the school yard in the shade of the almond trees. I was teaching my students about the physical geography of Trinidad and Tobago. The headmaster, Mr. Ganesh, came to my class in the school yard and told me that one of my former college friends wished to have a talk with me about a very important matter. I told the headmaster that he could send the person to my classroom at recess. I returned with my students to my classroom and waited for the recess bell. I recognised Raul instantly. I greeted him and we sat down to talk in my classroom.

Raul inquired, "Do you mind, Mitra, me asking you a very personal question?"

"It depends on the nature of the question, Raul."

"I have been watching you and Rangeela for a couple months, coming and going to and from this school almost every school day. Do you have any serious intentions of getting married to her?"

I looked at Raul, smiled, scratched my head and inquired, "Why are you asking this question?"

"I am interested in getting married to her if you are not interested."

"I am not interested in getting married to either Rangeela or any other woman."

"Why are you not interested in marrying her?"

"Raul, I wish to further my studies in mathematics. I need to have an excellent paying job so that I could have a happy and successful life. Marriage is not my priority at this time of my life. Raul, you can make a marriage proposal to her at any time. I do not own her marriage rights."

"Mitra thank you very much for making it so easy for me."

"Raul, I wish you the best of luck with her. She is a beautiful and wonderful person when you get to know her."

"Thank you again."

Raul got up, very pleased to learn that I was not an obstacle in his pathway to making Rangeela his bride. However, before Raul left the classroom, I kindly asked him not to tell anyone about the confidential dialogues that we had exchanged about Rangeela.

I did not mention the private meeting that I had with Raul to anyone — not even Rangeela. I wanted to learn whether Raul was serious about marrying Rangeela.

*****

The following Monday, Rangeela met me and told me about the marriage proposal that was offered to her on Sunday evening at her home. After telling her that I was very happy for her and congratulated her, she became annoyed to see my jubilant reaction. I apologized profusely and kindly begged her for details of the proposal.

She gave me a detailed account of the unexpected visit by a Mr. Surat and his family. She told me that on the Friday evening, her mother received a phone call from a Mr. Surat Singh. After a rather long telephone talk, her mother told Rangeela that Mr. Surat and his son, Raul, were coming to offer a marriage proposal to her on Sunday.

"Do you mean Raul from Benevelonce? I went to college with him. He is from a very wealthy family. You have struck a gold mine. Did you accept his proposal?"

Rangeela laughed and said that she wanted only me and that she had refused his proposal without hesitation because he was not too interesting. I had to promise her that I would not mention that marriage proposal to anyone and that we should not talk about it anymore.

Two months before the end of the academic year, Rangeela made mention of another marriage proposal offered to her by one of the very wealthy and prominent Thakurs' families from La Romain. The man was a young doctor who had recently returned from Ireland on vacation. He had seen Rangeela at one of the private parties for the affluent, filthy rich and famous personalities at his uncle's mansion located around Skinner Park

Savannah. The young doctor told her that he fell in love with her at first sight. He made inquiries about her and told his parents that he would like to marry her and take her back with him to Ireland. He offered to marry her during the month that he was holidaying with his friends and families. She refused his marriage proposal by claiming that she already had her marriage partner with whom she was passionately in love and would soon be married.

*****

One week later, Papa called me into his room and told me that Rangeela's mother phoned him yesterday morning and told him that she wanted to have a meeting with him on Sunday afternoon at two o'clock.

"Did she mention the reasons for the meeting?" I inquired.

"She gave no reasons. She said that she will be here, at our home."

Rangeela and her mother arrived at our home on time. They were in a very happy and cheerful mood. Her mother and Rangeela were cordially welcomed by my family.

They were led to the main living room where they were given refreshments of Trinidadian savories and freshly squeezed fruit juices. After exchanging a few pleasantries, Rangeela's mother proudly made the following announcement, "Brother Roshan, I am here to talk about Rangeela and Mitra. Everyone in the village knows that they are deeply in love. I am a single mother. Consequently, I have to look after the welfare and well-being, not only of myself, but also of all my six children. Rangeela has had two marriage offers within the last month from very wealthy and prominent families. She refused both of them. She wants to get married to Mitra as soon as possible. She loves him. At first, Rangeela did not realize that he was a kind, decent, and industrious person. She regrets offending him in public."

Papa questioned, "Rangella, do you seriously wish to get married to Mitra at this young age?"

Rangella responded, "I am madly in love with him. However, I do not want to continue rejecting marriage proposals until I am very positive that a marriage between Mitra and I will not materialize soon."

I sat very quietly as her mother pushed for an early marriage. Papa and her mother continued their talks about marriage and possible dates and financial affairs while Rangeela and I went into the kitchen for something to eat and to drink.

*****

Mother and daughter left, looking very happy as though their mission was successfully accomplished. As soon as they left, some very constructive and enlightening dialogues ensued between Papa and me in the privacy of his room.

Papa asked me, "Do you seriously want to marry Rangeela?"

"No, Papa."

"As soon as possible and before you break her heart, you should explain to her your decision not to marry her.

Son, let us analyze the impending scenario. Let us imagine a hypothetical marriage between Rangeela and you. You must have money to rent and furnish a place to live. You will need money for groceries, clothing, utensils, travelling expenses, entertainment recreation, medicals and many other sundries. Your salary is a mere one hundred and fifty dollars per month.

I assume hers is the same. You are working for an average of five dollars per day. Beggars earn more. Your salaries cannot sustain a marriage. You will have to be supported by me and that will not happen. So the anticipated marriage is doomed before it is hatched. I suggest that you and Rangeela go to university either locally or abroad. You should further your studies in the subjects where you excel. After you have earned your degrees and you have landed good paying jobs, then you can get married, that is, if you are still madly in love with each other. Presently, you can make love on hungry stomachs but not without money. No money, no love.

Analyze and interpret diligently what I have said. Make a reasonable decision that you will not regret later in your life. An excellent education, when applied efficiently and effectively, will open the doorways to a higher standard of living and a better quality of life. Good luck and God's blessings."

Papa left the room. I went to my own room and contemplated my future with Rangeela. I repainted the marriage financial scene in my mind.

After analyzing Papa's speech on the potential challenges of marriage, I decided to go to my neighbours, Vishal and Kareena. They were married for over ten years and could be able to enlighten me about the hidden cost of married life. I told them about the marriage proposal made by Rangeela's mother and the rational speech of Papa. They said that marriage was a very serious human relation contract. They concurred that Papa was right on target with his analyses and recommendations. They agreed that if they did not have family inheritance and other business enterprises that their teaching jobs would not earn them sufficient income to lead and enjoy their existing live. Although they were friends of Rangeela and had supported her in all her trysts with me, they alluded to the comments and insults she publicly hurled at me in his earlier encounter with her. They reminded me that she still had those pompous and mean streaks in her DNA, and that I should be very concerned that she would always be Rangeela the unpredictable. They reminded me of the Aesop's fable about the frog and the scorpion – the scorpion could not avoid stinging the frog in the middle of the stream, although he promised he will not. They repeated the pertinent question my Papa asked, "Do you want to get married to Rangeela?"

Having listened very carefully and intently to their analyses and explanations, they convinced me that I should not enter into a marriage contract with her at that stage of my life. They strongly recommended that I adopted the profound advice of my Papa.

*****

The following Monday morning as we were walking to school, Rangeela softly asked, "Are you going to marry me?"

"Rangeela, we have to talk. Marriage is a very serious life time commitment. We have to analyze all the different parameters of our marriage before we can make a firm and final decision."

She remained very silent and did not say another word to me until after the end of the school day. After we left the school premises and were on our way home, she said that she was going home with me to discuss the status of our marriage.

I was very startled at her bold statement, and became very confused at her sudden rush to get married.

First, her mother had come to our home with her to talk about marriage and second, her announcement that she was going home with me to talk about our imminent marriage.

I started to wonder what was beneath the sudden marriage gambit. Was she pregnant? Were they thinking that I was the father? I was very confident as I never had sexual intercourse with her. Was she harboring some serious disease? Were they trying to force a marriage on me because of family issues? Was she causing problems at home? Many puzzling thoughts were fluttering in my mind. She did accompany me to my home, much to the surprise of my grandfathers, my stepmother, Papa, my sisters, my brother and my cousin.

My youngest sister wanted to know whether we were already married and was I bringing her to live with us.

Papa approached us and wanted to know why I brought her home. He thought that I had decided to live with her in a common-law fashion as most of the young adolescents were doing. I told the watchful eyes, listening ears and stunned faces that we were there to have some serious discussions about the wherewithal that were necessary for a marriage to be successful.

I requested some privacy. Rangeela made a phone call to her mother to inform her about the hasty marriage discussions she had arranged at my home. We had a quick dinner of chicken pelau, watercress salad and cold grapefruit juice before we started our discussion. Afterward, we retreated to the front gallery, sat down on the basket shaped chairs and commenced our talks.

Rangeela listened very attentively to my explanations and rationalization for not getting married at this time of our lives. I convinced her that we should go to university and obtain at least one degree in a well-paying profession. The meeting did not last very long. She was very pleased with our final decision. I accompanied her to her home and kissed her good night as I left her at her front door. We courted for another few months in the great expectation that we would be happily married sometime in the future. On the day she was leaving to further her studies in England, I bade her farewell at the Piarco Airport in Trinidad. I never heard from her again.

I thought the most appropriate way to conclude my memoir would be with an excerpt from the ode, "Intimations of Immortality from Recollections of Early Childhood" written by the major English Romantic poet, William Wordsworth (1770-1850):

> What though the radiance
>
> which was once so bright
>
> Be now for ever taken from my sight
>
> Though nothing can bring back the hour
>
> of splendour in the grass,
>
> of glory in the flower,
>
> We will grieve not, rather find
>
> Strength in what remains behind.

DISCLAIMER

This work is a memoir. It is re-created to the best of my ability from the recollections of my personal experiences and the stories told to me by my grandfathers and father.

In order to maintain the anonymity, the names of people, places, institutions and some of the physical properties and places of residence have been changed to avoid litigation from them and from me.

All the characters and events are real. However, any resemblance of any actual person, alive or deceased, is entirely coincidental.

ACKNOWLEDGEMENTS

I am forever grateful to God for providing me with abundant energy, inspiration and determination to complete this challenging opus. I will always be deeply indebted to my grandfathers and my parents for courageously providing me with invaluable information of my ancestry.

To my wonderful, dedicated and energetic wife, Ambica (Rani), for continuously motivating, advising and supporting me throughout the arduous writing and editing stages.

I am also thankful to my special friends and associates, who shared their time, knowledge and energy during the gestation of the manuscript: Donald Adams, Myra Brezden, Irene Copp, Robert Janson, Martin Kofsky, Zaida Rajnauth, Kassandra and Robert Sawatzky, Kenneth Luginbuhl, and Sharon Wong.

Finally, I will always be grateful to Howard Aster for not only giving me, an unknown writer, this special opportunity to bring this book to the public, but also personally editing my manuscript. Honourable mention goes to the rest of the Mosaic Press support team.

ABOUT THE AUTHOR

Awadh Jaggernath was born in Trinidad where he was educated under the British education system. He taught in elementary and secondary schools, as well as for the extra-mural department of the University of the West Indies in Trinidad. In the 1960s, he immigrated to Canada to further his education at McMaster University, University of Toronto, Brock University and York University. For decades he taught mathematics and science at the collegiate level for the Toronto District School Board and the Halton Public and Separate School Boards. He is now retired and lives in Oakville.